MEMBERSHIP OF THE PUBLIC SCHOOLS COMMISSION

Chairman   Sir John Newsom, C.B.E.

Vice-Chairman D. V. Donnison, B.A.,
                 Professor of Social Administration,
                 London School of Economics.

Members   Dame Kitty Anderson, D.B.E., Ph.D.,
                 former Headmistress, North London Collegiate School.

                Lord Annan, O.B.E., D.Litt., D.U.,
                 Provost of University College, London.

                Kathleen Bliss, M.A., D.D.,
                 Lecturer in Religious Studies,
                 University of Sussex.

                J. C. Dancy, M.A.,
                 Master, Marlborough College.

                John Davies, M.B.E.,
                 Director-General, Confederation of British Industry.

                T. E. Faulkner, M.A., Ph.D.,
                 Convener, City of Dundee Education Committee.

                Dame Anne Godwin, D.B.E.,
                 former General Secretary,
                 Clerical and Administrative Workers Union.

                W. S. Hill, M.Ed., B.Sc.(Econ.).,
                 Headmaster, Myers Grove Comprehensive School,
                  Sheffield.

                T. E. B. Howarth, M.C., T.D., M.A.,
                 High Master, St. Paul's School.

                H. G. Judge, M.A., Ph.D.,
                 Principal, Banbury School.

                G. H. Metcalfe, M.A.,
                 Director of Education, Durham.

                John Vaizey, M.A.,
                 Professor of Economics, Brunel University.

                Bernard Williams, M.A.,
                 Knightbridge Professor of Philosophy,
                 University of Cambridge.

  Mr. Nigel Cook, who was Chairman of the City of Birmingham Education Committee, resigned from the Commission on health grounds in January, 1967.

Secretaries   G. F. Cockerill (Secretary)
                 G. Etheridge (Assistant Secretary)

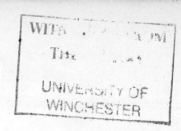
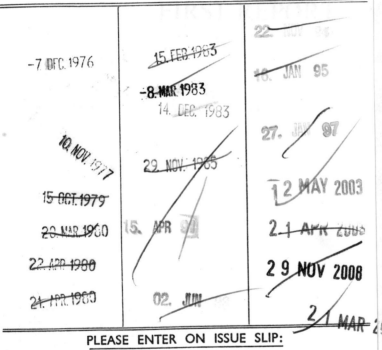
HER MAJESTY'S STATIONERY OFFICE

1968

The estimated cost of the preparation of the Report is £10,590, of which £6,265 represents the estimated cost of printing and publishing the Report.

SBN 11 270001 2

5th April, 1968

Dear Secretary of State,

Your predecessor (The Rt. Hon. Anthony Crosland, M.P.) appointed us following his statement in the House of Commons on 22nd December, 1965, with the terms of reference set out overleaf.

We now present to you a report on the principles which we think should govern the integration of independent boarding schools. We have not made recommendations about individual schools. We believe that the future of each school should be negotiated by a differently constituted body in the light of our recommendations.

We have not considered public day schools in this report. They are closely allied, in the type of education they provide, with direct grant and maintained grammar schools, and we think it essential that they should be looked at in the context of the developing pattern of secondary education in particular localities. We do not wish to delay our report on boarding schools while we consider the future of the day schools, and we have therefore decided to make them the subject of a second report. In our second report we shall also take account of the addition to our terms of reference (set out overleaf) which your predecessor (The Rt. Hon. Patrick Gordon-Walker, M.P.) made in October, 1967.

Three members who have not signed the report have appended a note of dissent, and there is a general note of reservation by one member who has signed the report.

Yours sincerely,

JOHN NEWSOM,

(*Chairman*).

The Rt. Hon. Edward Short, M.P.,
Secretary of State for Education and Science.

The main function of the Commission will be to advise on the best way of integrating the public schools with the State system of education. For the immediate purpose of the Commission public schools are defined as those independent schools now in membership of the Headmasters' Conference, Governing Bodies' Association or Governing Bodies of Girls' Schools Association.

The Commission will be expected to carry out the following tasks:

(a) To collect and assess information about the public schools and about the need and existing provision for boarding education; forms of collaboration between the schools (in the first instance the boarding schools) and the maintained system.

(b) To work out the role which individual schools might play in national and local schemes of integration.

(c) If it so wishes, and subject to the approval of the Secretary of State, to initiate experimental schemes matching existing provision with different types of need.

(d) To recommend a national plan for integrating the schools with the maintained sector of education.

(e) To recommend whether any action is needed in respect of other independent schools, whether secondary or primary.

In carrying out its tasks the Commission will be expected (while respecting the denominational character of the schools), to pay special attention to the following objectives:

(a) To ensure that the public schools should make their maximum contribution to meeting national educational needs, and in the first instance any unsatisfied need for boarding education in the light of the Martin[1] and Newsom reports[2].

(b) To create a socially mixed entry into the schools in order both to achieve (a) above and to reduce the divisive influence which they now exert.

(c) To move towards a progressively wider range of academic attainment amongst public school pupils, so that the public school sector may increasingly conform with the national policy for the maintained sector.

(d) To co-operate closely with local education authorities in seeking to match provision with need for boarding education.

(e) To ensure the progressive application of the principle that the public schools, like other parts of the educational system, should be open to boys and girls irrespective of the income of their parents.

---

[1] Report of the Working Party on Assistance with the Cost of Boarding Education, H.M.S.O., 1960.

[2] Half Our Future—A report of the Central Advisory Council for Education (England), H.M.S.O., 1963.

Additional terms of reference (*October*, 1967)

To advise on the most effective method or methods by which direct grant grammar schools in England and Wales and the grant-aided schools in Scotland can participate in the movement towards comprehensive reorganisation, and to review the principle of central government grant to these schools.

Table of Contents

VOLUME I

PART SIX

SCOTLAND; WALES

PART SEVEN

RECOGNITION AS EFFICIENT

List of Tables and Diagrams in this Volume

Introduction and recommendations

1. These terms of reference are explosive. No wonder. The "public schools" have long been a storm-centre of political controversy. That is why our terms of reference go beyond those usually given to Commissions. We were not asked simply to conduct an inquiry. We were asked to propose a plan of action. Whatever plan we devise will please neither the independent schools nor their sternest critics, neither the local authorities nor the teachers in the maintained schools with which we are told the independent schools must be integrated.

2. For this there is a simple reason. People hold beliefs about the nature of society. These beliefs colour their judgement of the public schools. Some will stress the value of independent institutions in a modern state; others will emphasise the duty of the State to regulate those institutions for the common good. It is of course beyond dispute that the State has the power to investigate and regulate the public schools. It first did so almost exactly a hundred years ago. But how far the State should use that power has always been contentious.

3. There is another reason why our proposals are bound to be controversial. Britain, in common with other European countries, is making a troubled and puzzling journey—the journey from a system of secondary and higher education designed to educate a small élite, to a system in which these kinds of education are to be made available to vastly greater numbers of boys and girls. The public school problem is only one aspect of this change, but in facing it we have had to plunge into the whirlpool of arguments about specialisation or breadth of study, diversity or uniformity, and ask ourselves how far equality of opportunity is compatible with academic excellence. So did those who submitted evidence to us. Both that evidence and our own discussions showed how profound is the conflict of ideals people discover when they consider the future direction which secondary education should take.

4. Thus, when we began to discuss how the independent schools were to become less socially divisive, the first problem to raise its head was: how far can they do so and remain independent? For years these schools have said that they are anxious to take children from different social classes and for the State or the local authorities to pay the fees. But until very recently, for reasons beyond their control, they have never had the opportunity of taking more than a comparatively small number of children in each school and have expected that those who came would be able to fit in without the schools changing their curriculum or their character. In our view it would be wrong for this situation to continue. If the public schools are to be paid from public funds to accept a large number of children of a different social class from that of their present pupils, the schools must in some sense be integrated with the pattern of State education. They cannot ignore what is happening in maintained schools and turn their back on the immense changes in national secondary education which are now taking place.

5. But when we came to study these changes another dilemma arose. At present the State system of secondary education is in flux. It is the policy of

1

the Government to move towards universal comprehensive education; but comprehensiveness, as the ship to carry all secondary education, is only beginning to get under way. Some comprehensive schemes for lack of school buildings are as yet comprehensive more in name than reality. Some local education authorities are still trying to retain some of their grammar schools, and through selection preserve the traditional curriculum and status of these schools. Should any secondary schools be exempted from the principle of comprehensiveness and remain selective? A strenuous debate is at present going on in public on this issue. Our own discussions on the topic were equally strenuous.

6. In this matter we encountered a further difficulty. The independent schools considered in this report are boarding schools: most of them are small, some of them tiny, when compared with the average maintained secondary school. Only a few of them are large enough to become comprehensive schools in the fullest sense of that term, and to take children of all levels of ability over a full age range. Whatever course we recommend must be practical; and that is why we shall propose that the schools should accept children of lower ability than many of them are accustomed to accept and should modify their curriculum, but without all becoming fully comprehensive. If this were done, the independent schools could help to provide places for a large proportion of children who need to go to a boarding school; and these schools would become less socially divisive. This proposal is in line with the present drive to abolish the secondary modern schools and to postpone for as long as possible the taking of irrevocable decisions about a child's future.

7. Yet there is a danger in this proposal. It is not only a compromise on the principle of full comprehensiveness but could also produce within a school the very divisiveness we want to eliminate. The scheme we propose involves introducing a substantial proportion of assisted pupils (at least a half) into the schools, the rest being fee-payers. But a school which consisted of the children of fee-payers selected for ability and assisted children who were nearly all of lower ability would be a bad school. It would be equally deplorable if a large proportion of the grant-aided places were filled by the kind of boys and girls who already go to public schools. If our compromise is to work, great trouble will have to be taken to get *both* the social mix *and* the spread of ability adjusted to each other.

8. That is not the only ground on which this proposal will be criticised. Some people will argue that to establish a system of assisted places in the independent schools will create, and not diminish, divisiveness. They will argue that we are advocating a system which could perpetuate far more effectively than any other means a permanent class division in our educational system. A policy designed to integrate could end in dividing the community. Our proposal will also be criticised by those at the other end of the spectrum of educational opinion. They will argue that the future welfare of the country depends on maintaining a small number of academically high grade secondary schools dependent on early selection. They will not accept that the wider spread of ability which our report envisages would make the best use of the special academic facilities which the public schools offer for a curriculum leading to intensive sixth form studies. This would apply whether or not the present sixth form curriculum is substantially modified.

9. We meet these criticisms in the report. While we agree that a great deal hangs on the sensitivity with which the scheme of assisted places in the public schools is administered, we have no fear that the scheme will lead to the creation of a new snob sector of semi-independent boarding and day schools drawing off the best pupils from the comprehensive schools. Nor do we think that the academic standards of the independent schools would be destroyed by admitting boys and girls who are less advanced than their contemporaries who got a better start in life. Practically every report or study about education during the past fifteen years has stressed that children of lower social classes may appear to be "less intelligent" on entering secondary school; but provided they are given the right opportunities many of them catch up by the time they leave school. What is more, the academic traditions of the public schools are not likely to be destroyed by accepting such children. The public schools are not all like Winchester. They vary immensely, in size, aim and achievement. A few of them have magnificent traditions of academic achievement, as have some of the maintained and direct grant schools. But the standard of ability demanded on entry differs from school to school. Some deliberately cater for children with little academic ability. That is why we offer a variety of alternatives to them. We offer alternatives to the pattern of the all-through comprehensive school—for example the opportunity to become sixth form colleges or to become schools admitting pupils at different ages, or even specialised academies. We suggest schemes for tiering and grouping the schools and other devices for exploiting the excellent sixth form facilities which some of these schools provide.

10. One matter, however, is not in doubt. There are more children in need of boarding education than can receive it. There are already 20,000 grant-aided boarders in the public and other independent schools (for example, children of diplomats and service personnel—mainly officers—serving overseas). There are also 11,000 boarders in maintained boarding schools and a further 9,000 in direct grant grammar schools. But there are many other children who need to be educated at boarding schools and who should be given assisted places.

11. Some people argue that "boarding need" is an illusion and that the child care service could deal with virtually all the cases which in our view require a place in a boarding school. We do not agree. Children's Departments, already short of staff, are going to have to carry heavier burdens in future; children in "long term care" frequently change foster homes and schools; their chances of academic success are correspondingly reduced, and very few of them go on to higher education. Boarding need is real.

12. Are the public schools the right place for these children? It is easy to say: here are a lot of children in need of boarding, and here are the independent schools in which they could be placed. But education is not solely a matter of supply and demand. It concerns the happiness and welfare of children. It ought to develop the intellect and the heart. There may be many children who would benefit from boarding education. But will they benefit from going to board in public schools?

13. Here we were helped by the research of the team under Dr. Royston Lambert which was given a grant by the Department of Education and Science to study boarding education before our Commission was appointed, and has since had further grants on our recommendation. Dr. Lambert has

told us that he and his colleagues fear that unless there are radical and immediate changes in the ethos of the public schools, they will be unsuitable for working-class boys and girls. We think this fear is exaggerated. We think the analysis that has been put before us is too static and does not take into account sufficiently the fact that a large entry into an independent school of children from the maintained sector with a different way of life will in itself change the school. The resultant changes could, indeed, be defensive and negative, but we see no reason to fear that they must be so. However, we have never doubted Dr. Lambert's contention that the ethos of the public schools will have to change if any scheme of producing a social mix is to work. We do not take the line that it is the duty of the children to "fit in" so that the school can "absorb" them. On the contrary: the independent schools, which have so much to give, have also much to learn and we have a good deal to say about the ways in which some of their hallowed traditions will have to be modified and some of their customs changed.

14. Plainly, if these children are to benefit from boarding in the public schools, and if the public schools are to benefit by becoming less socially divisive, the children should not be scattered in penny packets round all the schools. On the contrary, our proposal is that the schools should over a period make at least a half and then an increasing number of their places available for assisted pupils. All this will take time and it will be many years before all the independent schools worth while integrating are in fact integrated. It must be an advance in depth.

15. It will be a slow advance. It cannot be anything else. Not only have the independent schools got to be given time to change their curriculum and their customs. The speed at which schools can be integrated will be governed by the amount of money the Government can provide and the priority they give to the integration of the public schools above other kinds of expenditure. When the cost of providing such places is weighed against the needs of other sectors of school education—against the needs revealed by the Plowden and Newsom Reports—how far can the case for providing expensive places for boarding be justified? Any report on education which envisages adding to the total school budget must be realistic, and we do not believe that it would be responsible for us to advocate massive expenditure to provide places in boarding schools at this point in time.

16. Some people would take an even more stringent view. When about 400,000 parents pay school fees, why reduce their numbers and add still further to government expenditure? The question, of course, ignores our terms of reference. Also it could have been put just as forcefully in order to defend the privilege of parents to obtain places for their children in maintained grammar schools by paying fees. That privilege was abolished in the Education Act of 1944.

17. These, then, were conflicts of principle which troubled us; and these the major objections that we see (and try to answer more fully in this report) to the scheme of integration we have worked out. But why in any case put forward a scheme which is, in these various ways, a compromise? We indeed considered three other solutions to the problem either more or less radical than the one we propose, and we must explain what they are and why we have rejected them.

18. The first solution is to declare that the problem is insoluble, and to leave the public schools as they are. This view, in different forms, is held by those at opposite ends of the political spectrum. It is held by those who detest the notion of any State interference with the public schools and who are at best lukewarm in supporting any scheme to broaden their social entry. Those who hold this view believe that the public schools exist for those who can pay the fees: that the whole point of the schools is that they should be the places where boys and girls of the same class should go—together with those who through their parents' wealth have acquired the ability to enter that class. We cannot accept this view. It is directly opposed to our terms of reference. It totally disregards the extent to which public schools are already subsidised in one way and another from public funds. The State already pays wholly or partly for the education of over 40,000 children (day and boarding pupils) at independent schools i.e. nearly 10 per cent of all their pupils. To extricate the State entirely from its involvement in these schools would call for the withdrawal of all these pupils. This would be a negative act. We prefer to think of these pupils as the forerunners of a bolder measure of integration.

19. The view that the public schools are best left alone is also held by those who disapprove of them most strongly—and by those who, having read the numerous articles and reports on the future of these schools which have appeared since the Commission was set up, have formed the opinion that integration is neither worth the money nor the effort involved. Some believe that any scheme of integration will be thwarted by the governing bodies and heads of these schools so that they will remain as socially divisive as before and, worse still, more directly bolstered by State subsidies. Such people argue that the schools should be boycotted and subjected to every form of ostracism that wit can devise to strip them of their privileges. We have faced the issue of these privileges. We deal with the charitable status of the schools and the tax-avoidance schemes which undoubtedly enable many parents to afford the fees. We explore the extent to which independent schools employ more teachers than comparable maintained schools. We have suggested ways of meeting these problems; but they would be mainly negative actions unless we looked also to the integration of the schools. We do not believe that guerilla war waged against these schools is any substitute for recognising that they are an important part of the nation's secondary education system.

20. Moreover, those who oppose any scheme of integration should try to foresee what secondary education would look like if no attempt to integrate the public schools were made. Many of them are concerned that the development of comprehensive education will be jeopardized if places are taken up at schools outside the maintained system. They overlook the fact that our proposals would assist children over a very wide range of ability and would not take the form of academic selection. But, more important, they overlook the damage which may ultimately be done to comprehensive education if a whole sector of secondary schools is deliberately left outside the main stream. There would be a strong temptation for these schools to develop on increasingly selective lines, and to lose all sense of responsibility for boys and girls of lower ability, the late developers and those without private means. In our view, to believe that all the public schools will "wither away" through economic pressures in the foreseeable future is an illusion. So long as they exist as a separate sector, they will continue to stand apart from, and may well

cause harm to, the major educational movement of our times—the opening of opportunity to all children, whatever their background, to be given an education suitable to their talents. Is this what the opponents of the public schools really want?

21. Then there are others who have urged us to take a pragmatic view of the public schools. Surely, so the argument runs, they are so varied that no scheme can be devised to fit them all. Would it not be better to allow them to provide assisted boarding places for those in need and to allow the children filling these places to be selected solely by the school, as the best judge of the type of child it can educate? Each school could set its own standards, so the argument runs, and make what contribution it deemed fit. We cannot accept this as a solution. It would not be a scheme of integration but a fortuitous and haphazard set of arrangements. Under it no pressure would be put upon the schools to change their curricula, their relationships with the outside world, or their ethos. Such a scheme would neither integrate the schools nor make them substantially less socially divisive. Nor would it be fair to numbers of children in need of boarding education.

22. The other possible solution which we rejected is at first sight attractive because it would meet so many of the difficulties which have plagued us. This is to take the schools over and give them to local authorities to use as they see fit. The cost of taking all schools over simultaneously would be prohibitive, but they could be taken over individually or in groups over a period of years. There are many attractions in such a scheme. The problem of ethos disappears (assuming that the present staff and pupils would change); many schools could be grouped in "tiers" or become sixth form colleges or other types of school; local education authorities which at present would be reluctant (even if they had the powers) to contemplate building day school components in the grounds of independent schools sited in or near towns would no longer fear the administrative difficulties of co-operating with the governing bodies of independent schools; and authorities would be relieved of the cost of building their own boarding schools.

23. Why, then, have we rejected a scheme which disposes of so many of our troubles? First it is not clear that it would be either practicable or desirable to confine such a "take-over" to a somewhat arbitrary list of "public schools"; rather, it would have to extend ultimately to all independent schools. Those who do not object to this prospect on principle would have good reason to object to it on grounds of cost. The current cost alone would be at least £60 million a year in England and Wales. Even though it would be reached only over a period of years, we still think that the cost is too high when weighed against other educational needs in primary and secondary education. Second, there is no conclusive evidence that anything like the number of boarding places available in independent schools (130,000 in England and Wales) is needed by local education authorities. Third, local authority associations have shown little disposition to take over any of these schools. Fourth, considerable numbers of the staff in the independent schools would probably in these circumstances leave the teaching profession. Why incur net loss of valuable educational experience and capital?

24. Educational reform in this country is always an untidy patchwork. It is the result of give and take between the conflicting views of the teaching profession, parents, governing bodies, local authorities, universities and other

institutions of higher education, churches, and many other groups each with certain objects in view. It is influenced by reports of Commissions and Committees set up to examine specific problems; by research conducted by the Departments or in universities and colleges of education, and by the constant and increasing public debate about educational policy. Out of this debate come Acts of Parliament or administrative orders which reflect the conflict of opinion. The reforms often have effects which their authors could not have predicted. The Education Act of 1944 revolutionised secondary education. Less than twenty years later the Robbins Committee had to be set up to devise ways and means to cope with the cohorts of boys and girls qualified to go on to higher education. No doubt the country was slow to recognise that the one would follow inescapably upon the other. But educational reform moves by stages and everything cannot be done at once. We do indeed ask the independent schools to get on the move and to move fast. But they cannot be transformed overnight. We were asked in our terms of reference "to move towards" a progressively wider range of attainment so that the independent schools could "increasingly conform" with national policy. The course of action we recommend does exactly this.

25. Our scheme for the evolution of these schools is bound to be gradual. No one could advocate children being drafted to fill assisted places in the public schools. Their parents must want them to go there, and it may be some years before working class parents whose children are in need of boarding want to send their children to independent boarding schools. Indeed in the early years of the scheme disproportionately many of the assisted places may be sought by the parents of children whose social origins are not so very different from those of the fee-payers at these schools. But we believe that this will change. As the public schools change, prejudices against them may dissolve sooner than expected. The passage of time will lay the ghosts who have haunted us in our discussion. We believe that if our recommendations were adopted, the public schools would be transformed and would be regarded as part of the national system of education: open as the universities and so many professions and callings have become in the last fifty years to boys and girls from every class in society, and no longer the preserve of those who have money or social position, or both. But we do not leave it to time alone to effect these changes. We recommend that a Boarding Schools Corporation be set up to act as the mid-wife to our scheme.

26. That is why we believe that the wise course of action at this moment of time is to press ahead with a scheme which is indeed radical, but not so revolutionary as to make it virtually impossible for the independent schools to co-operate, nor so tepid as to have the appearance of change yet change little. We think that our scheme deserves the co-operation of the independent schools. We think so because in our discussions with the schools, the local education authorities and many other bodies who came to talk to us, we have sensed a willingness to admit that this was a genuine problem and that it ought to be tackled. We were given radical terms of reference: we have given a radical answer to them.

27. What is more, our scheme need not cost a great deal in the immediate future. The successors of the 20,000 assisted children who are at present spread over more than a thousand independent schools could be grouped to integrate a much smaller number of schools. This indeed will be an important

part of integration. But for real progress to be made towards abolishing social divisiveness in the schools, and at the same time meeting need for boarding, additional money would have to be spent on places for working class children. We shall show that, as the build-up would be slow, little additional cost would be incurred for several years. Although the net extra cost of a scheme affecting most independent boarding schools would eventually come to £12 million a year, more than a half of the places at well over 150 secondary schools and many preparatory schools (32,000 places in all, under the interim scheme we propose), could be taken up at a cost of £6·1 million.

Conclusions and recommendations

28. Our general conclusion is that independent schools are a divisive influence in society. The pupils, the schools and the country would benefit if they admitted children from a wider social background. We recommend a scheme of integration by which suitable boarding schools should make over at least a half of their places to assisted pupils who need boarding education. This change will take time, and not all schools can be brought within the integrated sector simultaneously. The details should be worked out school by school, by a body we shall call the Boarding Schools Corporation.

29. Our main conclusions and recommendations are as follows, (references to paragraphs in the report being shown in brackets):

I Integration

1. *Independent boarding schools suitable and willing to enter an integrated sector should be given every encouragement to do so. There should be a first condition that a school must admit assisted pupils from maintained schools to at least a half of its places—by the end of a build-up period of about seven years. (253)*

2. *Most schools, and especially boys' schools, should admit pupils of a wider range of ability. With very few exceptions, they should cater for pupils including those of an ability level corresponding with that required for courses leading to the Certificate of Secondary Education. They should be encouraged where possible also to admit children below this level of ability. Very few children with boarding need should be excluded from the opportunity of a place at an integrated school on grounds of low academic ability. It will be possible to achieve a wide range of ability within a smaller annual age group than in most maintained day schools because classes are normally smaller in boarding schools. (278, 279)*

3. *Where schools are too small to admit children of widely differing ability over the whole age range, they should adapt as far as possible to the comprehensive system by shortening their courses and adjusting their ages of admission. (264) For example, a group of schools having a common foundation or religious, educational or other bonds might between them cover the whole secondary age range and a very wide span of ability. (293)*

4. *Although the great majority of integrated schools should adopt these principles, there could be possible exceptions to the pattern:*

    (i) *A very small number of schools should be enabled to reorganise themselves to cater wholly or mainly for pupils at the sixth form level. (281 to 287)*

    (ii) *One or two schools might become "academies" catering for children with special aptitudes in music or ballet. (288)*

(*iii*) *Proposals to cater entirely for gifted children from an early age should be viewed with considerable caution, but are not excluded by our recommendations.* (*290*)

Association with maintained schools

5. *Independent boarding schools should be encouraged to work closely not only with each other, but with maintained day schools, with which they might share teaching resources and other facilities, and whose boarding needs they might help to meet.* (*295*)

Aided status

6. *For schools wishing to come within the maintained system there should be opportunities of "aided" status—that is, of a relationship with the State equivalent to that of voluntary aided schools, but possibly in association with a central body rather than a local education authority.* (*296, 297*)

Joint provision

7. *Local education authorities, in consultation with governing bodies, should where practicable plan new comprehensive schools to work closely with integrated boarding schools. It should be made legally possible for them to build by agreement on an independent school site and to arrange for joint responsibility for the resulting school.* (*272*)

Girls' schools

8. *Most girls' schools are (because of limitations of size and academic provision) less well poised for integration than boys' schools; even if they ____ all suitable they could provide only about a half as many places as boys____ therefore be necessary to take up places at schools not immed____ suitable integration until the integrated sector can accommodate al____ girls in need boarding education. Schools which are small but are otherwise suitable for ____ gration should be encouraged to make "tiering" or similar arrangements with other schools.* (*127, 128, 300*)

Co-education

9. *There should be more co-educational boarding schools, in order to meet the wishes and convenience of parents of both boys and girls, and also to extend opportunities of boarding education for girls. Some of the larger boys' schools in particular should be encouraged to adapt themselves for this role.* (*301, 302*)

Boarding for young children

10. *Where boarding at primary school age is essential, assisted places should first be sought in the junior schools or departments of integrating secondary schools and then in other preparatory schools. Preference should be given to preparatory schools which are willing to become co-educational and to enter into schemes of integration.* (*303*)

Holidays

11. *If there are children who cannot spend holidays at home or with relations, Children's Departments or other child care agencies should be invited to help. Failing this, it may be desirable for integrated schools to take it in turns to accommodate during holidays any children who have nowhere else to go.* (*307*)

Immigrants

12. The schools may have a valuable role to play in the education of immigrant children, and there should be no discrimination against them in allocating places. (308)

Exchange of teachers

13. An interflow of teachers should develop between the maintained and independent sectors in boys' schools to match that already taking place in girls' schools. In particular, a scheme should be established for the exchange of a hundred masters a year. (312)

Inspection

14. The inspection of boarding schools should in future take more account of the conditions and customs in the schools so as to judge how suitable they are as boarding communities for pupils of widely differing backgrounds. (311)

Governors

15. Governing bodies of integrating schools should include one third of members representing bodies or interests other than the Foundation. (314)

II. Denominational schools

16. Schools which are Christian foundations (as most public schools are) should be encouraged to accept pupils from denominations other than their own, as well as pupils of other religions or of no religion. (345)

17. There should be suitable safeguards for the conscience of parents in matters of religious worship and instruction. There is a case for extending choice in these matters also to senior pupils. (347, 348)

III. Changes at integrating schools

18. In order to meet the needs of assisted pupils, particularly those from maintained day schools, integrating schools will have to adapt themselves radically. This must not mean sacrificing important traditions and values, in particular those of hard work, good relations between pupils and staff and the wide variety of extra-curricular activities which many schools provide. But the style of life should be reconsidered. In particular: (233 to 241)

- *(i) There should be more women on the staffs of boys' schools and more men on the staffs of girls' schools.*
- *(ii) More opportunities should be provided for pupils to pursue their own personal interests in their leisure time.*
- *(iii) There should be more alternatives to Cadet Force activities and more choice and variety in games.*
- *(iv) Contacts with home, through weekly boarding where practicable, should be encouraged.*
- *(v) There could be greater freedom in forms of dress at some schools, particularly at weekends. Eccentric or unduly expensive school uniforms should be avoided.*
- *(vi) The prefectorial system may need to be modified so that excessive authority is not wielded by pupils; there should be no beating of boys by boys, and no personal fagging.*

IV. Subsidies for private education

19. By a majority we recommend that action should be taken to terminate the fiscal and similar reliefs of schools which are charities but which do not serve a truly charitable purpose. (366)

20. We suggest that Parliament should consider whether action should be taken to change fiscal policies which enable school fees to be paid otherwise than from parents' income[1]. (375)

V. Boarding need

21. The only justification for public expenditure on boarding education should be need for boarding, for either social or academic reasons. Social grounds would include circumstances in which a child is seriously deprived of reasonable possibilities of educational development because of the absence of a home in this country or because of adverse home or family conditions. Educational need may arise, whatever the home circumstances, if a child is unable to obtain education suited to his or her needs within daily travelling distance, or if the parents have to move home frequently in the nature of their work. These criteria should be interpreted rigorously. (156)

22. Applying a rigorous interpretation of need, we estimate that 80,000 children will require boarding places in schools of all kinds by 1980 (in England and Wales). We recommend that places for 45,000 of these pupils should be sought in independent schools. An addition of 2,000 places for Scotland would make a total of 47,000 assisted boarding pupils in independent schools. (210, 224, 225)

23. 20,000 places are already taken up wholly or partly at public expense in independent schools (out of a total of 138,000 boarding places, including Scotland). Our proposal is that a further 27,000 pupils should be assisted, and that all assisted pupils should attend schools approved for integration. About 38,000 of the 47,000 pupils might be in secondary schools or departments and about 9,000 in preparatory schools or departments. (224 to 226)

VI. Selection of assisted pupils

24. Guidance on boarding and placing policy should be given by the Boarding Schools Corporation to regional consortia of local education authorities, which (at any rate after the early stages) would handle the main volume of applications for pupils resident in this country. (323)

25. The Corporation would deal centrally with applications for sixth form colleges and academies (if any) and might also more conveniently receive applications from parents working overseas. (335 to 337)

26. The staffs of maintained schools and of welfare agencies should be encouraged to bring opportunities of boarding education to the notice of parents whose children might benefit from them. (321)

27. There should be no obligation upon parents to accept a place in a particular school, and alternatives should be suggested wherever possible. Similarly, heads of schools should not be obliged to accept a particular child, although this right should not be used as a means of preserving academic or social selection. (332, 333)

---

[1] The Chancellor of the Exchequer, in his Budget speech on 19th March, 1968, has now proposed measures affecting the taxation of minors' income and tax relief on certain kinds of insurance policy.

28. Places should be offered in schools as near as possible to pupils' homes. Where they are offered at a distance, it would be desirable for a group of children from the locality to go to the same schools. Flexible (i.e. weekly or other periodic) boarding arrangements should be encouraged. (327, 328)

29. Places in maintained and direct grant boarding schools should be regarded as the equivalent of places in independent schools; the aim is a boarding policy for all grant aided and integrated independent boarding schools. Local education authorities and governors of direct grant schools should be encouraged to make boarding places in their schools available to the Corporation and regional consortia. (329)

VII. Assistance to parents

30. All assisted pupils, whatever their parents' means, should be entitled to free tuition equivalent to the average cost of education in maintained day schools. (377 to 379)

31. Parental contributions should be made (according to means) towards the remaining cost of an assisted place. (380, 381)

32. Although the full cost of each place would be paid to the school by the Corporation, a standard cost—adjusted separately for primary (or preparatory) and secondary schools—should be attributed to each assisted place, so that the charge to parents would not vary according to the school attended. (380)

33. We recommend a scale of contributions identical in the lower ranges of income to the present university awards scale, but graduated more steeply at income levels exceeding £2,000 a year. (393)

34. We estimate an average net annual cost to public funds for each assisted secondary place of £408 at 1966/67 cost figures. This includes essential extras, administrative costs, and an allowance for capital development and for special assistance to parents at the lowest income levels. The equivalent preparatory school cost is £323. (410)

Cost of integration

35. The take-up of 38,000 secondary and 9,000 preparatory places would cost £18·4 million annually. (412)

36. A modified scheme for the take-up of 32,000 places as an interim measure would cost £12·5 million annually. (435)

37. There would be offsetting savings of £6·4 million a year now paid by government departments and local education authorities for pupils assisted under present arrangements, making the net costs of the full and interim schemes £12 million and £6·1 million respectively. (423, 435)

38. There would be further savings to public funds, of £2 to £3 million a year, resulting from our recommendation 19 above, and further substantial savings if Parliament decided to take action in the light of recommendation 20[1]. (421)

39. If the modified scheme were adopted as an interim measure, it should take the form of full integration of a smaller number of schools—not partial integration of a large number. (426)

---

[1] See footnote to recommendation 20 above.

40. Assistance from public funds for pupils (other than handicapped pupils) attending independent schools should, after a date to be decided, be restricted to those attending schools accepted for integration. (417,475)

41. The cost of assisted places (subject to parental contributions) should be met by local education authorities on a pooled basis. A variant of normal pooling would be to distribute the cost among authorities in such a way as to adjust their contribution in proportion to the number of pupils in their area not receiving education at the authority's expense. (442, 443)

42. The pooled expenditure should qualify for grant from the Exchequer, taking into account (in addition to normal rate support grant) any savings accruing to the Exchequer at 37 and 38 above. (441)

43. Future capital development at integrated schools should be subject to approval by the Boarding Schools Corporation, and should where necessary be met from loans amortised through fee income (the cost thus being borne by fee-paying and assisted pupils alike). (451, 452)

44. The Corporation should have the power to approve the level of fees to be charged at any integrating independent school, and a reserve power to approve the fees at other independent boarding schools in certain circumstances. (448 to 450)

VIII. Maintained schools

45. In areas where there is a shortage of boarding places which the integrated independent sector can only partially relieve, there should be provision for more maintained boarding schools, to be provided by local education authorities on a basis which would enable the capital cost to be amortised through fees and thereby pooled. (457, 458)

IX. Legislation and Administration

46. There should be an Education Act enabling an integrated sector to develop under the guidance of a Boarding Schools Corporation. The Corporation should have assurance of funds to facilitate forward planning. (463, 470)

47. Schools should be invited to submit development plans as a basis for negotiation; but no school would have a prescriptive right to be accepted for integration. (465)

48. The Secretary of State should have the power in the last resort to compel a school to enter into a scheme of integration if all efforts at negotiation and persuasion should fail, and if a school's refusal to enter the scheme would prejudice a successful integration policy. (478)

49. There should be provision for schools and parents to appeal against decisions of the Corporation or regional consortia. (480)

X. Scotland and Wales

50. We recognise that a scheme of integration appropriate to England and Wales may not be applicable to Scotland; a different kind of scheme would be acceptable provided it opened opportunities of boarding education to pupils who required it. (511)

51. We also accept that Wales, although subject to the same educational legislation and financial arrangements as England, has special problems which may call for different solutions. (527)

XI. Unrecognised schools

52. We endorse the Secretary of State's decision to require all independent schools with boarding pupils to reach an efficient standard. (537)

Part One

The Public Schools Today

CHAPTER 1

The starting point

30. The public schools are a unique British institution. For generations they have been extravagantly praised and extravagantly denounced, handsomely supported by benefactors and consigned to destruction by reformers. Foreign observers refer to them with a mixture of bewilderment and admiration. They themselves sometimes lament that they have become a legend, and they have certainly generated myths enshrined in literature. It is extraordinary that a particular type of school should have given rise to a recognisable literary genre. The public school novel, which began with *Tom Brown's Schooldays* and *Eric, or Little by Little*, is a regular feature in every decade. The school story, whether serious or fantastical, is itself a tribute to the fame of these schools. The public schools' house system, their discipline, their prefects, and their school colours and old school ties are to be found in vestigial form in many of the country's schools. People harbour the wildest notions about the life boys and girls lead in them. They are indeed a perennial topic of public discussion.

31. There are good reasons why this should be so. During the nineteenth century and until the beginning of the first world war the public schools dominated secondary education. While France and Prussia had established a system of national secondary education, England had relied on private enterprise. Partly through enlarging and reforming famous ancient endowed schools, partly by founding new ones, the upper class, the professional classes and wealthy businessmen provided schools to which they sent their children and to which parents aspiring to enter those classes in society tried to send theirs. Thus from Victorian times the public schools became the preserve of those who held a certain position in society or who could obtain entry by paying the fees. They attracted many of the best teachers and dominated the entry to Oxford and Cambridge.

32. This expansion coincided with the Railway Age. This enabled new public schools or old foundations in country towns to follow the pattern of Eton and Winchester and set themselves up as boarding schools. Public school education became almost synonymous with boarding education, and ancient schools, such as Charterhouse or Merchant Taylors', rather than remain in cramped surroundings, moved out of the centre of cities. Thus, although today the public schools educate less than three per cent of secondary school children, they provide more than half of the country's secondary boarding places and their splendid, sometimes historic, buildings stand in spacious grounds. By their nature they have remained the schools for the well-to-do. It could not be otherwise: their fees are so high. Yet even today, when taxation is high, numbers of parents are willing to pay, or find devices to pay, these fees; and some will scrimp and save to pay them.

33. Our evidence shows that people still believe—supporters and critics of the public schools alike—that children get social and educational advantages by

attending them. But there is more to it than that. By the turn of the century the boys' public schools developed a mystique, and it is this mystique, and the claims which are made for these schools, which mean much to their supporters and enrage their critics. The Edwardian public school with its fanatical zeal for team games and athleticism, its philistinism, its hierarchical system of prefects and boy-made customs reflecting seniority, gloried in cultivating what was called the public school spirit. This spirit defies definition because it has always meant different things to different people. To some it meant the Christian virtues, the patriotism and sense of duty, which was preached often from the pulpit by generations of headmasters and house-masters. To others, such as Kipling in *Stalky & Co.*, it meant the resourceful-ness, the freedom from cant, the rigid control of emotions and the refusal to betray comrades which boys learnt in their eternal conflict with the official rules of the school enforced by the masters.

34. Since Edwardian days the ideology of the public schools has changed immensely. In most cases the schools are now geared to academic success. In 1966-67, forty-five per cent of boys leaving H.M.C. schools obtained places in the universities. Their curriculum is wide, and enjoyment of the arts is no longer suspect but assiduously encouraged. But although the phrase "public school spirit" is often derided, it is still in its changed form very much alive. These schools believe in inculcating certain virtues—service to the community, leadership, initiative and self-reliance. There is nothing exceptional in this. All schools try to develop virtues in their pupils. But what is distinctive about the public schools is their claim that these virtues can be inculcated especially effectively through boarding and by protecting their pupils against malign influences in the outside world (including sometimes those in their families). How far they succeed is a matter of opinion. What is not open to question is that their clientèle take their claims to do so seriously, and their critics are as critical of their mystique as of their divisiveness.

35. Victorian Governments could hardly be described as strong advocates of State control, but they were not adverse to State intervention when they thought it necessary. Oxford and Cambridge had to be rescued by such inter-vention from their inability to reform themselves and from their ancient statutes which inhibited such reform. Similarly, nine of the ancient public schools were subjected to a scrutiny of their revenue and management by the Clarendon Commission (1861-64), while a few years later the Taunton Commission looked into the affairs of other endowed schools. But until the middle of this century the public schools were left to develop as they pleased and few questioned their right to do so or thought it odd that a set of private schools independent of the State and local education authorities should be the preserve of those whose parents could afford to pay the fees. Nor was it odd that the State did little more than try to ensure that no independent school should fall too far below the standards of schools maintained by local education authorities. From 1900, when effective central supervision of our educational system began, until the second world war, the State had enough on its hands to develop the complex of schools—county, voluntary aided, voluntary controlled and direct grant—which educate 94 per cent of our children.

36. Even as long ago as the nineteen-twenties, some thoughtful headmasters and others who had pondered over the future of the public schools began to

worry that they were the exclusive preserve of the sons of the well-to-do. These men had heard some of the great publicists on the Left, such as Shaw and Wells, call for the abolition of the public schools as citadels of privilege. Should not the schools throw open their doors through some financial device to a few gifted children from the poorer classes? The depression in the nine-teen-thirties and the second world war added a new anxiety. Who would in future be able to afford to pay the fees? These hopes and fears resulted in the Fleming Committee being appointed in 1942.

37. This body was asked how best to extend the association between the public schools and the national educational system. Its terms of reference were much less far reaching than our own. The Fleming Committee recommended[1] that boarding public schools wishing to enter their scheme should take a minimum of 25 per cent of pupils from grant-aided primary schools. These pupils (aged 11 or 13) would either have bursaries awarded by the Board of Education, or take up places reserved by local education authorities. Bursars would be interviewed by regional boards and paid for by the Board of Education, while local education authorities would receive grant aid from the Board for reserved places. The governing bodies of schools participating in the scheme were to include not less than three, and not more than one third, of their members nominated by the Board of Education. Every five years the scheme was to be reviewed "with a view to the progressive application of the principle that schools shall be equally accessible to all pupils and that no child otherwise qualified should be excluded solely owing to lack of means". When the proportion of children assisted from public funds exceeded 25 per cent, the requirement of previous attendance at primary school might be waived.

38. The recommendations of this scheme were never implemented nationally. The onus of taking up boarding school places was left with local education authorities. We shall examine the extent to which authorities have subsequently taken up places at independent boarding schools; but it is clear that, as an instrument of national policy, the Fleming Report rapidly became a dead letter. Up to the present time there has not been any nationally implemented policy for taking up places either at independent schools (day or boarding) or at any other type of boarding school, other than special schools. There were a number of reasons why this was so. It was certainly not the fault of the public schools which were anxious to implement the Fleming proposals. The proposals were made in 1944, at a time of great change in secondary education, and it is understandable that successive Governments and local education authorities regarded expenditure of this kind as having a low priority. On what grounds could local education authorities justify selecting a very few children and paying lavish fees for their education without any very clear criteria of need when the money spent on them could have been used in the maintained sector to improve conditions for so many others? The report posed extraordinarily difficult problems of selecting the pupils. Nor was it suggested that the public schools needed to change in order to educate these children.

39. If the Fleming scheme had been implemented, the changes it envisaged would have depended partly upon the criteria of selection and partly upon the number of bursars admitted. Regional boards were to be "guided by the

---

1 "The Public Schools and the General Educational System"; H.M.S.O.; 1944.

parents' choice of school and by the special needs and aptitudes of the pupils". If a significant number of bursaries had been awarded to children neither academically not socially attuned to the schools, changes in the schools might have been profound. But as the Fleming scheme assumed that the criteria for being awarded an assisted place were that the child should be suitable for a public school and that his parents wanted him to go there, this was unlikely to happen. Nor was there any certainty that the proportion of bursars would ever rise above 25 per cent. Had the Fleming scheme been fully implemented, despite these drawbacks, there might have been no need today to work out a scheme for integrating the schools fresh. A new initiative and governmental action could have done the job. But society has changed so greatly since the days when the Fleming Committee sat that their assumptions and solutions are today out of date; and in any case our terms of reference rule out the Fleming solution.

40. The terms of reference we have been given reflect the vast change in the assumptions which are made about society that have taken place since the first world war. The mass of the population which before that war were on the fringes of the nation have now been incorporated in it. They not only have the political rights which were won as the franchise was extended: they have a gradually but continually extending range of social rights in many fields. In education this has meant that not only is the State expected to provide schools for all children: it is expected to stop discrimination between them and to break down the barriers which class and home life erect. This is the strength behind the movement for comprehensive education and the revulsion against pronouncing on a child's future at 11. Formerly the public conscience was salved if any child of ability through gaining a scholarship or award could break into the élite institutions. Today it is different. Oxford and Cambridge, for instance, have come to recognise that their admissions procedures ought not in the future to be weighted against children who attend small maintained schools, and that it is not enough to demonstrate that there is no built-in prejudice in favour of public schoolboys. Just as university education is to be open through a system of grants to students from all walks of life and without regard to how rich their parents are, so doubt is being cast on the exclusive freedom of the well-to-do to buy a privileged form of secondary education for their children which is denied to others who may need it.

41. Our terms of reference are unusual because they made these assumptions explicit. We are asked to create a socially mixed entry to the schools in order both to meet unsatisfied needs for boarding education and also to reduce the "socially divisive influence which the schools now exert". This assumption has been a major cause of criticism of the terms of reference, and we shall therefore say how far we believe a divisive influence to exist. We are also asked to bear in mind the need "to move towards a progressively wider range of academic attainment amongst public school pupils, so that the public school sector may increasingly conform with the national policy for the maintained sector". This too has given rise to a good deal of misgiving. We shall argue how closely these two problems are related, and that in order to make the public schools less divisive, they will have to become more like maintained schools in their system of selection and entry.

42. At a comparatively early stage in our discussions we came to certain conclusions which differ radically from those of the Fleming Committee and

on which our whole report is based. Our first conclusion was that integration was meaningless if only 25 per cent of places in a school were available for children assisted from public funds. They should be there in large numbers if they came at all. Whereas the Fleming Report conveyed the impression that it was a privilege for assisted children to be able to enter a public school, we believe that the fee-paying children will benefit as much as the assisted children by the fact that they will be meeting, perhaps for the first time, their contemporaries from other strata in society. Whereas Fleming did not contend that the public schools should alter or adapt themselves to meet the needs of assisted pupils, we believe that the schools will have to change considerably and that the mere fact of very large numbers of assisted pupils being in the schools will help them to change.

43. Our second conclusion, which followed from the first, was that, by degrees, assisted pupils entering public schools in the future should be admitted only to schools accepted for integration. As the number of assisted pupils increased, so should more schools be integrated. Unless this was done, the assisted pupils would be scattered over the face of the public schools like confetti, and there would be no true marriage between the independent and the maintained sectors. To scatter them would be window-dressing; bad for the assisted children and useless for the schools. Indeed there are some independent schools which are not fitted for integration and which would have to be radically changed before any children were sent to them by the State.

44. Our third conclusion was that all independent schools recognised as efficient by the Department of Education and Science should be regarded as eligible for integration and not just those who happen to belong—or whose heads happen to belong—to the Headmasters' Conference or the other organisations named in our terms of reference. If our scheme were held to apply strictly to H.M.C. schools, for example, there might be some delightful manoeuvring whereby some schools pressed for admission to that body on the grounds that they were so hard up that they must integrate or go under, while others would gracefully find a pressing excuse for their heads to be relieved of the honour of belonging any longer to the H.M.C.

45. Our fourth conclusion was that integration of the public schools is impossible unless there is a general administrative settlement— a settlement which can be publicly debated and costed before legislation is passed. If there is not a central settlement, and the piecemeal arrangements between local education authorities and independent schools which have followed the Fleming Report continue, very little will change. If change is to be effective, it must be nationally accepted and nationally implemented. How else can the schools plan ahead for the new role which they should play?

46. For this reason we have decided that it is impracticable to carry out *at this stage* that part of our terms of reference which requires us to "work out the role which individual schools might play in national and local schemes of integration". There would be no purpose in our devoting considerable time and effort to negotiations with individual schools and local education authorities if at the end of the day we lacked power to reach agreement with them. There would be not only the risk of much wasted effort on all sides, but also an absence of reality and urgency in any negotiations which might take place.

If any scheme is to succeed, it must be worked out with a considerable number of individual schools. We regard this as a report on the administrative, financial and broad educational *principles* which should govern integration. We shall recommend that, if our proposals are thought to be on the right lines, a Boarding Schools Corporation should be set up to reach agreement with individual schools on the way in which they could be integrated.

47. This is a report on boarding schools only. Day schools will be the subject of our second report, when we also consider the direct grant schools, because they can be considered only in the context of the development of secondary education in their locality.

48. We describe briefly in Appendix 1 our method of working and the research we have set in train. We did not intend the whole of this research to be completed in time for our first report. Such parts of it as we required for immediate purposes were carried out as a matter of urgency. Other work which we sponsored was designed to help those who will conduct the detailed negotiations with individual schools.

CHAPTER 2

Facts and description

Public schools

49. Everyone uses the term "public school" and yet there is no generally accepted definition of these schools. Everybody would probably include the nine schools considered by the Clarendon Commission in their Report of 1864—Eton, Winchester, Westminster, Charterhouse, St. Paul's, Merchant Taylors', Harrow, Rugby and Shrewsbury. Most people would also include those famous schools which became prominent in the 19th century such as Marlborough, Wellington, Cheltenham, Clifton, Oundle, Uppingham and many other notable schools. Some use the term to mean any independent secondary school—a school not receiving grant from public funds. Our terms of reference specifically drew our attention to those independent schools which were (or whose heads were) members of the Headmasters' Conference (H.M.C.), the Association of Governing Bodies of Public Schools (G.B.A.) or the Association of Governing Bodies of Girls' Public Schools (G.B.G.S.A.). There were 288 such schools when we were appointed, including 11 in Scotland. They are listed in Appendix 2 and they are the schools referred to when the term "public school" is used in this report. There have been a number of changes in the membership of these three bodies and these are also shown in Appendix 2. The tables and diagrams in this chapter refer to 273 of the 277 public schools in England and Wales which were listed in our terms of reference; that is, omitting one school which has since joined the maintained system and three schools which closed in 1966. For convenience, we have grouped the tables and diagrams together at the end of the chapter. Particulars of schools in Scotland are given in Chapter 18 and Appendix 17.

Other independent schools

50. There are over 1,000 other independent schools for children mainly of secondary school age and over 1,800 preparatory and pre-preparatory schools. All independent schools in England and Wales have to apply for inclusion in the register of schools compiled by the Secretary of State under Part III of the Education Act, 1944. If a school wishes to be "recognised as efficient" under Rules 16, certain minimum standards of accommodation, staffing and instruction are required. All public schools are recognised but there are numbers of other independent schools which are not. We shall return to these in Chapter 19.

Direct grant schools

51. Direct grant schools are schools in England and Wales which receive grants from the Department of Education and Science and make available, either directly or through local education authorities, at least a quarter of places for which no fees are payable by parents. In practice, over 60 per cent of

upper school places have in recent years been allocated in this way. Fees are charged for the remaining places (in the case of day pupils, on the basis of an assessment of parental income).

Maintained schools

52. Maintained schools are schools whose running costs are met by a local education authority. In England and Wales they include schools provided by the authority (county schools) and "aided", "special agreement" and "controlled" schools established by voluntary bodies (voluntary schools).

Features of the public schools

53. The outstanding features of the public schools are that they are:

. . . mainly small schools

. . . mainly for pupils over 13 years old

. . . mainly for boarders

. . . mainly single sex and catering for more boys than girls

. . . mainly for private fee-payers

. . . and mainly in the south of England.

54. Nevertheless there is great variety. A few public schools are large, some are very small; although many are fully boarding, some admit only day pupils and there are numerous variations in between; some are urban, others are in the depths of the country; their age of admission varies. There is no such thing as a "typical" public school, and the independent sector as a whole has even greater variety. In the following brief description, amplified by the tables and diagrams at the end of the chapter, we shall compare the public schools, and where possible, other independent schools with maintained and direct grant schools.

Size of the sector

55. The public schools, and indeed all independent schools, are a small sector of the education system of England and Wales. Tables 1 to 6 show the numbers of schools and pupils in each category. 93 per cent of all pupils (disregarding for this purpose pupils in special schools) are in maintained schools, 1·5 per cent in direct grant schools and 5·5 per cent in independent schools. 3·9 per cent (within the 5·5 per cent) are at schools recognised as efficient; 1·4 per cent (within the 3·9 per cent) are at public schools. But to take the number of pupils in public schools as a percentage of the whole school population is misleading. Not only do they cater predominantly for pupils of secondary school age, but they admit most of their pupils later than do maintained secondary schools. It is therefore more relevant to take examples at ages at which pupils are attending secondary schools in both the maintained and independent sectors. At the age of 14 about 3 per cent of boys and 2 per cent of girls are in public schools. Because more pupils stay on after the age of 16 in the public than in maintained schools, the equivalent percentages at 17 rise to about 12 per cent for boys and 6 per cent for girls. The distribution of pupils between different kinds of school at varying ages is shown in Table 6 and illustrated in Diagram 2.

56. Not only is the total proportion of pupils in independent schools small; it is declining. In 1947 there were about 9 per cent of school children in independent schools; in 1957 the proportion had dropped to about 7 per cent; in 1967 it was 5·5 per cent. On the other hand, as more schools have applied for and received recognition as efficient, the proportion of all school children attending recognised efficient schools (including public schools) has risen from 2·9 per cent in 1947 to 3·9 per cent in 1967. Details are given in Appendix 5.

57. The numbers of pupils staying on at maintained schools have risen rapidly during the last twenty years. In this period the number of seventeen year olds in maintained schools has quadrupled while in independent schools it has less than doubled. The independent schools' share of the seventeen year olds at school has dropped from 27 per cent to under 15 per cent. This tendency seems likely to continue as children leave maintained schools later. Yet the numbers of pupils in independent schools has fallen in numerical as well as proportionate terms; the reduction is not, in other words, an apparent reduction accounted for wholly by increases in the maintained school population. For example, the number of pupils aged 14 in independent schools dropped from an estimated 47,000 in 1947 (about 8 per cent of the age group) to 37,600 in 1967 (5·8 per cent of the age group).

Sixth forms

58. Table 7 shows the average size of sixth forms in public schools, day and boarding. The boys' sixth forms average 157 pupils compared with 49 at girls' schools, and 74 at mixed schools. The equivalent maintained grammar school figures are 125, 96 and 107. At all schools, these averages mask considerable differences in the size of sixth forms.

59. A comparison of proportions of school leavers who go on to universities and other forms of higher and further education can be seen in Table 8 and Diagram 5. Especially noticeable is the proportion of independent school leavers who go on to the Universities of Oxford or Cambridge. Sample returns taken by the Department of Education and Science showed that, of all school leavers in the sample entering Oxford or Cambridge in 1966, some 45 per cent of boys and 25 per cent of girls came from independent schools.

Boarding education

60. It is in boarding education that the public schools make their biggest and most distinctive contribution. The number of all children boarding at school (other than in special schools) is a small proportion (about 1·9 per cent) of the school population of England and Wales. The figures are set out in Table 3. But the number of boarding places in independent schools (130,701) is more than six times the total in maintained schools (11,244) and direct grant grammar schools (9,318) combined. And within the independent sector, despite the fact that only 1·4 per cent of all children (day and boarding) are in public schools, public schools cater for 41 per cent of all boarding pupils. They provide 41,349 boarding places for boys and 21,635 for girls; these are almost entirely for secondary pupils, and account for over a half of all secondary boarding places in England and Wales.

Boarding houses

61. **Table 10** gives the range of sizes of the boarding community in schools with a quarter or more of boarding pupils. Boarding schools are usually organised in boarding houses. The normal size of senior houses is about 60 pupils; junior houses are usually about half as big. Within houses the majority share dormitories for seven or more pupils. About a tenth share dormitories for more than twenty pupils. The largest dormitory we have come across had 64 beds. Rather more than a tenth (usually the most senior pupils) sleep in rooms of their own. 68 out of 234 schools which answered the Commission's questionnaire on this point had no single rooms. More details are given in Appendix 6.

Links with home

62. A small number of public boarding schools allow their pupils to return home regularly at weekends. 6 boys' schools and 30 girls' schools have adopted weekly boarding and 2 boys' and 4 girls' schools allow visits home every other weekend. The majority of schools restrict the number of times parents can visit their children at school; the commonest arrangement is three visits a term. Details are given in Appendix 6, which also shows that the parents of some 17 per cent of boarding pupils entering public schools live, either temporarily or permanently, overseas.

Size of schools

63. **Table 9** shows the sizes of boys' and girls' public schools. The average size of schools wholly or mainly for boarders is 418 pupils at boys' schools and 259 at girls' schools. At schools wholly or mainly for day pupils the average sizes are 716 and 381 respectively.

Co-education

64. Among the 273 public schools in England and Wales, there are only 3 co-educational schools[1], with 1,162 pupils. Although a few of the remaining 270 schools have small numbers of pupils of the opposite sex (usually day pupils in their junior departments), they are all in effect single sex schools— 130 schools for over 62,000 boys and 140 schools for over 43,000 girls (counting day and boarding pupils). In the maintained sector 58 per cent of secondary schools are co-educational, catering for 60 per cent of secondary pupils.

Location

65. Large or small, boys' or girls', the great majority of public schools are found in the south of England. The distribution of boarding schools is shown in the map in Appendix 16. Only 13 per cent of the 63,000 public school boarding places in England and Wales are situated north of a line drawn through Chester and Lincoln, although 31 per cent of the population (of England and Wales) lives north of this line. Tables 11 and 12 compare the numbers of public schools and their pupils with other secondary schools and their pupils in each region.

---

[1] A fourth co-educational school was included in our terms of reference, but has since become maintained (see paragraph 49). Another co-educational school became a public school during 1967, but is not included in our figures.

Age of schools

66. Most public schools were founded before the twentieth century; only 3 boys' schools and 5 girls' schools have been established since 1939. Many have been refounded, reconstituted or changed in character very considerably, so that the original date may not be of particular significance. Diagram 6 shows the ages of schools in England and Wales.

Staffing

67. One reason often given by parents for choosing an independent school rather than a maintained school is the favourable teacher/pupil ratio of the independent schools. In 1967 the overall teacher/pupil ratio in schools recognised as efficient was 1: 12·7. The equivalent figure for all maintained primary and secondary schools was 1: 23·1. Out of 1,497 schools recognised as efficient, nearly three quarters had a ratio more generous than 1: 15, some 400 schools better than 1: 10 and about 100 schools better than 1: 7·5. The average ratio in public schools was 1: 11·6, compared with 1: 16·8 in maintained grammar schools.

68. But these figures taken in isolation would be misleading. They take no account of the complicating factors of boarding and the relative ages of pupils, nor do they differentiate between qualified and unqualified teachers. Boarding schools need more teachers than day schools—though opinions vary on how many more. A comparison of maintained boarding grammar schools with maintained day grammar schools shows that an average addition of about a sixth of the normal day school teaching staff complement is found in boarding schools. Research alone would show how valid such a staffing increment is; but in order to compare the staff ratios in the two sectors we have used this yardstick and applied a similar staff weighting to independent schools.

69. Secondly, account must be taken of the age of the pupils. For example, sixth formers generally require more staff than first formers because they are taught in smaller groups. To a lesser extent this applies to fifth formers as well, just as (whether rightly or wrongly) further down the age structure children in the maintained primary schools are taught in larger classes than those in secondary schools. Some weighting should, therefore, be given to allow for this when comparing staffing ratios.

70. In Table 13, to take account of boarding staffing needs, we have counted each boarding pupil as $1\frac{1}{6}$ pupils. To allow for the age differential, we have applied ratios similar to those reflecting the *relative* class sizes in maintained schools at different ages. It must be emphasised that, while over the whole range of schools these weightings probably provide a satisfactory comparison, they cannot be applied to individual schools. For example, a school with a large sixth form may be able to organise its pupils in sets of much the same size as the classes in the lower schools, whereas a small sixth offering a wide range of subjects will be very expensive in terms of teaching staff. It is, however, clear from Table 13 that the independent schools are substantially more generously staffed than the maintained schools.

Qualifications of teachers

71. It is necessary, however, to take account of the fact that not all teachers in

independent schools would be regarded as qualified teachers in the maintained sector. We attempted an analysis of the numbers of teachers in independent schools who would be regarded as qualified—for the public schools,
through our survey; for other recognised efficient schools, from a sample of
returns made to the Department of Education and Science. We found that
95 per cent of the teachers in public schools and 75 per cent of teachers (1966
figures) in a sample of other independent recognised efficient schools would
be regarded as qualified teachers in maintained schools.

72. Table 14 sets out the estimated numbers of teachers, qualified and
unqualified, who would be released if all recognised schools were staffed to
produce the same qualified teacher/pupil ratio (weighted by age of pupils and
for boarding pupils) as at present applies in maintained schools. The table
assumes that all unqualified teachers would be released first. The conclusion
is that there was, in 1966, a theoretical "surplus" in recognised schools of
1,532 qualified and 3,434 unqualified teachers. Taking the public schools
alone, the "surplus" was 1,317 qualified and 389 unqualified staff; this represents more than a fifth of all teachers, and about one sixth of all qualified
teachers, in the public schools.

Fees

73. Fees in the public schools vary considerably. The lowest annual tuition
fees in 1967 were under £100 and the highest over £300. Combined boarding
and tuition fees varied from less than £350 at some girls' schools to over £600
at four boys' schools and one girls' school. The average combined fee for all
boarding pupils was £510 for boys and £454 for girls. Details of the ranges of
fees are given in Tables 15 and 16. Lower fees are sometimes charged for
younger pupils and in other special circumstances at particular schools.

74. With fees of this order, the parents who meet them in full would be
expected to be mainly within Classes I and II of the five social classes defined
by the Registrar General. In the H.M.C. schools surveyed by Mr. Kalton, the
parents of over 80 per cent of the day boys and 92 per cent of the boarders
were in those classes, while the remainder were mostly in the non-manual half
of Social Class III. Our questionnaires to other boys' public schools (G.B.A.
members) and to girls' schools reveal a similar picture (see Appendix 6).

Curriculum

75. We next consider briefly the type of curriculum followed at public
schools. This is common to almost all boys' schools and would apply also to a
number of girls' schools; but there are significant differences in girls' schools,
which we examine in Chapter 4, referring meanwhile more specifically to boy's
schools.

76. Boys' public schools normally admit pupils at the age of 13 after an
examination designed to test their achievement (either the Common Entrance
or a more difficult scholarship examination). They have usually attended
preparatory schools in which much of the teaching is geared to these examinations. The public schools see their academic business as providing an
integrated five year course leading past the 'O' level examination to 'A' level
and beyond. Almost all boys stay on until they are over 17. Over 40 per cent
of the boys at any one time are in the sixth form.

77. There is no such systematic continuity in the curriculum of most maintained secondary schools. Their pupils, starting usually at 11, have come from primary schools in which the approach to the curriculum varies widely. Many of those who go to secondary modern or comprehensive schools leave at 15 or 16 without taking a sixth form course—although, particularly in comprehensive schools, there is a development of sixth form courses which are not directed to 'A' level.

78. The parents of public school boys tend to have in mind a much more specific range of careers for their sons than those of boys in maintained schools. With very few exceptions, they care greatly that their sons shall do well—and have had this in mind when making the considerable financial "investment" which is entailed. There thus tends to be a concentration of aim by public school staffs and parents alike, which is brought to bear on the boys. This has its counterpart, sometimes very strongly, in grammar schools, but even here the attitudes and aims of parents, staff and pupils tend perhaps to vary more widely than in public schools. The continuous interest of a boarding school housemaster or tutor in the work done by his boys can in particular be a powerful incentive towards effort and achievement.

79. The public schools, with a few exceptions, have traditionally accepted boys with a wide range of academic ability. In the past they educated both exceptionally able boys who passed with flying colours into the universities and others, some of whom failed even to collect 'O' levels. Both the clever and the far from clever followed much the same curriculum and were prepared, as far as possible, for the same examinations. In days gone by the wind was tempered to the shorn lamb by holding out to him ways of 'succeeding' in school life other than by academic prowess. Indeed, only a generation ago the tradition of 'character-building' and the obsession with excellence at games was still paramount in many schools and, in some, intellectual or artistic or scientific pursuits were suspect not only among boys but even among numbers of the masters.

80. But after the war the public schools made a drive for academic attainment, not only among the clever but among the average boys. The direct grant and maintained grammar schools had been greatly improved. The public schools were faced with fierce competition for university places and entry to careers dependent on qualifications rather than on family background and by the persistent influence of public examinations as the key to obtaining these qualifications. As a result, the best possible academic achievement is now held up as the goal for all boys and a number of the schools have deliberately raised the standard of academic attainment on entry.

81. But there is one essential difference between the public school system and the maintained system as a whole. The maintained system has always had to recognise that some children cannot cope with a specifically academic course. The introduction of the C.S.E.[1] type of examination is only the latest further

---

[1] The Certificate of Secondary Education; an examination reflecting the work of the schools and the needs of the pupils rather than entrance requirements for higher education. It is conducted regionally or locally, and there is teacher control of the syllabus and examinations. The standard is roughly that of pupils in the second and third fifths of the ability range, i.e. those 16 year olds who would not normally attempt the G.C.E. in four or more subjects. The aim is to reflect, and not inhibit, the originality of the work being done in the schools.

recognition of this fact. The public schools on the other hand have never overtly recognised that their least able pupils might have different needs. The range of ability in the public schools is not matched by a corresponding breadth in the curriculum, and the curriculum has not always been suitable for the less able boys.

The character of the public schools; their ethos

82. We shall not attempt to give a description of the character and ethos of the schools. Individual schools differ considerably, and any general description, if short, would be bound to be something of a caricature. Our detailed knowledge of a wider range of schools is in any case inevitably limited. Members of the Commission, usually in groups of two or three, have visited 44 public schools and have gained many valuable first-hand impressions, even if those impressions are sketchy. We have sampled the vast literature on the public schools. We have had the benefit of some of the recent research conducted by Dr. Lambert, and financed by the Department, which is partly based on long visits (lasting often over a period of weeks) which Dr. Lambert and other members of his team have paid to boarding schools, in the course of which, they have studied with an anthropological eye the social behaviour of the tribe. The evidence we received from outside bodies contained a great deal of material. From all this we have formed our own judgements, and these will be found in the body of our report.

83. While we do not attempt to describe the schools, there is a general point to be made about the kind of institution they are, which has a particular bearing on our recommendations, and to which attention is particularly drawn by the work of Dr. Lambert. Like any residential institution, of whatever kind, a boarding school exercises a pervasive influence on those who live in it; such influences of course particularly affect the young. Children learn from every aspect of their environment, and in the case of a boarding school that environment for quite long periods of time is provided almost totally by the school. They learn not only from teachers in the form-room, but from teachers out of it, from other boys, on the games field, and everywhere. The traditional public schools explicitly and purposefully seized this point, and fashioned the whole environment to produce a particular kind of learning experience, to inculcate particular sorts of values, and to form their pupils in a particular kind of culture.

84. In recent years, public schools have been changing their assumptions and aims, diversifying and opening up their culture. The change of emphasis to academic achievement, a decline in the importance of team games, a greater concern for the arts, and some dismantling of the complex disciplinary machine, are all, in many schools, conspicuous. Nevertheless, it remains true— and it could not but remain true—that their activities are based on the assumptions and aspirations of the British middle class, from which their pupils come and upon which their fees depend. The changes the schools are undergoing mirror, and no doubt to some extent are mirrored by, changes in the expectations and outlook of the middle classes; what has not changed is the existence of an intimate relation between the two.

Table 1

Number of public, independent, direct grant grammar and maintained secondary schools in England and Wales at January, 1967

	BOYS				GIRLS				MIXED				ALL SCHOOLS TOTAL
	Mainly boarding	Mainly day	Day only	Total	Mainly boarding	Mainly day	Day only	Total	Mainly boarding	Mainly day	Day only	Total	
Public schools	103	19	8	130	80	37	23	140	3	—	—	3	273
All independent recognised efficient secondary schools (including public schools)	173	43	34	250	156	131	96	383	44	31	39	114	747
Other independent secondary schools	62	27	44	133	17	34	55	106	15	55	225	295	534
Direct grant grammar schools	14	26	42	82	1	20	74	95	—	1	1	2	179
Maintained secondary schools	12	63	1,126	1,201	1	23	1,185	1,209	6	34	3,279	3,319	5,729
Totals	261	159	1,246	1,666	175	208	1,410	1,793	65	121	3,544	3,730	7,189

Source: Department of Education and Science returns for January, 1967.

Notes: 1. A school having pupils predominantly of one sex and under 12 pupils of the opposite sex, or which is mixed in its junior department only, is classified according to the sex of the majority of its pupils.

2. A mainly boarding school for the purposes of this table is taken as a school in which 50 per cent or more of the pupils are boarders. A mainly day school is a school with some boarders but less than 50 per cent and a day school is one which has no boarders.

3. Independent schools have been classified as secondary if they make provision for pupils aged 15 or over even though they may have some pupils of primary school age.

4. The figures for independent recognised efficient schools include those for public schools.

Table 2

Number of independent preparatory (or pre-preparatory) and maintained primary schools in England and Wales at January, 1967

	Boys Schools				Girls Schools				Mixed Schools				All Schools Total
	Mainly boarding	Mainly day	Day only	Total	Mainly boarding	Mainly day	Day only	Total	Mainly boarding	Mainly day	Day only	Total	
Independent recognised efficient schools	272	96	71	439	15	9	35	59	14	39	199	252	750
Independent non-recognised schools	27	22	69	118	—	1	30	31	4	53	882	939	1,088
Maintained primary schools	1	1	223	225	—	—	239	239	1	9	22,357	22,367	22,831
Totals	300	119	363	782	15	10	304	329	19	101	23,438	23,558	24,669

Source: Department of Education and Science returns for January, 1967.

Notes: 1. A school having pupils predominantly of one sex which has less than 12 pupils of the opposite sex is classified according to the sex of the majority of its pupils.

2. A school has been classified as primary if it admits below the age of 11 and makes no provision for pupils aged 15 or over.

Table 3

Pupils in different types of school in England and Wales at January, 1967
(both Primary and Secondary)

	Day pupils only			Boarders only			Total day and boarding			Totals as percentage of Head 1
	Boys	Girls	Total	Boys	Girls	Total	Boys	Girls	Total	
1. Number of pupils in all schools (excluding special schools)	3,939,971	3,788,166	7,728,137	104,248	48,337	152,585	4,044,219	3,836,503	7,880,722	100
2. Number of pupils in maintained schools	3,750,386	3,566,480	7,316,866	8,610	2,634	11,244	3,758,996	3,569,114	7,328,110	93·0
3. Number of pupils in direct grant institution, technical and grammar schools	49,755	57,172	106,927	8,487	2,153	10,640	58,242	59,325	117,567*	1·5
4. Number of pupils in all independent schools (including pupils at 5, 6 and 7 below)	139,830	164,514	304,344	87,151	43,550	130,701	226,981	208,064	435,045	5·5
5. Number of pupils in independent schools recognised efficient (including pupils at 7 below)	81,204	103,121	184,325	80,342	40,512	120,854	161,546	143,633	305,179	3·9
6. Number of pupils in non-recognised independent schools	58,626	61,393	120,019	6,809	3,038	9,847	65,435	64,431	129,866	1·6
7. Number of pupils in public schools	22,002	22,279	44,281	41,349	21,635	62,984	63,351	43,914	107,265	1·4

Source: Department of Education and Science returns for January, 1967.

*The total includes 1,322 pupils at direct grant institutions which are not within our terms of reference.

Table 4

Secondary² pupils in different types of school in England and Wales at January, 1967

	Day pupils only			Boarders only			Total day and boarding			Totals as percentage of Head 1
	Boys	Girls	Total	Boys	Girls	Total	Boys	Girls	Total	
1. Number of pupils in all schools (excluding special schools)¹	—	—	—	—	—	—	1,607,369	1,528,249	3,135,618	100
2. Number of pupils in maintained schools	1,447,723	1,374,256	2,821,979	8,370	2,502	10,872	1,456,093	1,376,758	2,832,851	90·3
3. Number of pupils in direct grant institution, technical and grammar schools	43,996	47,100	91,096	7,850	1,963	9,813	51,846	49,063	100,909	3·2
4. Number of pupils in all independent schools (including pupils at 5, 6 and 7 below)¹	—	—	—	—	—	—	99,430	102,428	201,858	6·4
5. Number of pupils in independent schools recognised efficient (including pupils at 7 below)	32,065	50,635	82,700	51,917	34,573	86,490	83,982	85,208	169,190	5·4
6. Number of pupils in non-recognised independent schools¹	—	—	—	—	—	—	15,448	17,220	32,668	1·0
7. Number of pupils in public schools	17,731	14,600	32,331	39,674	20,267	59,941	57,405	34,867	92,272	2·9

Source: Department of Education and Science returns for January, 1967.

¹ The ages of boarding pupils in non-recognised schools are not available, and we cannot therefore analyse either boarding or day pupils in these schools into primary and secondary categories.

² For the purpose of this table the term 'secondary pupil' includes:
   (i) all pupils in maintained secondary schools, in the upper schools of direct grant schools and in independent secondary schools.
   (ii) in the case of independent schools with both primary and secondary departments, all pupils aged 12 and over together with two thirds of those aged 11 years.

Table 5

Primary[2] pupils in different types of school in England and Wales at January, 1967

	Day pupils only			Boarders only			Total day and boarding			Totals as percentage of Head 1
	Boys	Girls	Total	Boys	Girls	Total	Boys	Girls	Total	
1. Number of pupils in all schools (excluding special schools)[1]	—	—	—	—	—	—	2,436,850	2,308,254	4,745,104	100
2. Number of pupils in maintained schools	2,302,663	2,192,224	4,494,887	240	132	372	2,302,903	2,192,356	4,495,259	94·7
3. Number of pupils in direct grant institution, technical and grammar schools	5,759	10,072	15,831	637	190	827	6,396	10,262	16,658	0·4
4. Number of pupils in all independent schools (including pupils at 5, 6 and 7 below)[1]	—	—	—	—	—	—	127,551	105,636	233,187	4·9
5. Number of pupils in independent schools recognised efficient (including pupils at 7 below)	49,139	52,486	101,625	28,425	5,939	34,364	77,564	58,425	135,989	2·9
6. Number of pupils in non-recognised independent schools[1]	—	—	—	—	—	—	49,987	47,211	97,198	2·0
7. Number of pupils in public schools	4,271	7,679	11,950	1,675	1,368	3,043	5,946	9,047	14,993	0·3

Source: Department of Education and Science returns for January, 1967.

[1] The ages of boarding pupils in non-recognised schools are not available, and we cannot therefore analyse either boarding or day pupils in these schools into primary and secondary categories.

[2] For the purpose of this table the term 'primary pupil' includes:
 (i) all pupils in maintained primary schools, in the lower schools of direct grant schools and in independent primary schools.
 (ii) in the case of independent schools with both primary and secondary departments, all pupils aged 10 years and under together with one third of those aged 11 years.

Table 6

Number of pupils in various age groups in different types of school (England and Wales), 1967

	Pupils aged 6			Pupils aged 10			Pupils aged 14			Pupils aged 17		
	Boys	Girls	Total	Boys	Girls	Total	Boys	Girls	Total	Boys	Girls	Total
Public schools	153	754	907	1,885	2,332	4,217	10,837	6,043	16,880	7,744	2,849	10,593
% of Total	0·04	0·21	0·13	0·55	0·71	0·63	3·31	1·91	2·63	12·30	5·62	9·32
All independent recognised efficient schools	5,663	6,959	12,622	13,466	10,780	24,246	15,810	15,154	30,964	9,802	5,786	15,588
% of Total	1·47	1·90	1·68	3·95	3·30	3·63	4·83	4·80	4·82	15·56	11·41	13·71
Other independent schools	8,078	7,226	15,304	5,236	5,709	10,945	3,029	3,581	6,610	730	565	1,295
% of Total	2·10	1·97	2·04	1·54	1·75	1·64	0·93	1·13	1·03	1·16	1·11	1·14
Direct grant grammar schools	301	1,188	1,489	2,145	2,258	4,403	7,572	7,700	15,272	5,289	4,901	10,190
% of Total	0·08	0·32	0·20	0·63	0·69	0·66	2·31	2·44	2·38	8·40	9·66	8·96
Maintained grammar schools	—	—	—	245	281	526	55,066	57,233	112,299	34,000	29,056	63,056
% of Total	—	—	—	0·07	0·09	0·08	16·83	18·12	17·47	53·99	57·29	55·46
All maintained schools	370,853	351,098	721,951	319,995	308,130	628,125	300,720	289,411	590,131	47,154	39,462	86,616
% of Total	96·35	95·81	96·09	93·88	94·26	94·07	91·93	91·63	91·78	74·88	77·81	76·19
Total	384,895	366,471	751,366	340,842	326,877	667,719	327,131	315,846	642,977	62,975	50,714	113,689

Source: Department of Education and Science returns for January, 1967.

Notes: 1. The figures exclude pupils in special schools and approved schools and children educated otherwise than at school.
2. The figures for direct grant grammar schools include pupils in their lower schools.

Table 7

Sixth form numbers in public schools (*England and Wales*) at January, 1967

No. of pupils in sixth forms	Number of schools			
	Boys' schools	Mixed schools	Girls' schools	All schools
0 – 29	3	—	46	49
30 – 59	13	—	56	69
60 – 89	23	3	23	49
90 – 119	14	—	8	22
120 – 179	33	—	6	39
180 – 239	17	—	1	18
240 or more	27	—	—	27
Total	130	3	140	273
Average size of sixth form of public schools	157	74	49	101
Average size of sixth form of maintained grammar schools	125	107	96	109

Source: Department of Education and Science returns for January, 1967.

Table 8
Destination of leavers from different types of school in 1966 (England and Wales)

Numbers and percentages

Types of schools	All destinations			Oxford and Cambridge			Other Universities			Total Universities			Colleges of Education			Other full-time Further Education			Employment		
	Boys	Girls	Total	Boys	Girls	Total	Boys	Girls	Total	Boys	Girls	Total	Boys	Girls	Total	Boys	Girls	Total	Boys	Girls	Total
1. Public schools Number of leavers	10,578	5,170	15,748	1,491	141	1,632	3,145	933	4,078	4,636	1,074	5,710	97	421	518	2,179	2,710	4,889	4,551	1,609	6,160
Percentage[1]	*3·29*	*1·70*	*2·52*	*38·13*	*18·92*	*35·05*	*14·64*	*9·02*	*12·81*	*18·25*	*9·69*	*15·65*	*2·11*	*2·76*	*2·61*	*8·60*	*8·19*	*8·37*	*1·71*	*0·66*	*1·21*
2. All independent recognised efficient schools Number of leavers	15,972	14,328	30,300	1,771	191	1,962	3,486	1,467	4,953	5,257	1,658	6,915	219	1,029	1,248	3,418	5,175	8,593	7,078	6,466	13,544
Percentage[1]	*4·98*	*4·74*	*4·86*	*45·29*	*25·64*	*42·15*	*16·23*	*14·20*	*15·57*	*20·70*	*14·47*	*18·96*	*4·78*	*6·77*	*6·31*	*13·50*	*15·65*	*14·72*	*2·67*	*2·66*	*2·66*
3. Direct grant grammar schools Number of leavers	7,934	6,934	14,868	610	261	871	2,522	1,487	4,009	3,132	1,748	4,880	273	1,276	1,549	1,384	1,287	2,671	3,145	2,623	5,768
Percentage[1]	*2·47*	*2·29*	*2·39*	*15·60*	*35·03*	*18·71*	*11·74*	*14·39*	*12·60*	*12·33*	*15·78*	*13·38*	*5·96*	*8·39*	*7·83*	*5·47*	*3·89*	*4·51*	*1·18*	*1·08*	*1·13*
4. Maintained grammar schools Number of leavers	60,009	58,983	118,992	1,446	290	1,736	13,303	6,728	20,031	14,748	7,018	21,766	3,102	10,293	13,395	7,545	10,455	18,000	34,614	31,217	65,831
Percentage[1]	*18·70*	*19·50*	*19·09*	*36·98*	*38·93*	*37·29*	*61·93*	*65·11*	*62·96*	*58·08*	*63·35*	*59·68*	*67·68*	*67·67*	*67·68*	*29·80*	*31·61*	*30·83*	*13·04*	*12·85*	*12·95*
5. All maintained schools Number of leavers	296,896	281,115	578,011	1,529	293	1,822	15,474	7,380	22,854	17,003	7,673	24,676	4,091	12,905	16,996	20,520	26,610	47,130	255,282	233,927	489,209
Percentage[1]	*92·55*	*92·97*	*92·75*	*39·10*	*39·33*	*39·14*	*72·03*	*71·41*	*71·83*	*66·96*	*69·29*	*67·66*	*89·26*	*84·85*	*85·87*	*81·04*	*80·45*	*80·71*	*96·15*	*96·26*	*96·20*
Total leavers	320,802	302,377	623,179	3,910	745	4,655	21,482	10,334	31,816	25,392	11,079	36,471	4,583	15,210	19,793	25,322	33,072	58,394	265,505	243,016	508,521

Notes: [1] Figures in ordinary type represent the number of leavers from each category of school going to each destination. The figures in italics represent those numbers expressed as a percentage of the total number of leavers from all categories of school going to each destination.

[2] Leavers entering temporary employment before continuing their education have been counted under the appropriate category of continued education. Those entering university following temporary employment have been divided between "Oxford and Cambridge" and "Other Universities" in the same proportions as those going direct to universities from school.

[3] Employment includes pupils whose destinations were not known and those who left for other reasons.

[4] Head 2 of the Table includes head 1 and head 5 includes head 4

Source: Questionnaires to schools (see Appendix 6).
Department of Education and Science returns for a 10 per cent sample of school leavers in the academic year 1965/66.

Table 9 Size of public schools in England and Wales at January, 1967. No. of schools of different sizes by pupil numbers

	Total No. of schools	Average size	All pupils						Pupils of 11 years and over only					
			Up to 200	201–400	401–600	601–800	801–1000	1001 or more	Up to 200	201–400	401–600	601–800	801–1000	1001 or more
BOYS														
Mainly boarding	103	419	6	48	33	12	3	1	8	51	32	10	1	1
Mainly day	19	683	—	3	3	7	5	1	1	4	5	8	—	1
Day only	8	796	—	1	—	5	1	1	—	1	1	5	—	1
GIRLS														
Mainly boarding	80	258	24	46	9	—	1	—	31	42	6	—	1	—
Mainly day	37	379	5	18	11	3	—	—	11	21	5	—	—	—
Day only	23	385	1	12	8	1	1	—	10	10	3	—	—	—
MIXED														
Mainly boarding	3	388	—	2	1	—	—	—	—	2	1	—	—	—
Mainly day	—	—	—	—	—	—	—	—	—	—	—	—	—	—
Day only	—	—	—	—	—	—	—	—	—	—	—	—	—	—
TOTALS	273	393	36	130	65	28	11	3	61	131	53	23	2	3
Totals as percentage of all public schools			13·2	47·6	23·8	10·2	4·0	1·1	22·3	48·0	19·4	8·4	0·7	1·1
Equivalent percentage of all maintained secondary schools			6·4	31·4	36·7	17·1	5·0	3·4	6·4	31·4	36·7	17·1	5·0	3·4

Source: Department of Education and Science returns for January, 1967.

Table 10   *Number of boarders at independent recognised efficient schools with 25 per cent or more boarders at January, 1967*

		Numbers of schools having the following numbers of boarding pupils										Total No. of schools	Total No. of pupils	Average No.
		0–50	51–100	101–150	151–200	201–250	251–300	301–400	401–500	501–600	Over 600			
BOYS	Public schools	—	2	9	8	16	20	23	15	10	11	114	40,151	352
	Independent recognised efficient secondary schools (including public schools)	17	27	26	16	25	21	25	15	10	11	193	49,051	254
	Independent recognised efficient primary schools	79	184	51	4	2	—	—	—	—	—	320	23,520	74
GIRLS	Public schools	—	11	19	24	16	7	9	7	—	1	94	19,960	212
	Independent recognised efficient secondary schools (including public schools)	22	69	44	31	23	8	9	7	—	1	214	31,167	146
	Independent recognised efficient primary schools	6	11	4	—	—	—	—	—	—	—	21	1,531	73
MIXED	Public schools	—	—	—	—	1	—	1	1	—	—	3	946	315
	Independent recognised efficient secondary schools (including public schools)	10	21	9	3	4	—	3	2	—	1	53	7,037	133
	Independent recognised efficient primary schools	21	6	2	—	—	1	—	—	—	—	30	1,462	49

Source: Department of Education and Science returns for January, 1967.
Note: The boarders include pupils below secondary school age attending schools classified as secondary and pupils of secondary school age attending those classified as primary.

Table 11

Number of public schools, recognised efficient independent secondary schools, direct grant grammar schools and maintained secondary schools in each region at January, 1967

	Public schools			*Independent secondary schools recognised as efficient[1] (including public schools)*		*Direct grant grammar schools*		*Maintained secondary schools*		*Total*
	Boys	*Girls*	*Total*	*% Col. 11*	*No. of schools*	*% Col. 11*	*No. of schools*	*% Col. 11*	*No. of schools*	*% Col. 11*	*Total of Cols. 5, 7 & 9*
	1	*2*	*3*	*4*	*5*	*6*	*7*	*8*	*9*	*10*	*11*
Northern	4	7	11	2·1	38	7·1	11	2·1	483	90·8	532
Yorkshire & Humberside	7[2]	7	14	2·3	29	4·7	18	2·9	569	92·4	616
North West	4	5	9	0·9	36	3·9	55	5·9	844	90·2	935
East Midland	10	4	14	2·9	31	6·5	8	1·7	439	91·8	478
West Midland	12	13	25	3·5	58	8·2	10	1·4	640	90·4	708
East Anglia	5	4	9	3·6	29	11·8	10	4·1	207	84·1	246
Wales	4	4	8	2·0	33	8·2	4	1·0	364	90·8	401
South East	61[3]	73	134	6·3	339	16·0	42	2·0	1734	82·0	2115
South West	26	23	49	8·5	108	18·7	21	3·6	449	77·7	578
Total	133	140	273	4·1	701	10·6	179	2·7	5729	86·7	6609

Source: Department of Education and Science returns, 1967.

Notes: [1] Schools making provision for pupils aged 15 or over.

[2] Includes 1 mixed school.

[3] Includes 2 mixed schools.

Table 12

Number of pupils in public schools, recognised efficient independent
secondary schools, direct grant grammar schools and maintained
secondary schools in each region at January, 1967

	Public schools		Independent secondary schools recognised as efficient (including public schools)		Direct grant grammar schools		Maintained secondary schools		Total
	Pupils	*% of Col. 9*	*Pupils[1]*	*% of Col. 9*	*Pupils*	*% of Col. 9*	*Pupils*	*% of Col. 9*	*Total of Cols. 3, 5 & 7*
	1	*2*	*3*	*4*	*5*	*6*	*7*	*8*	*9*
Northern	3,622	1·6	8,909	4·0	6,842	3·0	208,051	93·0	223,802
Yorkshire & Humberside	4,652	1·5	6,334	2·0	12,391	4·0	292,396	94·0	311,121
North West	5,029	1·1	10,419	2·4	39,091	8·9	388,142	88·7	437,652
East Midland	5,563	2·5	7,662	3·5	5,535	2·5	207,115	94·0	220,312
West Midland	11,038	3·3	14,359	4·3	6,715	2·0	312,629	93·7	333,703
East Anglia	3,213	3·3	6,128	6·2	5,148	5·2	86,967	88·6	98,243
Wales	2,035	1·1	5,788	3·1	1,710	0·9	178,304	96·0	185,802
South East	54,484	5·1	86,690	8·2	27,613	2·6	945,430	89·2	1,059,733
South West	17,629	7·0	25,396	10·1	11,200	4·5	213,817	85·4	250,413
Total	107,265	3·4	171,685	5·5	116,245	3·7	2,832,851	90·7	3,120,781

Source: Department of Education and Science returns, 1967.

[1] Pupils aged 11 or over in secondary schools (as defined for Table 11 Note 1).

Table 13

Teacher/pupil ratios in different types of school at January, 1967 (England and Wales)

Category	Number of schools	Number of pupils				Number in sixth form	All boarders	Number of teachers (part-time as full-time equivalent)	Un-weighted teacher/pupil ratio	Weighted teacher/pupil ratios	
		2–10	11–14	15	16+						
1	2	3	4	5	6	7	8	9	10	11	12
Maintained primary and secondary schools (including grammar schools)	28,560	4,300,370	2,374,635	372,199	280,906	181,760	11,244	317,507	1 : 23·08	1 : 19·84	1 : 19·14
Maintained grammar schools	1,236	529	412,295	108,034	174,040	135,163	6,862	41,369	1 : 16·80	1 : 21·90	1 : 20·09
Direct grant grammar schools	179	16,034	58,266	14,852	27,093	23,743	9,318	7,033	1 : 16·53	1 : 20·55	1 : 19·37
Independent schools recognised as efficient (including public schools)	1,497	110,737	120,160	29,447	44,835	37,132	120,854	23,983	1 : 12·72	1 : 14·30	1 : 13·57
Independent schools not recognised	1,622	91,314	27,710	5,786	5,056	not available	9,847	9,367	1 : 13·86	1 : 11·54	not available
Public schools	273	13,186	48,676	16,627	28,776	27,565	62,984	9,221	1 : 11·6	1 : 16·0	1 : 15·3

Source: Department of Education and Science returns for January, 1967.

Note: Weightings applied as follows:

Column 11
(i) Boarders multiplied by seven sixths.
(ii) Pupils aged 10 years or under multiplied by two thirds.
(iii) Pupils aged 15 years multiplied by four thirds.
(iv) Pupils aged 16 years or over multiplied by two.

Column 12
(i) Boarders multiplied by seven sixths.
(ii) Pupils aged 10 years or under multiplied by two thirds.
(iii) Pupils in the sixth form multiplied by two.

Table 14

Ratios of full-time qualified teachers to pupils in different types of school at January, 1967 (England and Wales)

Category of school	Number of teachers in schools		Teacher/ pupil ratio[2]	Number of teachers released if pupil/ teacher ratios as for maintained schools	
	qualified	unqualified	(qualified full-time teachers only)	qualified	unqualified
All maintained schools	297,023	5,379	1:21·2	—	5,379
Public schools	7,788	389	1:17·6	1,317	389
All independent recognised efficient schools[1] (including public schools)	16,764	3,434	1:19·3	1,532	3,434

Source: Department of Education and Science annual returns for January, 1967.
Notes: [1] Numbers of teachers in independent schools estimated on a 1 in 14 sample.
[2] Weighted for boarding pupils and by age of pupils as in Column 11 of Table 13.

Table 15

Fees for day pupils at public schools, January, 1967 (England and Wales)

£	Number of schools		
	Boys	Girls	Mixed
Under 100	2	4	—
100 – 149	3	13	—
150 – 199	22	42	—
200 – 249	33	31	1
250 – 299	18	6	2
300 or more	15	1	—
Average fee per pupil	£213	£172	£201

The average fee for day pupils in all public schools was £192.

Source: Department of Education and Science returns for January, 1967.
Notes: 1. Tuition fees were not available for 6 boys' and 12 girls' schools with day pupils.
2. Average fee calculated by multiplying the numbers of day pupils at each school by the annual fee charged at January 1967 and then dividing the aggregated total for all schools by the total number of day pupils.

Table 16

Fees for boarding pupils at public schools, January, 1967

£	Number of schools		
	Boys	*Girls*	*Mixed*
Under £300	—	5	—
300 – 349	—	3	—
350 – 399	7	22	—
400 – 449	22	33	1
450 – 499	38	32	1
500 – 549	31	14	1
550 – 599	18	4	—
600 or more	4	1	—
Average fee per pupil	£510	£454	£472

The average fee for boarding pupils in all public schools was £491.

Source: Department of Education and Science returns January, 1967.

Notes: 1. Boarding fees were not available for 2 boys' schools and 3 girls' schools with boarding pupils.
2. Average fee calculated by multiplying the numbers of boarders at each school by the annual fee charged at January 1967 and then dividing the aggregated total for all schools by the total number of boarders.

Diagram 1

PROPORTIONS OF PUPILS IN VARIOUS AGE GROUPS AT DIFFERENT TYPES OF SCHOOL AT JANUARY, 1967   (ENGLAND AND WALES)

BOYS

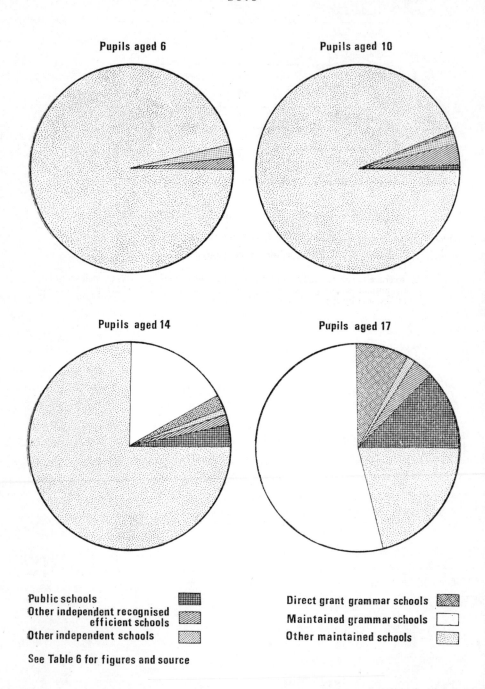

Pupils aged 6

Pupils aged 10

Pupils aged 14

Pupils aged 17

Public schools

Other independent recognised efficient schools

Other independent schools

Direct grant grammar schools

Maintained grammar schools

Other maintained schools

See Table 6 for figures and source

Diagram 1

PROPORTIONS OF PUPILS IN VARIOUS AGE GROUPS AT DIFFERENT TYPES OF SCHOOL AT JANUARY, 1967 (ENGLAND AND WALES)

GIRLS

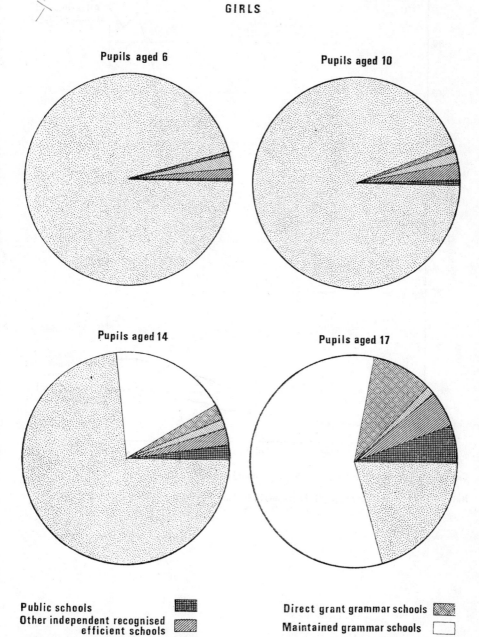

Pupils aged 6

Pupils aged 10

Pupils aged 14

Pupils aged 17

Public schools

Other independent recognised efficient schools

Other independent schools

Direct grant grammar schools

Maintained grammar schools

Other maintained schools

See Table 6 for figures and source

1—c

Diagram 2

NUMBERS OF 17 YEAR OLDS IN ALL MAINTAINED SECONDARY SCHOOLS, DIRECT GRANT GRAMMAR SCHOOLS AND INDEPENDENT RECOGNISED EFFICIENT SCHOOLS   (1947 —— 1967)

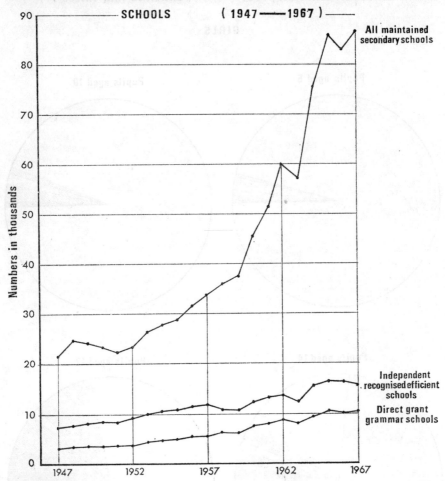

Source : Department of Education and Science annual returns

Note   : The figures relate to pupils in schools in England and Wales only (excluding those in special schools)

Diagram 3

PERCENTAGE OF 17 YEAR OLDS TO 14 YEAR OLDS 3 YEARS EARLIER FOR MAINTAINED SECONDARY, DIRECT GRANT GRAMMAR AND INDEPENDENT RECOGNISED EFFICIENT SCHOOLS   (1951—1967)

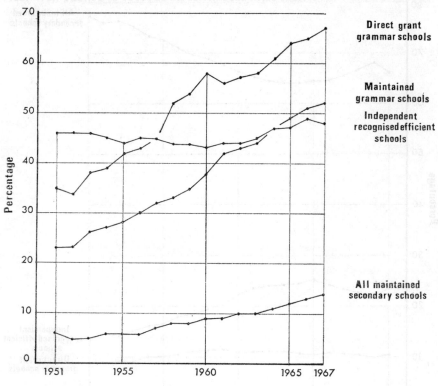

Source : Department of Education and Science annual returns

Note   : The percentages relate to pupils in schools in England and Wales (excluding special schools)

Diagram 4

17 YEAR OLDS IN ALL MAINTAINED SECONDARY SCHOOLS, DIRECT GRANT GRAMMAR SCHOOLS AND INDEPENDENT RECOGNISED EFFICIENT SCHOOLS SHOWN AS PERCENTAGES OF THE TOTAL 17 YEAR OLDS IN ALL THREE TYPES OF SCHOOL (1947–1967)

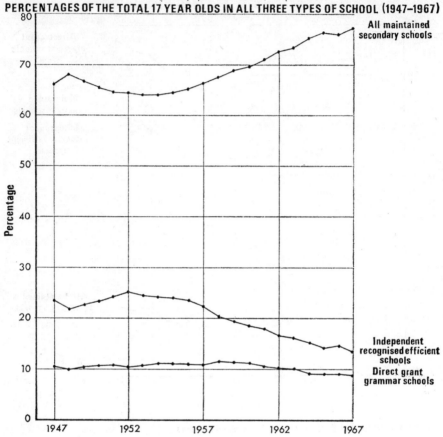

Source: Department of Education and Science annual returns

Note   : The percentages relate to pupils in schools in England and Wales (excluding special schools)

Diagram 5

DESTINATION OF LEAVERS FROM VARIOUS TYPES OF SCHOOL, 1965 — 66

BOYS

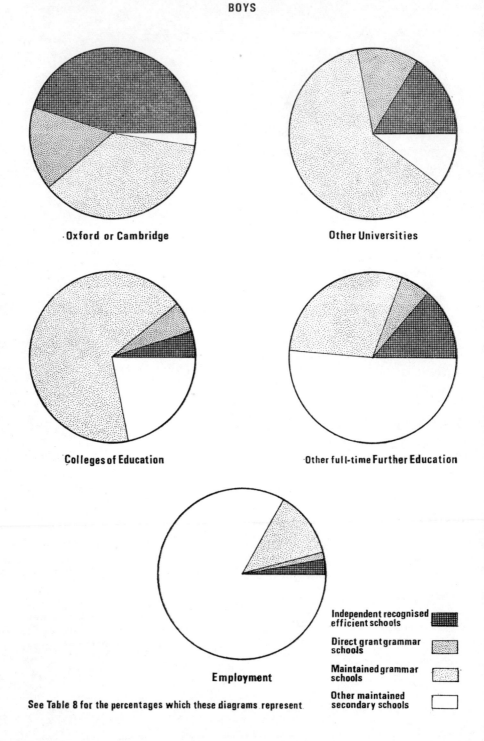

Oxford or Cambridge

Other Universities

Colleges of Education

Other full-time Further Education

Employment

Independent recognised efficient schools

Direct grant grammar schools

Maintained grammar schools

Other maintained secondary schools

See Table 8 for the percentages which these diagrams represent.

Diagram 5

DESTINATION OF LEAVERS FROM VARIOUS TYPES OF SCHOOL, 1965 — 66

GIRLS

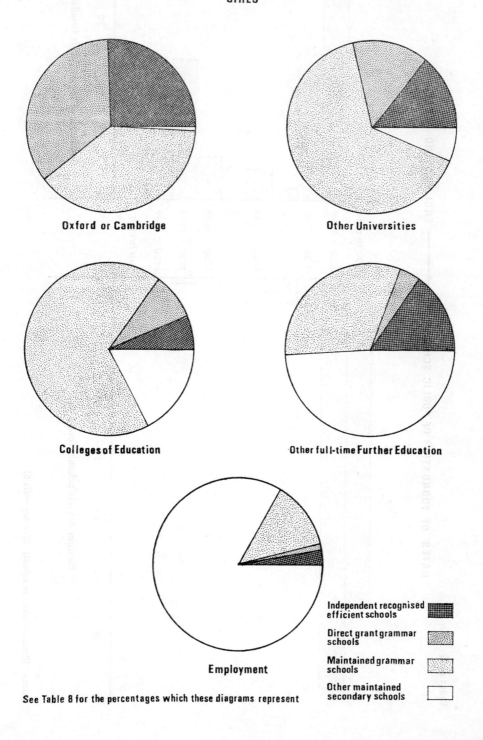

Oxford or Cambridge

Other Universities

Colleges of Education

Other full-time Further Education

Employment

Independent recognised efficient schools

Direct grant grammar schools

Maintained grammar schools

Other maintained secondary schools

See Table 8 for the percentages which these diagrams represent

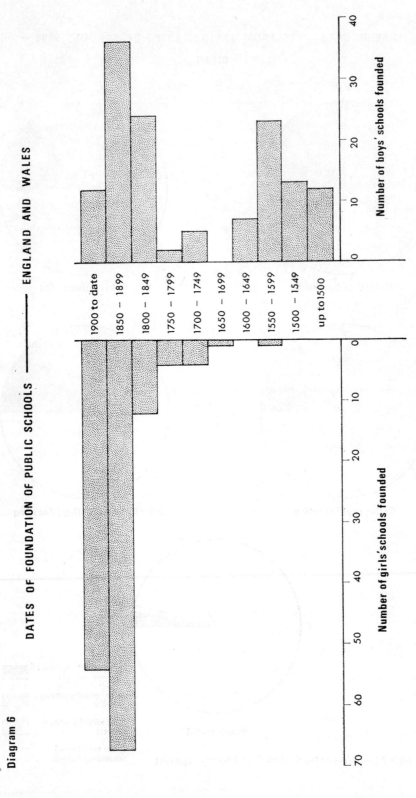

Diagram 6

DATES OF FOUNDATION OF PUBLIC SCHOOLS ——— ENGLAND AND WALES

Number of boys' schools founded

Number of girls' schools founded

Source : Questionnaires to schools (See Appendix 6)

CHAPTER 3

Divisiveness—boys' schools

85. Some people have objected to the assumption made in our terms of reference that the public schools are a divisive influence. One answer to this objection is that the public schools themselves think they are. Since 1921 more and more of them have said in public that they want to broaden their entry. As the G.B.A./H.M.C. Joint Working Party said in their evidence, "only the better off can afford to send their sons to us, and our parents therefore nearly all come from the upper income brackets and follow the occupations normal to those in those brackets". The case for broadening the entry has been advanced by the Bow Group and the Fabian Society alike, and by individuals within all the main political parties. But in what ways are the schools divisive? The following seem to us to be the most important.

School age

86. The most striking division between the children of this country occurs at eight or nine years old. For that is the age at which so many public school children start to board at preparatory schools. From then on they rarely get the chance of meeting their contemporaries in other social classes, as they would do if they went to a maintained school. They do not mix with them in term time and not often in the holidays. And this lasts for ten years. What is more, the traditions of the public schools reinforce, rather than diminish, this division. For though some of them have made efforts in the last few years to increase their contact with the local community during term time, they remain self-contained societies. Even day boys in these schools are kept within the orbit of the school. The G.B.A./H.M.C. say in their evidence: "for real parity day boys should really be day-boarders, i.e. take their full part in all the day's activities and return (home) only to do their preparation and sleep". Public schools play games chiefly against other public schools: they rarely exchange pupils or fraternise with maintained schools in their area. They belong, in a remarkable degree, to a world of their own. The schools may not seek this status; but it is thrust upon them partly by their history and partly by the class consciousness which surrounds them.

The masters

87. The masters in these schools are no less isolated from their colleagues in the nation's schools. Mr. Kalton's survey[1] showed that, in 1962-63, seventy per cent of masters at H.M.C. schools with boarding pupils had themselves been educated at H.M.C. schools, and not more than one master in five in H.M.C. independent boarding schools had taught in secondary schools, other than H.M.C. They stick in the public schools, as pupil and master, just as the masters in the maintained system stick in those schools; and neither system learns from the other.

---

[1] Tables 4.10 and 5.13 of "The Public Schools—A Factual Survey", by Graham Kalton: Longmans, Green & Co. Ltd., 1966.

Ability and class

88. The public schools educate a number of exceedingly clever boys. They also educate a number who—at any rate when they arrive—are of no more than average ability. They take pride in doing so, and it does them credit that, as Mr. Kalton's survey showed, boys of modest abilities at 11 have been able to succeed academically[1]. It would be wrong to attribute this wholly to boarding: "failure" at 11 can be similarly retrieved in comprehensive schools. Boarding probably helps. No doubt another factor is the high proportion of masters to boys. But probably the most important reason is the assured background of most of the boys. There is a well-documented body of evidence that children's educational attainment is related to home background, and that children from poor homes generally do less well than those of equivalent ability from better-off homes. One has only to read the Supplement to the Ministry of Education Annual Statistics for 1961, the Report of the Committee on Higher Education, 1963, and successive reports of the Central Advisory Council for Education[2], as well as the findings of a number of research workers[3]. Over ninety per cent of boarding pupils in boys' public schools (excluding children of armed forces personnel, who are not allocated to any social class in the official classifications) had parents in the professional or managerial classes[4]. Most of them would have been away to a good start whatever school they went to. Yet these are the children who are put into separate schools for up to ten years of teaching in small classes—at a time when teachers are in short supply.

89. It would be perfectly fair to argue that the children in maintained grammar schools are divided not only from those in the public schools but also from those in the secondary moderns—though the latter division does not begin until the age of 11. Even when the division between grammar and secondary moderns has been abolished by comprehensive education—and it will not be abolished overnight—the children of the well-to-do and the poor may still be separated by going to schools in different neighbourhoods. The better teachers may congregate in the "good" neighbourhood schools and they will stay there longer than teachers in more depressed areas. But the fact that schools will always vary in quality is not an argument for perpetuating deliberate and unnecessary forms of social and academic selection. Great

---

[1] (i) 11+ results of 32 per cent of entrants to H.M.C. independent boarding schools were known to Mr. Kalton. 18 per cent of all entrants had passed the examination and 14 per cent had failed. Only 10 per cent of pupils leaving the schools in the same year (1962–63) had failed to obtain at least four 'O' level passes in G.C.E.

   (ii) In H.M.C. day schools 11+ results were known for 72 per cent of pupils. 10 per cent of all entrants had failed the examination; 20 per cent of leavers (in the same year) had failed to obtain at least four 'O' level passes in G.C.E.

   (iii) See footnote to Chapter 10, paragraph 263, for reference to intelligence levels of public school entrants.

[2] Central Advisory Council Reports: "Early Leaving" H.M.S.O. (1954).
                                          "15 to 18" (1959).
                                          "Half our Future" (1963).
                                          "Children and their Primary Schools" (1967).

[3] For example:
   J. W. B. Douglas—"The Home and the School" MacGibbon and Kee (1964).
   Stephen Wiseman—"Education and Environment" Manchester University Press (1964).

[4] For full details of social class at al lpublic schools, see Appendix 6.

efforts are now being made to reduce these inequities and the loss of talent they entail. Progress in that direction would be frustrated if the public schools opened their doors only to those who reached high academic standards at 11 or 13. An entry of this kind from the maintained schools would produce a wider rift as the maintained schools grow more comprehensive. This is why some people argue that the public schools should be taken over to educate the under-privileged.

School buildings and grounds

90. Many public schools have the advantage of fine physical facilities. Their sites are very large: the average acreage of a boys' public boarding school is 113. Some of the living accommodation, in ancient or 19th century buildings, is Spartan, and some of the equipment and classroom facilities compare unfavourably with those of a modern maintained school. But nearly all public schools have well-stocked libraries, spacious playing fields, and new or modernised laboratories, often provided by the loyalty of old boys or parents, or by the Industrial Fund to which British firms contributed £3 million to re-equip public school laboratories a decade ago. This is greatly to the credit of those who have endowed the schools and those who have run them. At the same time, it is true that various forms of tax concessions have meant that the State has indirectly contributed to these improvements. The physical advantages of these schools contribute to setting them apart (in some cases quite literally) from other schools.

Co-education

91. A single sex boarding school must enforce another kind of divisiveness, and a common criticism of the public school system has been that, from 8 to 18, boys are cut off from girls except during the holidays. We have no evidence that, when a public school boy meets a public school girl, they behave as if each belonged to a separate species. Teen-age culture has lapped over the moats of even the most staid schools, and some have tried to encourage joint functions with neighbouring girls' schools, though still in a gingerly fashion. But there is one marked difference. In most maintained day schools boys and girls learn to work together and in all they can go out with each other if they choose in their leisure time. In boarding public schools they can rarely do so, and few of these schools are co-educational. Only one per cent of pupils aged 11 and over at public schools attend co-educational schools, compared with 36 per cent at maintained grammar schools and 60 per cent at all maintained secondary schools. Even in the small maintained boarding sector, six out of nineteen mainly boarding secondary schools admit boys and girls. There are many views on the merits and demerits of co-education, and it is not a subject on which we want to take a dogmatic stand on either side. Parents are entitled to say whether they prefer one type of school or the other. But parents should be able to choose what type of boarding they prefer and this will not be possible unless there are more co-educational schools. Many parents would prefer their sons and daughters to go to the same schools—particularly if they have special needs for boarding education due to the absence of parents abroad or other circumstances that make it harder to maintain the unity of the family. The segregation of boys from girls in boarding schools for ten of their most formative years must have a socially divisive effect.

Maintained boarding schools

92. The segregation of the sexes has its divisive effect, of course, not only in independent boarding schools; it operates also in those maintained boarding schools which are not co-educational. But, more generally, the ethos of maintained boarding schools is different from that of public schools. They are less confined by tradition, they are not fee-paying (except in the form of graduated parental contributions towards boarding costs), they do not draw many pupils from preparatory schools, and their parents have rarely been to boarding schools themselves. Their style is more like that of the maintained system as a whole and does not isolate their pupils from that system.

Who gets to the top?

93. The public schools are accused of hogging all the most important positions in the country. Is this true? We have little evidence about careers in industry and commerce. The following diagram gives some illustration of the present influence of former public school pupils in various walks of life; but the predominance of public school men *today* is no guide to what it will be thirty years from now when the present generation of public school boys are competing for the top posts against those who are now at school in the greatly improved maintained sector.

94. Yet some of the evidence which we have received on this point seems to us to be a trifle simple-minded. Some people seem to regard opportunities in various professions and senior positions as being fairly distributed if up to a half of new entrants have been at maintained schools, or if less than a half of new entrants were at public schools. But the entire independent recognised efficient sector has provided in recent years less than 19 per cent, and the public schools less than 16 per cent, of entrants to universities[1]. These are more nearly the yardsticks by which one should measure the proportions of new entrants to professions and executive positions. It is naïve to take 50: 50 as the yardstick[2].

95. The simplest case to take, since it is well documented, up to date, and should be free from any suspicion of deliberately biased selection, is recruitment to the public services, and in particular to the Administrative Classes of the Home Civil Service and the senior branch of the Diplomatic Service. The proportion of successful candidates for the Administrative Class who had been at public schools (as defined) was 35 per cent in 1936, 39 per cent in 1956 and 43 per cent in the years 1963-67 taken together. The entry from maintained schools in the years 1963-67 was 30 per cent; the remaining 27 per cent of successful candidates were almost all from direct grant schools or independent schools other than public schools. The Diplomatic Service entry in the same five year period comprised 88 successful candidates from public schools, 27 from maintained schools and 26 from other schools. For the Administrative Class, competitors from independent and maintained schools were roughly equal; in the case of the Diplomatic Service, there were about 70 per cent more candidates from independent than from maintained schools.

---

[1] See Chapter 2, Table 8.

[2] For example, the Franks Report (University of Oxford: Report of Commission of Inquiry; Vol. 1, paragraph 189) says: ". . . of the closed awards made for entry in 1965–66, only 45 per cent went to boys from independent boarding schools".

Diagram 7

THE PROPORTIONS OF INDEPENDENT AND DIRECT GRANT SCHOOL PUPILS AT VARIOUS STAGES OF EDUCATION COMPARED WITH THE PROPORTIONS FROM THOSE SCHOOLS IN A SELECTION OF PROFESSIONS AND POSITIONS

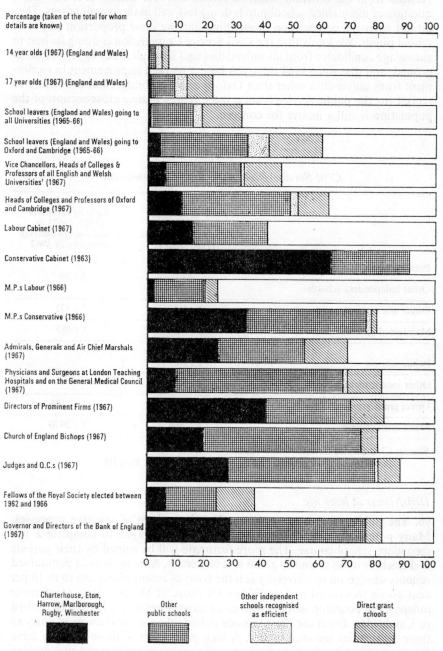

Percentage (taken of the total for whom details are known)

14 year olds (1967) (England and Wales)

17 year olds (1967) (England and Wales)

School leavers (England and Wales) going to all Universities (1965-66)

School leavers (England and Wales) going to Oxford and Cambridge (1965-66)

Vice Chancellors, Heads of Colleges & Professors of all English and Welsh Universities[1] (1967)

Heads of Colleges and Professors of Oxford and Cambridge (1967)

Labour Cabinet (1967)

Conservative Cabinet (1963)

M.P.s Labour (1966)

M.P.s Conservative (1966)

Admirals, Generals and Air Chief Marshals (1967)

Physicians and Surgeons at London Teaching Hospitals and on the General Medical Council (1967)

Directors of Prominent Firms (1967)

Church of England Bishops (1967)

Judges and Q.C.s (1967)

Fellows of the Royal Society elected between 1962 and 1966

Governor and Directors of the Bank of England (1967)

Charterhouse, Eton, Harrow, Marlborough, Rugby, Winchester

Other public schools

Other independent schools recognised as efficient

Direct grant schools

Notes

1. In this and the following professions or positions former pupils of Scottish schools are included. Pupils at Scottish schools have not, however, been included in the totals of those at present receiving education because the categories of school in Scotland do not come within the same definitions as those in England and Wales. Inclusion of Scottish figures would not in any case significantly alter the diagram.

2. For sources and detailed figures see Appendix 8.

Details are given in Appendix 8 but the following table shows the relative success ratio in the Administrative Class and Diplomatic Service competitions from different types of school in the period 1963-67. It also shows the ratio of success in these examinations to the total number of pupils going to universities from the different kinds of school in 1962. Clearly it is not just a question of maintained school pupils doing less well in the examinations. They do not enter the competition in anything like the same proportion as public school pupils. We know that the Civil Service Commission is doing its best to encourage candidates from all universities and from all kinds of school background, and that since 1964 there has been a marked improvement in recruitment from universities other than Oxford and Cambridge; but the failure to recruit for the public service from a more representative cross-section of the population is still a matter for concern.

Table 17

Civil Service/Diplomatic Service recruitment

	Ratio of successes to competitors Administrative Class (1963–1967)	Ratio of successes (1963–1967) to school leavers entering university in 1962
Public schools	1 : 4·6	1 : 99
Other independent schools	1 : 7·8	
Direct grant grammar schools	1 : 4·4	1 : 171
Maintained schools	1 : 7·5	1 : 483
	Diplomatic Service	
Public schools	1 : 9·3	1 : 287
Other independent schools	1 : 23·3	
Direct grant grammar schools	1 : 10·8	1 : 1106
Maintained schools	1 : 20·6	1 : 2970

Source: Civil Service Commission evidence.
          Department of Education and Science Statistics 1962, Part III.

Divisiveness in later life

96. The public schools are only one link in a chain of selective processes. Many potentially able children are still not encouraged to complete a full secondary school course. The more fortunate will be helped by their parents and teachers to do so and to go on to a university. Among those at maintained schools who go on to university (on the basis of recent years) less than 10 per cent go on to Oxford or Cambridge. Of those at Headmasters' Conference independent boarding schools who go to universities nearly half go to Oxford or Cambridge. From the most famous public schools, the chances of entry to these universities are even higher. A high proportion of those entering these famous public schools come from a small number of well-known preparatory schools. Thus the hold of public school men on senior posts in many fields is

the outcome of a process which begins in the home and leads through preparatory school and public school to the universities and beyond. The public schools play a central part in this process. Their success in securing entry to Oxford and Cambridge is one of the biggest advantages they offer to those who pay their fees, and one of the main reasons for the subsequent success of their pupils. While they recruit from so limited a section of the population, these advantages will remain a divisive influence.

97. Even if the success of public school boys is due largely to the personal qualities and social advantages of pupils who might have got to the top whatever school they went to, the question still remains whether it is good for anybody that so many of these boys should be segregated at a small number of schools.

98. But in fact most people believe that their education does make a contribution to these young people's later success. The public schools themselves claim to provide in some sense a "better education", whether they base their claim on more and better teachers or on superior facilities or on the advantages of boarding. Fee-paying parents presumably accept this claim. And employers, in their evidence to us, have rung endless variations on the theme: "Public school boys have more self-assurance (or self-reliance)". If that is so, if this type of education materially improves life-chances, the further question has to be answered: can it be right for these advantages to be reserved for those who, being already richest, usually need them least?

99. Some have expressed a more extreme view to us. Britain, they say, cannot flourish without leaders, and leadership could not flourish without the public schools. Public school headmasters are among those who blush for the philosophical, historical and sociological naïveté that such a proposition enshrines. Have other nations without such a system of education—the Israelis, the Japanese, the Swedes—no leaders? Have we no other source of leaders? The Robbins Report is only one of the more recent studies to demonstrate the abundant reserves of talent in this country. Much of this talent is only gradually beginning to surmount the handicaps imposed, first, by home circumstances and, secondly, by a restrictive system of secondary schooling. Justice and efficiency both demand that nobody of character and ability should be denied the chance of achieving professional competence which is the prerequisite of leadership. Our country would prosper more if greater efforts were made to attain this ideal.

General

100. Indeed, the biggest single disadvantage of having two sectors of education —one fee-paying and privileged in the matter of class sizes, the other subject to teacher rationing—is that those who can afford to opt out of the maintained system care less about its development. People who are themselves professionally concerned with education—whether as politicians, administrators, or even as members of the Public Schools Commission—do not always make use of the maintained se   for their own children. If all influential parents had children in maint   they would have brought pressure to bear on Parliament and   better than they are.

101. Some peop   t schools are pace-setters:
that their high academi   al work give the lead to the

maintained sector. There was some truth in this at the beginning of the century when the network of maintained grammar schools was being woven. But it is no longer true as a generalisation today. Each sector can point to its centres of excellence and its pioneers in the secondary field, while in the opinion of most judges the maintained schools, and not the preparatory schools, are the leaders in primary education.

102. The public schools are not divisive simply because they are exclusive. An exclusive institution becomes divisive when it arbitrarily confers upon its members advantages and powers over the rest of society. The public schools confer such advantages on an arbitrarily selected membership, which already starts with an advantageous position in life. There is no sign that these divisions will disappear if the schools are left alone. They themselves deplore this. It is time we helped them to change a situation which was not of their making.

CHAPTER 4

Girls' schools

"The movement for education for girls did not pre-date the social
and democratic revolution of the last hundred years. They have
developed together, and this factor has affected the ethos of girls'
education. Historically, boarding schools for girls were not widely
established before good day schools, charging very moderate fees.
Nor were these good day schools in existence for long before the
State entered the field, giving grants to existing girls' secondary
schools, and providing others. Hence, there has never been an
entrenched superiority either of boarding schools over day schools,
or of independent schools over grant-aided and state-provided schools
for girls. The concept of the 'girls' school giving a good education'
has embraced all types of school—boarding, day independent,
grant-aided, maintained. It has not adhered to the independent school
as such".

(*Evidence from the Girls' Public Day School Trust, 1966*)

103. This statement seems to us to be true. It is one of the many ironies of the
present situation that the national weakness in providing for girls' education
in the nineteenth century helps to explain why the "public school problem"
is generally regarded (with some justification) as applying only to the education of boys. For the boys, the prosperous and self-confident middle classes
had within fifty years of Arnold's death virtually completed the construction
of a system of independent, fee-paying, boarding secondary education which
was revolutionary in its day and unique in Europe. When the maintained
boys' secondary schools began to gain strength after 1902, they found themselves competing with the efficient and well-established public school system
into which the sons of the most influential members of society were automatically recruited. The development of girls' education was different. The
pioneers were inevitably middle class women such as the famous Miss Buss and
Miss Beale. Although they first created and improved independent schools,
they were as much concerned with day as with boarding education. Former
pupils of independent and endowed schools went to work within the maintained sector, and both the independent and the maintained girls' schools
fought together for the same objective of equality of opportunity for girls and
for freedom to enter the great middle class professions of law, medicine,
teaching and the public service.

104. But in the next expansion of careers women were not so fortunate. When
the boys' schools expanded their curriculum to meet the requirements of
science and technology, the girls' schools found themselves once more facing
the barriers of closed careers. Their dilemma was and is a real one. A career
leading to the highest positions in the main fields of industry and commerce is
virtually closed to girls, even with high educational qualifications.

63

105. This has had the effect of depressing pure science and applied science in girls' schools and consequently they have too few good mathematics and science teachers. The majority of girls follow courses in the humanities in the sixth form. It should not be forgotten that girls have, and ought to have, other objectives than university entrance in mind. They enter colleges of education, nursing, medical auxiliary training and secretarial colleges, and in doing so they make an important contribution to the welfare of the nation. Nevertheless the Robbins Report[1] urges that more girls should stay on at school "if only from the national point of view of making better use of what must be the greatest source of unused talent", and there has in recent years been a drive to get married women whose families have grown up to return to teach in the schools.

106. Early marriage has changed the old notions of career for girls. They can follow a professional career before marriage and in the early years of married life and hope to return to that career when their family responsibilities lessen. But these hopes are not always fulfilled. In 1958 an eminent sociologist[2] wrote:

". . . the apparent conflict between motherhood and wage-earning . . . now has to be viewed in relation to the earlier and much more compressed span of life during which the responsibilities of motherhood are most intense. With an expectation of another thirty-five to forty years of life at the age of forty, with the responsibilities of child upbringing nearly fulfilled, with so many more alternative ways of spending money, with new opportunities and outlets in the field of leisure, the question of the rights of women to an emotionally satisfying and independent life appears in a new guise.

    Yet, at present, practically all forms of educational and vocational training, along with entry to many pensionable occupations, are shut to the woman who has reached the age of forty. Motherhood and date of birth disqualify her . . ."

Some progress has been made. Colleges of Education now provide refresher courses for women returning to teaching and for mature students, but the number of such refresher courses in the professions is at present inadequate. If there is a shortage of women in professional jobs, there is all the more reason why more girls should go on from school to higher education.

The independent girls' schools

107. Can the independent girls' boarding schools help achieve this? There are 140 girls' schoo   ithin our main terms of reference. They provide fc   upils (roughly a half as many as in boys' public scl   y pupils aged 11 and over and for about 1,400 bo   s aged 10 and under. The sizes and organisation of the schools (of which more than two thirds are in the south of England) are shown in the following tables. The comparable sizes of boys' schools are shown in Chapter 2 (Table 9).

---

[1] Report of the Committee on Higher Education, H.M.S.O. 1963.

[2] Professor Richard M. Titmuss—"Essays on 'The Welfare State' "—George Allen and Unwin, 1958.

108.

Table 18

Number and size of girls' public mainly boarding schools
(schools with half or more of their pupils in residence)

January, 1967

Total pupils	Schools	Pupils aged 11 and over	Schools
up to 200	24	up to 200	31
201–400	46	201–400	42
401–600	9	401–600	6
601 and over	1	601 and over	1

Source: Department of Education and Science returns for January, 1967.

Table 19

Number and size of girls' public mainly day schools
(schools wholly for day pupils or having less than half their pupils in residence)

January, 1967

Total pupils	Schools	Pupils aged 11 and over	Schools
up to 200	6	up to 200	21
201–400	30	201–400	31
401–600	19	401–600	8
601 and over	5	601 and over	—

Source: Department of Education and Science returns for January, 1967.

Table 20

Number and size of sixth forms in girls' public schools

January, 1967

	0–50	51–100	101–150	151–200	over 200	Total
Mainly boarding schools	50	24	5	—	1	80
Mainly day schools	38	16	6	—	—	60

Source: Department of Education and Science returns for January, 1967.

109. With these facts before us we asked ourselves the same questions as we had asked about the boys' schools when we considered how they should be integrated with the maintained sector. We asked how far they were divisive and whether there was some built-in superiority in prestige which enhanced the ability of public school girls to get better jobs. But, although the fact that

their parents pay fees divides their daughters to some extent from contemporaries in the maintained sector, the answers we got were different.

Are the girls' schools divisive?

110. There is one curious administrative fact which makes the girls' schools less divisive than boys'. There is no organisation of headmistresses comparable to the Headmasters' Conference. The Association of Head Mistresses represents heads of all types of secondary girls' schools. Not only the heads of independent and direct grant schools (which are in membership of the Association of Governing Bodies of Girls' Public Schools) belong; so do heads of maintained secondary schools of all kinds—grammar, comprehensive, secondary modern and others—as well as heads of multiracial schools overseas. The senior mistresses of mixed schools are also affiliated to branches of the Association. Whatever differences exist between girls' independent and maintained schools, they have not been crystallised by the creation of rival powerful professional organisations.

111. Furthermore women, during the course of a teaching career, move very much more freely than men from one type of school to another. They evidently do not accept the existence of two mutually exclusive sectors of education, and there is cross-fertilisation going on all the time.

112. To these two considerations there should be added a third. The age and the system of entry to girls' schools are much more flexible than is the case with boys' schools. The girls' Common Entrance examination permits pupils from primary schools to enter at the age of eleven, and older girls to transfer from preparatory schools. Girls at boarding schools come from more varied educational backgrounds than boys at H.M.C. schools. Many of them have spent several years at maintained primary or secondary schools; many of them have had no previous experience of boarding; many of them would fall below the minimum academic standard acceptable to H.M.C. schools; many will complete their secondary education in the sixth forms of day schools or in colleges of further education.

113. Moreover, the girls' public schools charge lower fees. The annual fees for boarding and tuition averaged £454 per pupil in January, 1967 (varying from £235 to £615) compared with £510 (varying from £300 to £614) at boys' schools. The average figures including compulsory additional charges were £467 and £528 respectively. More is spent on optional extras at girls' schools— £19 compared with £11 at boys' schools. Taking all these extras into account but ignoring scholarships, bursaries and allowances, the boys' schools received in 1967 an average of £53 more per pupil in fees than the girls' schools. Not only are their fees lower, they are also far less heavily endowed than boys' schools, and must to a great extent provide for capital as well as current expenditure out of fee income. They have less resources to call upon for staffing and for capital developments than the boys' schools.

114. Parents choose to send their girls to boarding public schools for many reasons. One reason is obvious. The long waiting list at certain schools famous for their academic distinction speaks for itself. Another reason is that the girls' public schools have a certain social cachet. The clear tones of the distinctive upper class accent echo down their corridors, and this may be one not entirely insignificant reason why some girls are sent there by their parents.

A survey of social mobility in England and Wales in 1954[1] showed that in a sample group of marriages over 83 per cent of spouses were of similar social origin or educational level; a former public school girl will usually marry someone of her own social class.

115. But these schools are not as divisive as the boys' schools. Their pupils are few in number and they do not later wear an old school tie—literally or metaphorically. The tie would be of no use to them in their future careers. No magic doors to careers are opened at the mention of any school's name, however socially distinguished the school may be. The academically distinguished schools obviously help their pupils to a place in the universities— but so do those in the maintained and direct grant sectors.

Career prospects

116. There is yet another reason why a girl will not gain the same advantage as a boy through going to an independent school. Most girls' schools are not as strong academically as boys' schools and do not prepare girls as adequately for higher education and the careers which go with that education. Girls are often receiving an education which is inadequate in length, variety and relevance. The same criticism could be made of maintained grammar schools for girls. Within the sixth forms of England and Wales boys outnumber girls by 4 to 3, and the Department of Education and Science, in making its projections and predictions for the Robbins Committee, assumed that this ratio would remain constant. The following table shows the proportions of pupils leaving various kinds of school before the ages of 16 and 17 respectively. It will be seen that there is a marked contrast not only between boys' and girls' independent schools but also between girls' public and other independent schools.

Table 21

Percentage of pupils leaving below 16 and 17 years of age

| | GIRLS | | | | BOYS | | | |
| | 1 Maintained grammar schools | 2 Direct grant schools | 3 All Independent recognised efficient schools (including public schools) | 4 Public schools | | 5 Maintained grammar schools | 6 Direct grant schools | 7 All Independent recognised efficient schools (including public schools) | 8 Public schools | |
Age of leaving				Boarders	Day pupils				Boarders	Day pupils
Below 16	8·2	2·9	8·9	3·0	5·7	6·4	4·7	3·9	2·2	2·7
Below 17	43·4	25·6	43·3	28·5	29·3	33·5	21·7	19·0	13·0	17·3

Source: Columns 4 and 8: Commission Questionnaire and "The Public Schools—A Factual Survey" by Graham Kalton.
Columns 1 to 3 and 5 to 7: Department of Education and Science returns (10 per cent sample of leavers).

Note: The figures relate to the academic year 1965–66 with the exception of those for H.M.C. public schools which are for the year 1962–63. The difference in dates is explained in Appendix 6.

[1] "Social Mobility in Britain" edited by D. V. Glass—Routledge and Kegan Paul Ltd. (1954), p. 337.

117. A similar imbalance is reflected in the figures for the G.C.E. 'A' level examination. A comparison of the 1966 'A' level entries for various types of school shows that nearly twice as many boys as girls entered for this examination in all subjects taken together. The ratios of boys to girls leaving school with two or more passes in the examination (adjusted to allow for the varying numbers of boys and girls leaving in 1965-66) were:

1·4: 1 in maintained grammar schools (24,630 boys, 17,460 girls)

1·3: 1 in direct grant schools (4,450 boys, 3,080 girls)

2·1: 1 in independent recognised efficient schools (including public schools) (7,640 boys, 3,240 girls).

The percentages of boys leaving different kinds of secondary school in the academic year 1965-66 who had obtained two or more 'A' levels were:

Maintained grammar schools	Direct grant schools	Independent recognised efficient schools	Public[1] schools
41	56	47·8	49·8

The equivalent percentages for girls were:

29·6	44·4	22·6	30·9

118. It follows that many girls either do not have 'A' level opportunities or are not taking them. Of the girls who do complete an 'A' level course, few choose courses in science, mathematics and technology. The career prospects for girls in these fields, particularly for those returning after a break, may be a deterrent. The ten most popular subjects, for girls and boys respectively, were in 1966:

Table 22

G.C.E. Advanced Level Summer 1966

Number of Pupils

Girls	Summer 1966	Boys	Summer 1966
English Literature	25,433	Mathematics	49,411
French	15,067	Physics	36,115
History	13,614	Chemistry	24,853
Geography	9,504	English Literature	17,998
Mathematics	8,742	History	17,429
Art	8,106	Geography	15,885
Chemistry	6,461	Economics	14,511
Physics	6,011	French	11,220
Biology	5,624	Biology	7,549
German	3,911	British Constitution	6,823

Source: Statistics of Education 1966, Volume 2.

119. The most important, and already familiar, conclusion to be drawn from these figures is that the nation as a whole is failing to identify and develop its "greatest source of unused talent". There is, as yet, no evidence that co-

---

[1] These figures relate to the results in 1965–66, with the exception of those for boys' public schools in membership of the H.M.C., which relate to the year 1962–63. This difference in dates is explained in Appendix 6. The figure for boys' public schools should therefore be treated with caution, as the proportion of leavers from H.M.C. schools with two 'A' levels has probably increased since 1962–63.

educational schools are proving any more successful than girls' schools in establishing the truth that the education of girls matters—in the same way and for the same reasons—as much as the education of boys. The provision of an education which is adequate in terms of length, quality, variety and relevance is therefore a problem not only for girls' boarding schools but for all girls' schools, and not only for all girls' schools but for all schools with girls in them.

120. Nevertheless the problem seems to be accentuated in the independent schools, and particularly in the smaller schools. As the figures in Tables 18, 19 and 20 show, many schools are very small in total numbers and are catering for too few pupils at the sixth form level to be able to provide a wide range of 'A' level subjects in addition to general courses. To this there are a few notable exceptions, but the generalisation holds good. The sixth form general courses, which many schools provide, have virtually no parallel in the boys' schools. These courses vary from school to school and enable them to cater for the less academic girls. But, despite this advantage, the small school may be too small to cater effectively for both the clever and the less able, and the clever girl in such a school is restricted in her choice of subjects in the sixth form and below.

121. Table 21 shows that girls in independent schools leave school earlier than boys, the difference being more marked than in other kinds of school. We suspect that in some cases the explanation is that the aim of the school is social rather than academic. But whatever the causes, the fact is that only 57 per cent of the girls attending independent secondary schools are still there after reaching the age of 17, compared with 81 per cent of boys. The proportion of leavers obtaining two or more 'A' levels is smaller than the proportions among girls from either maintained or direct grant grammar schools. We do not want to make too much of these figures, because it is difficult to compare the independent with the grammar schools. Most independent schools admit girls of a much wider range of ability than grammar schools[2].

122. Nevertheless the analysis of leavers from girls' public boarding schools in 1966 is disturbing. The destinations of the 3,667 boarding pupils for whom details are available were:

619 (17%) universities in the United Kingdom
59 (2%) universities abroad
364 (10%) other schools (excluding those leaving under 15)
201 (5%) colleges of education (teacher training)
696 (19%) colleges of further education (including art and music)
531 (14%) secretarial colleges
106 (3%) finishing schools
351 (10%) other continued education in the United Kingdom
94 (3%) other continued education abroad
364 (10%) nursing (including child nursing and medical auxiliary services)
174 (5%) other employment
108 (3%) elsewhere

---

[1] If the boarders in girls' public schools only are taken, the proportion is about the same as in maintained schools, but still less than in direct grant schools.

[2] On the other hand, a number of girls—357 in 1965–66—enter boarding public schools at the sixth form level, and this makes them more comparable with grammar schools at this level.

123. These figures suggest that substantial numbers of girls leave school after taking 'O' level and take their 'A' levels from day schools or colleges of further education. This impoverishes the sixth forms of many of the boarding schools, and it is therefore questionable whether they are the right place for girls in need of boarding education, who would have to rely on the academic strength of the school at which they boarded, at sixth form level as well as before.

124. Thus this tendency to early leaving faces us with a problem when we ask how the independent girls' schools are to be integrated. Some schools are adapting themselves in various ways to make a boarding school a more attractive place for girls over 16, but the fact has got to be faced that many girls appear to find the restrictions of boarding school life intolerable, and this problem looms over us.

Prospects for integration

125. In general, therefore, the girls' boarding public schools by comparison with boys' schools, suffer from very severe limitations. They are small in size, with inadequate sixth forms, and they lack financial resources, in terms either of endowment funds or response to appeals. There is a sense in which the smaller schools suffer from the effects of their own virtue. Many boys' schools, calculating the effects of an intake restricted in numbers upon the size and quality of the sixth form, would have selected only high fliers. The girls' schools do not appear to have adopted such a policy—or it may be that they have had less competition for places from clever pupils—and many of them could be described as suffering from the difficulties of being at once small and academically comprehensive (or something near it).

126. What troubles us is the effects rather than the causes of the present situation. The schools already admit girls of widely differing ability, and the heads have declared themselves willing to admit girls from a much wider social range. At first sight integration with the maintained sector would appear to be relatively easy. But all is not as easy as it looks. On the one hand, there are a large number of small schools, able to provide an environment which is not so large as to be forbidding for pupils who are new to boarding. On the other hand, the schools appear in many cases unable, for one reason or another, to take more than a relatively small proportion of girls through to university entrance. As we have said, there are reasons why this should be so— the relatively narrow range of employment open to university-trained women and the alternatives open to many girls who find work as teachers, secretaries, nurses, social workers, and in the world of the arts and entertainment, more attractive. Nevertheless, parents of assisted pupils should have the assurance that the schools to which their girls go should open the way to a wider range of careers. We cannot recommend that girls should be sent at public expense to those schools which:

  (i) appear to lack the means to encourage a high proportion of abler girls to continue their studies

  (ii) are too small to provide an adequate range of courses for *both* academically inclined and less academically inclined girls

  (iii) are remotely situated and likely to face increasing staffing difficulties.

To say this, however, is not to exclude the possibility that, for some children in need of boarding, the small school may provide the most congenial background and atmosphere, and we shall take account of this in our recommendations.

127. The number of girls' boarding places in all kinds of school (excluding special schools) in England and Wales is so much less than that for boys (48,337 girls compared with 104,248 boys) that, if a significant additional need occurs, it will be necessary to increase the number of places substantially. But not by providing more small schools. As the nation's need of specialist teachers becomes even more intense, small schools will either be unable to attract staff or will attract more than they ought to in relation to the numbers of pupils. The best way forward for the schools is for them to expand, and, if that is impossible, for them to combine. In either case they should try to provide day as well as boarding places. Another way, to which we shall return, is to extend co-education[1].

128. The prospects for integrating many of the existing schools in their present form are thus at first sight not very promising. The excellence of some girls' boarding schools (although the total of places they provide is few) is not in question; but the other considerations we have outlined mean that the number of schools which could be regarded as suitable for integration will inevitably be limited. In many cases major changes of organisation and of age range will be necessary to enable the schools to help to meet a future need for boarding and to provide that quality and variety of academic education to which girls have as good a right as boys.

---

[1] We do not assume that co-education will automatically lead to an immediate increase in the number of girls taking mathematics and science subjects, welcome though this would be. Experience in the maintained sector suggests that girls in mixed day schools tend towards the arts more if anything than in girls' day schools. But, quite apart from the other advantages of co-education, girls should as a matter of right be able to attend schools which are equipped to teach them mathematics and science to the highest level. If they do so, at least it will be possible, as it otherwise would not be, to tackle the problem of encouraging more girls to take these subjects.

Part Two

The Choices Open

CHAPTER 5

Options and constraints

129. What options are open? In what ways could the independent schools be integrated with the maintained sector?

130. Let us look at the background against which integration would take place. The great majority of local education authorities have already decided their long-term plans for comprehensive reorganisation and a number of them are already implementing their schemes. Out of 162 authorities in England and Wales, 73 had at the end of 1967 had their schemes of reorganisation approved in full and 27 in part. 70 of the schemes approved will provide "all-through"[1] comprehensive schools, 71 include breaks at various ages to provide "two tier" schemes (including 27 middle school schemes) and 16 include sixth form colleges. In Scotland, the 35 education authorities have all submitted schemes of reorganisation which have been wholly or substantially approved.

131. Progress with reorganisation depends to a large extent on the provision of the necessary buildings. Although each year's capital investment programme makes a contribution to an ultimately complete pattern of reorganisation, the full process will be a long one, and the rate at which individual authorities will complete the implementation of their plans will vary considerably. It will be many years before the reorganisation of all maintained secondary schools is complete; and it is only by degrees that all maintained schools will cease to have a competitively selective intake.

132. Nevertheless time is running out. The fact that local education authorities are beginning to implement their plans makes it all the more important that, if the independent sector is to be integrated with the maintained sector, time should not be lost. Authorities may have to be prepared to amend their plans and building programmes, and the independent schools to be associated with these plans if they are to be integrated.

133. There is also a sombre cloud in the background. As we write this report, the raising of the school leaving age to 16 has been postponed and cuts have had to be made in educational programmes. Any committee of inquiry which makes recommendations to spend more public money must take into account the state of the economy and make proposals which are reasonable and not extravagant. We believe that the dilemma in which the public schools find themselves in relation to the maintained educational system cannot be resolved unless public money is spent. It will be for the Government to judge what priority should be given to implementing our recommendations. In

---

[1] This includes authorities with schemes which have some schools catering for pupils aged 11–16 years and some schools for pupils aged 11–18 years, and schemes which include all-through comprehensive schools alongside other forms of comprehensive organisation. Only 36 authorities have schemes which, in the long term, consist exclusively of schools catering for pupils aged 11 to 18 years.

making them, however, we have tried to keep before our eyes the paramount needs of public education; and the scheme we ultimately put forward is costed and planned so as to be as flexible as possible and so as not to put too heavy a burden upon the Exchequer, particularly in the early years.

OPTIONS

134. There are those who are opposed to any scheme which would cost money because they hold that the independent schools should be left strictly alone. People who hold this view fall into two camps. The first are those defenders of the public schools who object to any interference by the State with private institutions or with the freedom to buy and sell education. The second camp of those who want to leave the problem strictly alone contains the bitterest critics of the public schools. They regard them as thoroughly bad institutions, on which no public money should be spent, which should attract no tax reliefs and to which no children should be sent at public expense. They also hold the conviction that the public schools' days are numbered, and that it is only a matter of time before they will either wither away or cease to be of any importance. The conclusion they reach is that all available resources should be devoted to the maintained school system.

135. We do not agree with these views. The public schools are part of the nation's educational heritage. As long ago as 1861, in writing to the then Public Schools Commission, Mr. Gladstone described the Commission as "dealing with what in a large sense is certainly public property". We do not believe that the more prominent schools will either go bankrupt or cease to have a divisive influence if they are left unchanged. Also, it would be wrong to ignore the important contribution which they and other independent schools, as institutions of real educational value, might make to national education. We agree with the "wither away" approach only in one sense—that we would not be prepared to recommend token schemes of integration which would achieve none of our main purposes. There is nothing to be gained by spending public money in order to subsidise pupils in independent boarding schools unless they are pupils in need of boarding education and unless it is done in such a way as to bring the two sectors closer together. We would much sooner preserve the *status quo* than encourage this kind of development. Nor need it happen. The genuine desire for integration which we have found among many of those working in the public schools, and much of the evidence we have received, suggests that this line of development does not command support.

Take-over

136. The next possibility, at the opposite extreme from taking no action, is that of a take-over. It is arguable that all independent schools, or at any rate those which are recognised as efficient and might have some contribution to make towards the maintained system of education, should be taken over and run by local education authorities. This is by no means impossible. Local education authorities are well capable of maintaining and running, with the help of suitable governing bodies, any type of school, and to take over the

independent schools in their areas would in most cases be no more than a marginal addition to their responsibilities. Indeed, in the very long term, this might well ultimately happen to many independent schools, if no steps were taken to integrate the two sectors. If there were a lengthy economic recession in the country they might fail to weather the storm; and as costs rise to meet increasingly heavy demands for scarce manpower and sophisticated equipment (educated manpower in a labour-intensive "industry", teaching machines, laboratory equipment and computers), so education, especially at the sixth form level, will become more expensive and difficult to provide. Futhermore, by the end of this century, the importance of education in determining life chances will be even greater than it is today, and public interest in the way it is organised will be correspondingly stronger.

137. A deliberate policy for taking the schools over would have to be carefully worked out; but there is no intrinsic difficulty. A single measure of legislation would enable all acceptable independent schools to be maintained by local education authorities either as county or voluntary schools as from a given date. The case of boarding schools would be more complex than that of day schools only in the sense that they would continue to draw pupils from a regional or national catchment area. But many institutions run by local education authorities—for example, colleges of education and boarding special schools—already do this. There would be no constitutional difficulty in arranging the administration of every boarding school by the local education authority in whose area it is located, with boarding places offered to other authorities on the usual basis.

138. There are attractions in this solution, and most of us would not regard it as being in principle wholly wrong, either morally or educationally. Having said this, we must explain why we nevertheless do not regard it as the right solution to propose at this stage. There are four reasons which, taken together, have persuaded us to rule out take-over as a solution.

(i) We doubt whether public opinion as a whole is ready to support the total abolition of independent schools.

(ii) If the entire independent sector were to be taken over the cost would be considerable. It would of course be no more than a marginal addition to the gross national education bill. It would be no more expensive, for example, than a very welcome decision to stay on at school by some of the children who now leave maintained schools as soon as they can. Nevertheless, as a deliberate act of policy, to be pursued as an alternative to other ends of policy, it would be expensive[1], costing at least £60 million a year in current costs alone. Expenditure of this order would be absurd if it led to the postponement of other action such as the implementation of the recommendations of the Newsom and Plowden Councils.

---

[1] *Take-over* (figures refer to England and Wales only).

(1) Various alternative costs of take-over are possible, based on different assumptions of what it would entail. We do not see that it would be defensible to take over boarding schools only, if it were proposed (as we do not) to take over any schools at all. It would, furthermore, be impracticable to do so because of the large number of schools which admit both day and boarding pupils. The following estimates of annual cost therefore apply to boarding and day schools alike, the only distinction drawn being between independent schools recognised as efficient and all independent schools regardless of recognition.

(*footnote one continued on next page*)

(iii) With one exception[2], none of the local authority associations which have given evidence has shown any disposition to take over all (or for that matter, any) independent schools.

(iv) Although (as will be argued later in Part III) there is a need for boarding places for children who cannot otherwise be suitably educated, there is at present no evidence that pupils with such needs could fill *all* the places the schools could offer even if their parents wanted them to do so. There is thus no reason why local education authorities should take over all these places.

A pragmatic solution—experimental schemes

139. Some suggest that, if only negligible funds are available, a start might be made by conducting experiments in co-operation between the independent and the maintained schools. Some experiments are already being made. There are a number of schools with a modest (in the case of some day schools, substantial) intake of pupils from local education authorities. There are also highly desirable experiments in local co-operation between some public and maintained schools. Desirable as all this may be, such schemes do not integrate the public schools or make them significantly less divisive. A school cannot afford to embark on major changes in its teaching, recruitment of pupils and other arrangement in response to an experiment which may be brought to an end at short notice. We do not believe that the main centres of

---

(2) The costs are as follows:

(i) At current local education authority cost levels for tuition only, assuming either no use of boarding facilities or their use wholly without cost to public funds:

(a) Recognised efficient schools	£47 million
(b) All independent schools	£63 million

(ii) At current local education authority tuition cost levels and maintained school levels of boarding cost, assuming full use of boarding facilities at no cost to parents:

(a) Recognised efficient schools	£72 million
(b) All independent schools	£89 million

(iii) At prevailing independent school fee levels—tuition plus boarding:

(a) Recognised efficient schools	£78 million
(b) All independent schools	£95 million

(3) Later in the report (Chapter 8), we conclude that there will by 1980 be a need for 80,000 boarding places—13,000 of which would be available (for "need" pupils) in maintained and direct grant schools without further building. Assuming an average boarding cost per pupil equal to the 1967 average boarding fee at maintained boarding schools of £210 (which is probably rather less than the full cost) and an average parental contribution towards that cost of £90 per pupil, the 67,000 places which could, under a take-over scheme, be made available in independent schools, would result in a boarding charge of £8 million per year to public funds. This assumes that the schools could be run at the same level of cost as the present maintained schools. It also assumes that the remaining boarding places in the schools would be occupied by full fee payers; the schools could not function economically as boarding schools unless all places were filled. Added to the tuition cost of £63 million at 2(i)(b) above, this produces a minimum total annual cost of £71 million a year. From this can be deducted some £9·4 million which is now spent by government departments and local education authorities in grants or allowances for children attending independent schools (day and boarding). In round figures, therefore, and on the most optimistic assumptions of cost, a complete take-over of independent schools would cost at least £60 million a year. This figure takes no account of annual loan charges appropriate to the capital costs of bringing many school premises up to standard. In practice, we believe that the cost might be much higher than £60 million a year.

2 The Welsh Joint Education Committee (see paragraph 519).

power and influence in the independent sector—the major public schools— could be tempted to make radical changes on this basis[1].

Short-term boarding

140. A number of those giving evidence have stressed the importance of providing a short period of boarding education for children during their secondary school life. This is in line with much recent educational thinking (for example in "Half our Future") that arrangements of this kind should be made; some authorities are already making them, and others intend to do so. Independent schools willing to take on a special role rather than to continue as schools in the normally accepted sense would be doing a useful service. Valuable though this role would be, it presupposes a total change of function. The schools concerned would cease to exist in any recognisable form as schools—i.e. as providing instruction for pupils over a period of years. While endorsing the need for more short-term boarding, and expressing the hope that some schools might adapt themselves to provide it—in holiday time if not during term—we do not feel that to ask independent schools to take this on as a permanent function would be anything other than abolition under a different guise.

Our own proposals

141. In part Four we set out the middle course which we believe ought to be adopted in order to integrate the independent schools. But before charting this course, we must point out the constraints, partly psychological and partly material, which are bound to affect what can be achieved in the next ten to fifteen years. These constraints arise partly from the difficulties facing the teachers in the independent schools and of their governing bodies; and partly from the attitude of those who we hope will want their children to be given assisted places.

CONSTRAINTS

The right to private education

142. We have already argued that the public schools, which we understand are all trusts under charitable jurisdiction and which receive considerable indirect help from the Exchequer, cannot claim to be exempt from State intervention. But should any proposals to change these schools be constrained by the right of parents to choose whatever education they wish for their children? Local education authorities are required "to have regard to the general principle that, so far as is compatible with the provision of efficient instruction and training and the avoidance of unreasonable public expenditure, pupils are to be educated in accordance with the wishes of their parents" (Education Act, 1944: Section 76). This Section bears on an authority's general arrangements for admission to schools. The rights of parents to choose a particular school are covered more specifically by the provisions of

---

[1] If money were not available for a proper scheme of integration, on a national basis, some schools might wish to run pilot schemes of their own, in the spirit of this report, rather than do nothing. We would applaud their motives, in circumstances which we no less than they would regret, and our rejection of the *ad hoc* approach is not intended to prejudice such pilot schemes—but only to point out that they cannot be regarded as a substitute for an integration policy.

Section 37, in that they can select the school to be named in a school attendance order; in which case the final decision rests with the Secretary of State and not with the authority.

143. Nevertheless choice is in practice limited in most areas, as it is bound to be if too many children want to attend the same school. For fee-paying parents also the choice is frequently limited by their income, their child's level of ability, or the competition to enter particular schools. To reduce the freedom of the small number of potential public school parents would not limit the total freedom of choice if by so doing there would be greater choice for others. Increased scope for pupils to receive boarding education would be exactly equal to the curtailment of this option for others.

144. The Declaration of Human Rights, which was ratified by the United Kingdom in 1951, has been invoked as supporting the case against any modification of the existing arrangements for independent education. The relevant part of the Declaration, which says that "parents should be free to choose the kind of education to be given to their children", has been more recently underlined by a 1966 Covenant of the General Assembly of the United Nations. The relevant Article[1] is reproduced below. The Covenant has not yet been ratified by the United Kingdom. The Article does not conflict with our proposals. It deals with the rights of parents and children. We accept the right of parents to choose schools, and wish to extend this right to as many parents as possible. The Article does not equate freedom of choice with the freedom to pay fees. The reference in paragraph 2(b) of the Article to the "progressive introduction of free education" makes this clear. If fee paying

---

[1]ARTICLE 13

1. The States Parties to the present Covenant recognize the right of everyone to education. They agree that education shall be directed to the full development of the human personality and the sense of its dignity, and shall strengthen the respect for human rights and fundamental freedoms. They further agree that education shall enable all persons to participate effectively in a free society, promote understanding, tolerance and friendship among all nations and all racial, ethnic or religious groups, and further the activities of the United Nations for the maintenance of peace.

2. The States Parties to the present Covenant recognize that, with a view to achieving the full realization of this right:
  (a) Primary education shall be compulsory and available free to all;
  (b) Secondary education in its different forms, including technical and vocational secondary education, shall be made generally available and accessible to all by every appropriate means, and in particular by the progressive introduction of free education;
  (c) Higher education shall be made equally accessible to all, on the basis of capacity, by every appropriate means, and in particular by the progressive introduction of free education;
  (d) Fundamental education shall be encouraged or intensified as far as possible for those persons who have not received or completed the whole period of their primary education;
  (e) The development of a system of schools at all levels shall be actively pursued, an adequate fellowship system shall be established, and the material conditions of teaching staff shall be continuously improved.

3. The States Parties to the present Covenant undertake to have respect for the liberty of parents and, when applicable, legal guardians, to choose for their children schools, other than those established by the public authorities, which conform to such minimum educational standards as may be laid down or approved by the State and to ensure the religious and moral education of their children in conformity with their own convictions.

4. No part of this article shall be construed so as to interfere with the liberty of individuals and bodies to establish and direct educational institutions, subject always to the observance of the principles set forth in paragraph 1 of this article and to the requirement that the education given in such institutions shall conform to such minimum standards as may be laid down by the State.

were the issue, the freedom of public authorities to buy places for children in need of them whose parents cannot afford school fees must be reckoned as a desirable freedom alongside that of individual parents. These freedoms, like others, are in competition. To recognise only the rights of individual fee-payers would be to restrict the freedoms of the poor in order to extend those of the rich.

Waiting lists

145. Another constraint standing in the way of any scheme of integration was frequently mentioned by schools in their evidence. They consider themselves committed to children already on their waiting lists. How then can they find places for assisted children? These commitments extend in some cases as far as the end of the 1970's, though not all schools take names so far ahead. Schools vary in the number of their places that have been so committed, and also in the degree to which they are subject to the "vanishing effect", a well known hazard of the system by which a parent who has entered his child for a given school does not ultimately send him there. The usual form of under-taking given by a school is that a child will be admitted at a given future date subject to his or her reaching a required academic standard and subject to the availability of a place. But these are not legal obligations. If the number of places available were, for example, drastically reduced, a school would not be obliged in law to provide a place. If our recommendations are accepted, this will certainly occur at a number of schools. We would like to enable schools to honour their existing commitments as far ahead as possible; but we do not think this should be the overriding consideration when we come to consider the timing of our proposals for integration. As a working premise, we suggest that the Secretary of State should not regard as inviolable any undertaking to admit a pupil who has not at the time of legislation following this report attained the age of eight. Pupils younger than this have not yet been com-mitted in an irrevocable sense to fee paying education, and their future would be in no way jeopardized if, as an alternative to independent schooling, they entered maintained schools. If they have a special need for boarding education, they will be able to secure places under the scheme we propose.

Parental attitudes

146. A further constraint, which will be overcome only by degrees, is the reluctance of many people who are not accustomed to boarding education to send their children to boarding school, however well suited these may be to meet their needs. We say more about this point—which we take very seriously —later in the report. Unless there is a massive increase in boarding provision, the corollary will be the need for a growing acceptance of day school places by parents accustomed to using boarding schools.

Local education authority attitudes

147. Local education authorities may, as we have suggested, need to revise their plans. They may also need to change their attitudes. Understandably enough, they have in the past regarded the independent sector as none of their concern. But if the independent schools are to be integrated, the authorities will have to look at the matter afresh. For instance, as we shall argue later (in

paragraph 272), an independent boarding school with large grounds on the outskirts of a town could increase its size and overcome the difficulties of providing a comprehensive curriculum if the local education authority would erect school buildings and add a sizeable proportion of day pupils— the authority joining with the existing governing body in the management of the enlarged school. Thus authorities could enable something to be done at relatively little cost in the early stages by being willing to share in the enlargement and adaptation of independent schools as part of their normal secondary school provision.

Educational considerations

148. We have already mentioned that there are more co-educational schools in the maintained than in the independent sector. Whether this is because the parents who send their children to independent schools dislike co-education, or whether it is because the schools themselves prefer to stay as they were founded, is far from clear. We have encountered arguments against co-education which, if valid, would show that co-education even in day schools was highly undesirable. This we cannot accept—for if we did we would be condemning 58 per cent of maintained secondary schools. We have already said that we believe that the problem of integration to some extent depends on a number of schools being willing to become co-educational. But we realise that such a change of heart will take time and that this is one of the constraints which we are facing.

149. Most public schools are at present too small to become all-through comprehensive schools. Small schools cannot go comprehensive over the whole age range (from 11, 12 or 13) and at the same time retain good sixth forms. If schools are to have as wide an ability range as possible, as well as a good sixth form, some may need to cover a shorter age range. This change will take time.

150. There is one last major constraint which is bound to affect any scheme put forward for integration. Any scheme in the interest of both assisted and the fee-paying children must bring into the public schools teachers with experience of teaching in the maintained schools; similarly some of the existing staff may need to learn, for example, how to teach children taking the Certificate of Secondary Education. These changes cannot take place overnight or they will disrupt the schools. They will have to wait in part upon the normal process of retirement. Those who advocate change must not expect the public school problem to be solved by the stroke of a pen.

Part Three

The Need for Boarding

CHAPTER 6

Need for boarding

151.   (i) "There is a danger that by concentrating attention on the methods used to select children for secondary education, we may fail to appreciate the importance of other ways in which talent is lost or diverted" . . . "There is evidence that extreme poverty of the environment leads to a progressive deterioration in academic ability".

"The Home and the School"; J. W. B. Douglas
(MacGibbon & Kee, 1964).

(ii) " . . . many heads, especially of schools in difficult urban areas, leave us in no doubt at all that under the conditions in which some families are obliged to live, it is asking the impossible of parents and children to expect homework to be done satisfactorily. Even where housing conditions are good, large families and small living rooms, or the open plan design of many houses and flats, may make it extremely difficult for boys and girls to have reasonable privacy and quiet in which to concentrate on their work".

"Half our Future"; Report of Newsom Council, 1963.

(iii) "Despite the Service education allowance many servicemen cannot afford boarding schools unless local education authorities assist. It is desirable that all ranks, who have the same need, should be able if they so wish to provide boarding education for their children".

Evidence from Ministry of Defence, 1967.

(iv) "Two girls have been sent to us at short notice this term by the . . . Authority. The parents are divorced, father is a very sick man, grandmother has begun to have 'blackouts' and falls in the street. The younger girl yelled for three days on arrival because she wanted her father. We therefore allowed him to bring his caravan into the school grounds, the school sister gave him the daily injections he requires, and after only a fortnight the girl is settled".

Letter from Headmistress, 1967.

(v) "Rises in the numbers coming into care in 1965-66 compared with 1962-63 were particularly marked in the following circumstances:
    (a) Abandoned or lost—up 50 per cent
    (b) Family deserted by mother, father unable to care for children —up 31 per cent
    (c) Children illegitimate, mother unable to care—up 38 per cent and
    (d) Unsatisfactory home conditions—up 81 per cent."

Home Office—Report on the Work of the
Children's Department: 1964-66.

(vi) "The Association is of the opinion that it is desirable that there should be boarding schools, as the needs of certain children can best be met through this type of education.

. . . for many children whose home or parental background is incomplete or faulty, boarding school is usually more acceptable at all levels of society than any other substitute for parental care, such as a children's home. Other children, even though they have satisfactory homes, may benefit from education in boarding schools because of the possibility of providing in such schools a more flexible and at the same time structured education than in ordinary day schools".

Evidence of The Association of Children's Officers, 1967.

(vii) "1,420,000 children are living in overcrowded conditions . . ."

Ministry of Social Security, 1967.

(viii) "For the present generation, tackling a wide range of social and economic objectives, a further broadening of opportunity at all stages of the educational process is imperative. There is a general awareness of this; and the road to further educational advance lies not so much in appeals to the public conscience as in the exploration of the use of resources . . ."

"Education in 1965"; Department of Education & Science.

152. Many children live in conditions of social and thus of educational deprivation. It would be absurd to suggest that all deprived children need to live away from home in order to receive suitable education; and for those who do need to live away from home, it does not follow that a boarding school is necessarily the right place. Nevertheless, the need of many children for an alternative home for the whole or part of the year may be held to include, as one of its elements, boarding schools as the best answer for a proportion of children. So long as even a small proportion of deprived children fall within this category, they will represent in numerical terms a formidable challenge to public authorities to provide or assist them with boarding education.

The present position

153. Responsibility for boarding where there is an acute social or educational need is already accepted by public authorities:

(i) Where there is a need for special educational treatment which cannot be provided suitably in an ordinary school or a day special school, boarding education is provided wholly at the expense of local education authorities in boarding special schools or sometimes in independent schools which cater for handicapped children (about 25,000 pupils in England and Wales).

(ii) Where any child cannot be provided with suitable education within daily travelling distance of his home, the local education authority have a duty to meet the full costs of boarding education (about 2,000 pupils in England and Wales).

(iii) Where a child is found to be unsuitable for education at school (under Section 57 of the Education Act, 1944, as amended) local health authorities make provision which is in some cases residential (about 30,000 children of compulsory school age in England and Wales).

(iv) Where a child has no home or a very unsatisfactory one, he or she may come "into care" under the Children Act, and be placed by the local authority either with foster parents or in one of a variety of voluntarily or statutorily provided institutions while attending day school (about 22,000 children in England and Wales of compulsory school age came into care in 1966-67—some for very short periods).

(v) Approved schools accommodate about 5,500 children of compulsory school age in England and Wales.

154. Where there is neither medical nor physical incapacity, serious delinquency nor social or educational need of a degree which makes boarding away from home imperative, local authorities have a much more difficult judgement to make in deciding whether children should be provided or assisted with boarding education. In recent years they have been guided by the Report of the Working Party on Assistance with the Cost of Boarding Education, 1960[1], in which the categories of need which should "most readily be entertained" by authorities were defined as follows:

(i) Cases in which both parents are abroad.

(ii) Where the parents are in England and Wales but are liable to frequent moves from one area to another.

(iii) Where home circumstances are seriously prejudicial to the normal development of the child.

(iv) Where a special aptitude in the child requires special training which can be given to the child only by means of a boarding education.

Categories of need

155. We accept the Working Party's definitions as general lines of guidance; but we think they might with benefit be elaborated, and this we shall attempt. But the decision whether a child should be offered a place at public expense in a boarding school can only be made in the full knowledge of individual circumstances; and we do not want, by attempting too rigid a set of definitions, to inhibit the work of those who will implement our report. They should have all possible discretion in reaching their decisions. We shall not, therefore, try to prescribe exactly the range of circumstances in which a child might be considered as eligible for education in a boarding school. It will be particularly important not to do so if there should be more candidates than there are places available, as we believe may be the situation once the availability of places under a national scheme becomes widely known. Only those with access to the children and their families will be able to decide whether, for example, the needs of a particular motherless child are greater than those of a child of a large family in a crowded home trying to do homework against overwhelming odds. But within the broad band of those eligible *to be considered* for boarding education as assisted pupils, we would include the following categories, which elaborate but do not go beyond the Working Party's criteria. They are drawn partly from suggestions made by Dr. Royston Lambert[2] which are reproduced in full in Appendix 9.

---

[1] Referred to in our terms of reference as the Martin Report.
[2] In "The State and Boarding Education": Methuen, 1966.

1—D*

156. The categories are as follows:

(i) If both parents are dead or have abandoned their children. Children in such circumstances might be better settled with relations, with foster parents or in a residential home. However, for some children, boarding school would be the right answer, provided holidays could be spent with relations or alternative arrangements made either by the local authority or the school.

(ii) If the child is living with a lone parent having full responsibility for the family; for example, a parent widowed, divorced, separated or deserted. At the time of the 1961 census (Table 31 of the Household Composition Tables) there were 661,700 children in this category, either below the age of 15 or in full time education over that age. A considerable proportion of these children would be of an age (i.e. 8 upwards) to be considered for education while living away from home. For many of them attendance at a boarding school might be irrelevant to their needs and could be positively damaging if it meant breaking up the family group still further. Nevertheless, this group quite certainly includes some children who are neglected because a single-handed parent cannot give them sufficient attention, or for other reasons, and whose needs should entitle them to be considered for boarding school places.

(iii) If the child's parents are too ill, mentally or physically, to provide a tolerable home background.

(iv) If both parents live abroad in the course of work (subject to paragraph 168 below).

(v) If there is a reasonable certainty that the nature of the parents' employment will involve the child in frequent and educationally disruptive changes of school. The justification for boarding might depend upon the child's course of study and the stage he had reached; but as a broad guide we think the case would be made out if a child would otherwise have to change schools once every two years, or more frequently, during the remainder of his or her school life.

(vi) If travelling between home and school imposes undue strain or fatigue on the child. This must depend upon the child's age and physical condition, and the length of the school day, rather than upon an absolute time factor. The Department of Education and Science, in a Manual of Guidance (revised 1960) suggested that a journey which took more than three quarters of an hour for primary age pupils, or more than one and a quarter hours for secondary pupils (including time spent waiting for transport) would be unreasonable; but we do not think this should be interpreted rigidly.

(vii) Where conditions of housing are so exceptionally grave as to impair a child's proper educational development. Boarding education is no substitute for good housing; but society cannot ignore its *educational* responsibility to those children living in the worst conditions.

(viii) If the child's aptitude or intended course of study requires some special educational provision not available in an accessible day school or college of further education.

(ix) If there is extreme tension in personal relationships within the child's home, and the child would benefit by being away during term time.

157. It is not difficult to think of family circumstances which would not be covered by these criteria, but which might be equally serious in their impact on a child. We therefore attach great importance to a final criterion, which we deliberately do not try to elaborate, because to do so would inevitably limit the range of its application. It is:

(x) Where there are any other exceptional circumstances which severely impede a child's educational progress.

158. It may be desirable to distinguish, insofar as this can be done, between those categories of boarding need which call for a substitute home for the whole year and those in which boarding is required only during term time. The first three listed, and possibly the last one, presuppose circumstances in which attendance at a boarding school would or might have to be combined with suitable arrangements for spending holidays with relations or friends, in a foster home or children's home, or at the school.

Alternatives

159. As we have said, it would not be right to regard whole-time education in boarding school as being more than one among many possible ways of meeting the needs of a child who may have no home (at any rate in this country) or whose home circumstances may be grossly prejudicial to his or her educational development. Which type of provision would be most suitable is, and should remain, a matter for decision by all who are concerned with an individual child's needs—the parents, education authorities, and social and welfare authorities and organisations. We have no wish to stimulate a demand for boarding education by suggesting that it is necessarily to be preferred to any of the following alternatives:

(i) It may be right for a child to make the best of existing circumstances, with such help as he or she can be given. For example, an extended school day at a day school may be an answer where both parents are out at work or where homework is impossible at home. This might be linked, where possible, with short term boarding to broaden the child's horizon, and to provide a complete change of environment, particularly for children in socially deprived areas.

(ii) Boarding with relations, friends or foster parents or in a children's home while attending day school might suit many children better than going away to boarding school—particularly if the home difficulties are likely to be temporary.

(iii) A boarding wing attached to a day school may provide the right combination of substitute home and educational opportunity for many children.

(iv) Boarding hostels not under the control of, or closely associated with, a day school are another possible alternative, but are in our view less satisfactory than a boarding wing which is an integral part of the school.

(v) If the difficulty arises from limitations of curriculum in the existing school, every effort should be made to remedy the deficiency by attendance (part-time if appropriate) at another school or a college of further education.

160. The second of these possibilities—boarding with foster parents or in children's homes—deserves special consideration. The primary task of the children's authorities which do most of this work is to support the family and, whenever possible, to keep or reunite children with their parents. Most of the children coming into their care in the course of a year go home again very soon. The arrangements made for those who stay longer must take account of many other things besides educational needs, and when children are moved from one foster home or children's home to another, a change of school is often entailed. The number of children who take their education to the stage of G.C.E. 'A' level or beyond while still in public care is very small. The children's authorities already have a great deal of work to do in extending their services to encompass the duties laid on them by Section 1 of the Children and Young Persons Act of 1963, and action which may follow from the report of the Seebohm Committee could throw even heavier burdens on them. This is not the time to call for another major extension of their work. It should not be assumed that the educational needs of children and their need for a secure family life can be clearly distinguished or separately dealt with. Some children who now go to boarding schools might have fared better in foster care, but some in foster homes might have fared better in a boarding school. Cases quoted to us show that families undergoing a period of stress sometimes find it easier to cope with their difficulties and care for their children if the children can go to a boarding school: the alternative of placing a child in someone else's home can be more disruptive of family unity. We hope the education and children's services will co-operate very closely in making arrangements for individual children, and it is for this reason that we shall propose that the Boarding Schools Corporation and the consortia of local education authorities working under its supervision should include people experienced in the work of the child care service.

Boarding education—good or bad?

161. Whether a child should be enabled to live away from home while continuing his or her education is bound to depend upon a number of factors affecting the individual child. But there is a further question to be borne in mind in considering whether boarding should be at a boarding school rather than elsewhere. Do boarding schools provide the right sort of environment for healthy development? It is generally accepted that the schools differ very widely. Nevertheless, we think it worth while to summarise below the arguments for and against boarding education which have been presented to us in evidence. We would emphasize that while some of these statements may be true of all schools, others may be true, if at all, only of a minority.

Arguments for

162.   (i) Absence from home helps the development of independence, mental toughness, a spirit of enterprise and a sense of responsibility.

    (ii) Training in community life leads to ease in social contacts, ability to lead and also to accept the authority of others.

    (iii) A stable environment, with regular sleep, planned diet and ordered routine (safeguarded from distractions) is not only healthy but encourages concentration and serious study.

(iv) Living, working and playing in one place avoids waste of time and effort in travelling.

(v) There is more scope for purposeful activity than in most homes.

(vi) There is the stimulus of constant contact with good adult minds and examples of high standards.

(vii) Levels of discipline and behaviour can be achieved which would not be accepted by a pupil at home.

Arguments against

163. (i) The loss of the warmth and affection of home can cause emotional problems, especially for the sensitive and immature.

(ii) Removal from the neighbourhood environment leads to isolation, lack of friends during the holidays and makes for social divisions in the home community.

(iii) Where standards and values of the home and the school are different, the more total commitment demanded by a boarding school can lead to serious conflicts and problems of adaptation.

(iv) Lack of privacy may be a real deprivation for many children.

(v) Pupils' time is over-organised.

(vi) There is too much conformity of thought and behaviour.

(vii) The school is too artificial and isolated a community, limited in the age of the great majority of its members, and usually containing pupils of one sex only.

(viii) The effectiveness of the boarding school in inculcating standards and attitudes is harmful if these standards are low or the vision is limited.

164. In attempting to balance these views there are a number of factors to take into account. It is obvious that children differ widely in their needs and that schools also vary widely in what they are able to offer. There are also special considerations affecting different types of schools, which we mention at a number of points in the report. Many children's individual needs are not within the power of society to change; children will continue, for example, to be orphaned, or to have parents working overseas. Yet the most significant factor, looking ahead, is that, while these needs may not change, the schools' capacity to meet them might well be changed. Schools are organic, and capable of adapting themselves to meet changing needs and attitudes in society, just as they have responded to the changing demands of parents over the past century. The ways in which they might do so, without sacrificing any of their essential values, are complex and varied, and we return to them later in the report; but it is important to establish at this point that we are not considering a static situation. It is not a case of considering whether a few children from slum homes would benefit from being admitted tomorrow to traditional public schools; but of whether, with suitable safeguards and preparation, a substantial number of children, with different kinds of need for boarding, could be admitted to a wide variety of schools in a few years' time.

Need and desire

165. We are asked to consider what contribution independent schools might make towards meeting any unsatisfied *need* for boarding education. By need is clearly meant need of a kind sufficient to justify public expenditure—the spending of much more on certain children than on the great majority of their contemporaries. A desire for boarding education for a child who is or who would be at no substantial disadvantage in a day school would not be sufficient.

166. Yet, to be successful, boarding education requires that need be accompanied either by desire on the part of the parents and child for a boarding education, or at least a clear willingness and readiness to co-operate. It would be not only an infringement of liberty to remove children to boarding school against their wishes or those of their parents, but would be foredoomed to failure, and would be greatly to the detriment of the schools they attended.

167. The demand for boarding education is not clear cut or easily predictable. The vast majority of parents—more of them than ever before—are keenly and responsibly concerned about the education of their children. But the answers they give to questions about the demand for boarding are likely to depend heavily on the forms of boarding education proposed, and on the experience and attitudes of parents themselves. All these things could change very quickly, and we want to ensure that all parents are enabled to make the wisest possible decisions for their children within the limits of choice which resources permit. Once the decision is taken to open the public schools to a wider range of children in need of the education they can provide, the greatest care must be taken to explain the opportunities to parents and to show them what the schools have to offer. If the initiative is left entirely to parents, without sympathetic guidance, the opportunities available will not reach some of those in greatest need of them. We cannot overstress the importance of the part to be played by primary and secondary school heads and teaching staff, on whose guidance so many parents rely.

British nationals overseas

168. We have included in our criteria of need the children of parents working or serving overseas. The question may arise whether children should be assisted if their parents, although British, are resident overseas more or less permanently, or at any rate for very long periods. This is a difficult problem, and is one on which we do not feel competent to make a firm recommendation. An arbitrary line may have to be drawn between those overseas pupils who should be eligible for assistance and those who should not. The present situation is, we understand, that local education authorities vary widely in their treatment of applications for boarding education from Britons working for long periods abroad (as has been represented to us, for example, by the India, Pakistan and Burma Association), and we feel that it is a matter in which greater consistency would rightly be expected to follow our recommendations.

CHAPTER 7

The number of boarding places needed

169. We have been asked "to ensure that the public schools should make their maximum contribution to meeting . . . any unsatisfied need for boarding education". It is not our task to make plans to meet the country's total need for boarding education, but we must consider what is likely to be the scale of future need, before deciding what part the independent schools might play. We begin, therefore, by setting out the numbers of pupils in boarding schools of various kinds and the numbers who are helped from public funds.[1] We then consider how the need for assisted places is likely to change in the future.

EXISTING BOARDING PROVISION

England and Wales

170. 151 maintained schools in England and Wales (other than special schools) have boarding facilities. In January, 1967, 21 had more than half of their pupils in residence. These 21 schools (including 2 primary schools) accounted for 4,764 of the 11,244 pupils boarding at maintained schools. The total comprised 8,610 boys and 2,634 girls; 372 pupils of primary school age and 10,872 of secondary school age.

171. Of the 179 direct grant grammar schools in England and Wales, 62 take boarding pupils. In January, 1967, 15 of these schools had more than half of their pupils in residence, accounting for 4,249 of the total of 9,318 boarders in direct grant grammar schools. This total included 7,201 boys and 2,117 girls.

172. By far the largest proportion of boarding places is in independent schools. As they are central to our terms of reference, we asked the Department of Education and Science to analyse the January, 1967 returns from recognised efficient independent schools in England and Wales to show the age structure of boarders. When we were subsequently asked to consider direct grant schools, a similar analysis of their boarding pupils was made. The results for both recognised efficient and direct grant schools are set out in Table 23 following together with the equivalent figures for the public schools only. Pupils in the main school or its preparatory department have been included in the public school figures, but not pupils in separate though associated preparatory schools.

173. Table 24 following shows the distribution of boarding pupils between those recognised efficient independent schools which are mainly for primary or preparatory age pupils, those mainly for secondary pupils and those which have both primary and secondary departments.

---

[1] Details of boarding schools in England and Wales are given in Appendix 14, and equivalent details for Scotland in Appendix 17.

Table 23

Ages of boarding pupils in recognised efficient independent schools[1] and direct grant grammar schools in England and Wales at January, 1967

Age	1 Direct grant grammar schools			2 Independent recognised efficient schools (including public schools)			3 Totals			4 Public schools only (included in 2 and 3)		
	Boys	Girls	Total	Boys	Girls	Total	Boys	Girls	Total	Boys	Girls	Total
7 or under	10	6	16	838	423	1,261	848	429	1,277	27	24	51
8	96	20	116	3,359	705	4,064	3,455	725	4,180	241	105	346
9	184	42	226	5,228	1,327	6,555	5,412	1,369	6,781	500	286	786
10	283	72	355	6,167	2,033	8,200	6,450	2,105	8,555	651	656	1,307
11	631	205	836	7,489	4,053	11,542	8,120	4,258	12,378	1,248	1,895	3,143
12	780	319	1,099	8,315	5,293	13,608	9,095	5,612	14,707	1,688	2,969	4,657
13	1,011	276	1,287	9,789	5,995	15,784	10,800	6,271	17,071	6,090	3,493	9,583
14	1,133	327	1,460	10,219	6,281	16,500	11,352	6,608	17,960	7,887	3,595	11,482
15	1,056	305	1,361	10,325	6,164	16,489	11,381	6,469	17,850	8,022	3,582	11,604
16	944	255	1,199	9,408	4,939	14,347	10,352	5,194	15,546	7,565	2,988	10,553
17	732	212	944	6,899	2,618	9,517	7,631	2,830	10,461	5,710	1,693	7,403
18 or over	341	78	419	2,306	681	2,987	2,647	759	3,406	1,720	349	2,069
Total	7,201	2,117	9,318	80,342	40,512	120,854	87,543	42,629	130,172	41,349	21,635	62,984

Source: Department of Education and Science returns, 1967.

[1]. There are also 9,847 boarding pupils in independent schools not recognised as efficient (6,809 boys, 3,038 girls). The ages of these pupils are not available, but 2,068 (1,721 boys and 347 girls) were at primary schools, 3,425 (3,112 boys and 313 girls) at secondary schools and 4,354 (1,976 boys and 2,378 girls) at schools with both primary and secondary departments.

Table 24

Independent schools recognised as efficient

Boarders by age at January, 1967

Age	Primary schools			Secondary schools			Primary and secondary schools			Totals		
	Boys	Girls	Total	Boys	Girls	Total	Boys	Girls	Total	Boys	Girls	Total
7 and under	686	175	861	—	—	—	152	248	400	838	423	1,261
8	2,976	298	3,274	—	1	1	383	406	789	3,359	705	4,064
9	4,474	503	4,977	2	5	7	752	819	1,571	5,228	1,327	6,555
10	5,090	601	5,691	96	145	241	981	1,287	2,268	6,167	2,033	8,200
11	5,324	506	5,830	854	1,167	2,021	1,311	2,380	3,691	7,489	4,053	11,542
12	5,307	265	5,572	1,452	2,049	3,501	1,556	2,979	4,535	8,315	5,293	13,608
13	1,830	38	1,868	5,522	2,582	8,104	2,437	3,375	5,812	9,789	5,995	15,784
14	33	—	33	7,361	2,744	10,105	2,825	3,537	6,362	10,219	6,281	16,500
15	—	—	—	7,525	2,617	10,142	2,800	3,547	6,347	10,325	6,164	16,489
16	—	—	—	6,905	2,083	8,988	2,503	2,856	5,359	9,408	4,939	14,347
17	—	—	—	5,100	1,117	6,217	1,799	1,501	3,300	6,899	2,618	9,517
18	—	—	—	1,468	220	1,688	643	337	980	2,111	557	2,668
19	—	—	—	140	48	188	55	76	131	195	124	319
Total	25,720	2,386	28,106	36,425	14,778	51,203	18,197	23,348	41,545	80,342	40,512	120,854

Source: Department of Education and Science returns.

Definitions: Primary schools—schools at which a substantial proportion of pupils start below the age of eleven and normally do not remain beyond the age of thirteen. (Small numbers of fourteen and fifteen year olds have been included in the figures for these schools).

Secondary schools—schools at which pupils normally start over the age of eleven. (Small numbers of nine and ten year olds have been included in the figures for these schools).

Primary and secondary schools—schools with pupils below the age of eleven and over the age of thirteen, which cannot be classified as either primary or secondary.

Scotland

174. Details of boarding pupils in Scotland are given in Chapter 18 and Appendix 17. There were (in 1967) 1,594 boarding pupils in maintained schools (including pupils living in hostels), 1,492 in grant-aided schools and 7,155 in independent schools (in Scotland there is no recognition as efficient).

ASSISTANCE FROM PUBLIC FUNDS

175. Many children at boarding schools are already helped from public funds, either because they qualify for grants from local education authorities or because their parents get allowances from the government departments which employ them. We consider these forms of assistance in turn.

Local education authorities (England and Wales)

176. All pupils in maintained boarding schools and hostels attached to schools get free tuition and are eligible for assistance with the cost of boarding according to their parents' income. (Chapter 15 explains the scales of assistance used by authorities.) In the 19 maintained secondary schools which in 1967 had a majority of boarding pupils, it appears that about one third of the pupils (339 of the 1,005 who entered in 1966-67) enter by choice rather than because they need to board. If these figures were typical of the other 132 maintained schools (primary and secondary) in England and Wales which have boarders, about 7,500 of the total of 11,244 boarders would be pupils with a need for boarding. But the proportion of boarders who need boarding education is likely to be higher in schools which are not primarily boarding schools. As a rough estimate, we shall assume in our calculations that there are 8,000 pupils in need of boarding who are already boarding at maintained schools.

177. Children are also assisted by local education authorities at boarding schools which are not maintained. The Department of Education and Science at our request sent a questionnaire to local education authorities in England and Wales asking how many pupils (other than handicapped pupils receiving special educational treatment) they assisted at non-maintained boarding schools in 1966. The numbers are shown below:

Table 25

Numbers of boarding pupils assisted by local education authorities at non-maintained schools in England and Wales on 20th January, 1966

Age	Direct grant grammar			Independent recognised efficient			Independent non-recognised			Total non-maintained schools		
	Boys	Girls	Total	Boys	Girls	Total	Boys	Girls	Total	Boys	Girls	Total
12 or under	267	148	415	1,819	1,098	2,917	86	33	119	2,172	1,279	3,451
13	163	88	251	774	523	1,297	38	12	50	975	623	1,598
14 and 15	398	158	556	1,675	1,040	2,715	80	35	115	2,153	1,233	3,386
16 or over	352	131	483	1,689	802	2,491	53	16	69	2,094	949	3,043
Totals	1,180	525	1,705	5,957	3,463	9,420	257	96	353	7,394	4,084	11,478

Source: Questionnaire to local education authorities.

Scotland—equivalent assistance

178. In Scotland pupils are helped at non-maintained schools mainly by the Scottish Education Department, which makes awards for children whose parents are overseas or who do not belong to the area of any education authority. 118 of these central awards were made to boarding pupils in 1966-67. There were also 10 boarding pupils assisted directly by education authorities.

Central Government

179. The Government as employer makes education allowances to substantial numbers of employees' children. The rates of allowance are given in Chapter 15. In the Diplomatic Service, staff who are serving abroad or, having served abroad, are liable to be stationed overseas again within five years, are eligible for assistance. There are similar arrangements in the Civil Service, except that allowances after return from overseas are paid only if there is a liability for service abroad again within three years. Members of the Armed Services may apply for boarding allowances if they are serving overseas or, when in this country, if they are liable to be moved within four years. The following estimates of numbers are taken from figures supplied by Departments.

Table 26

Numbers of boarding pupils assisted by government departments at different categories of school in England and Wales (1966)

	Public schools	Other recog- nised schools	Non- recog- nised schools	Direct grant grammar schools	Main- tained schools	Other and not known	Total
Diplomatic	495	497	48	31	23	162	1,256
Home Civil Service	128	118	25	51	68	1	391
Overseas Aid Service[1]	727	670	142	290	387	6	2,222
Total Non-Forces Departments	1,350	1,285	215	372	478	169	3,869
Officers	2,737	3,909	576	2,075	1,736	645	11,678
Other Ranks	103	819	342	273	1,200	103	2,840
Total for Forces[2]	2,840	4,728	918	2,348	2,936	748	14,518
General Total	4,190	6,013	1,133	2,720	3,414	917	18,387

Source: Enquiry of government departments.
Notes: [1] The distribution between schools for children of Overseas Aid Service staff is not known. The figures have therefore been divided in the same proportions as the known figures for the Home Civil Service.
[2] The distribution between schools for children of Royal Navy and Army personnel is also not known. The figures for the Armed Services as a whole have therefore been divided in the same proportions as the figures for the Royal Air Force, details of which were provided for us.
[3] The figures affected by the estimates at [1] and [2] are shown in italics.
[4] Pupils are also assisted by public corporations and nationalised industries but the numbers are too small to affect our calculations; for example, B.O.A.C. assisted 80 children as boarders in 1966.
[5] As our calculations in this chapter will relate to England and Wales, we have excluded an estimated 400 boarding pupils assisted by government departments at schools in Scotland, and a further 400 attending schools outside Great Britain.

Overlap

180. Some pupils are helped by both local and central government, each taking into account assistance given by the other. We have found out from local education authorities how many pupils are helped twice, and have made the appropriate deductions to show, in Table 27 following, the net total of boarding pupils assisted at schools in England and Wales. Pupils at public schools (as defined in our terms of reference) are included in those attending independent recognised schools.

Future need—England and Wales

181. Thus there are already about 35,000 pupils helped from public funds at boarding schools in England and Wales (excluding handicapped pupils). We now have to estimate how many places should be taken up in the future. We first consider the future need for boarding education, and then how far it might be met in independent schools.

182. The task is formidable because there are a number of unknown factors, and we know of no method by which accurate estimates can be made. We shall explain some of the difficulties. On the other hand, we shall be expected to give reasonably firm estimates of the cost of integration, and these will depend directly on the number of pupils to be assisted, so that the problem must be tackled.

183. It is not necessary to arrive at exact figures. We were not asked to make recommendations for meeting the whole of the country's needs for boarding education—but rather, in considering the integration of the public schools, to ensure that they "make their maximum contribution to meeting in the first instance any unsatisfied need for boarding education". It would be sufficient for our purposes to establish that there is a boarding need part of which can be suitably met by admitting pupils in substantial proportions to public and other independent schools.

184. It is important not to overestimate boarding need. Boarding is an expensive form of provision. But neither must we underestimate it. There is always a temptation to assume that the existing level of provision is about right. Yet there has been shown in the past to be no merit in underestimating future educational needs, for example in the field of teacher supply or of the number of places required in higher education; and we do not see that any service would be done by playing down the need which may exist for boarding education.

185. We have used two separate methods for estimating future boarding need:

(i) We have ourselves made projections based on the current practice of local education authorities, to take account of increases in the total school population, making adjustments only for changes of policy which we consider essential.

(ii) We invited Dr. Royston Lambert, who was already engaged in research into boarding education when we were appointed, to study boarding need and demand on our behalf and to arrive at his own conclusions. With the exception of additions which we have made to his figures to allow for

Table 27

Total of pupils assisted with boarding education in England and Wales

	Direct grant grammar	Independent recognised efficient	Non-recognised	Maintained	Total for all schools
Pupils assisted by local education authorities	1,705	9,420	353	11,244[2]	22,722
Pupils assisted by government departments[1]	2,863	10,739	1,192	3,593	18,387
Total	4,568	20,159	1,545	14,837	41,109
Pupils assisted by both l.e.a.'s and central government	314	1,586	88	3,593	5,581
Net total of pupils assisted from public funds	4,254	18,573	1,457	11,244[2]	35,528

Source: Special enquiries of local education authorities and government departments and returns of the Department of Education and Science.

[1] For the purposes of this table, pupils in the category "Other and not known" in Table 26 have been distributed among the various types of school in proportion to the total numbers assisted in these schools.

[2] This figure represents the total number of boarders in maintained schools in January, 1967. All such pupils received free tuition, and boarding fees were charged according to an income scale. All the other figures relate to 1966.

pupils already assisted at boarding schools and forward projections for anticipated increases in the total school population, his results have been arrived at by methods quite independent of our own.

Difficulties

186. We shall set out the results of both these approaches to the problem. But before doing so we describe some of the difficulties which soon became apparent, and which demonstrate that any figures arrived at can be no more than approximations.

187. First there is the question of parents' attitudes towards boarding education. To many parents, boarding education is at present a remote and unreal concept, associated with delinquency or handicap rather than with educational opportunity. Some may consider boarding to be desirable, but regard the independent schools at present as having social or other features which they would find unfamiliar or objectionable. Also there is a big difference between parents' willingness to consider boarding education in principle and in practice. Although they can be—and have been—asked for their views about it by Dr. Lambert's team, their behaviour could not be confidently forecast unless we were able to offer them places for their children in particular boarding schools and ask them to pay contributions appropriate to their incomes. Even then, their behaviour would reflect current attitudes towards boarding education and the public schools rather than the attitudes which may prevail in ten or fifteen years' time. It would be unrealistic to forecast future demands from current behaviour, and equally rash to assume that people will quickly become more willing to use the public schools.

188. As the time span of integration will extend over the next two decades, we must consider the effect of the anticipated rise in the school population upon the numbers in need of boarding education. It would be simplest to assume that the proportion of children in need of boarding will remain the same as the numbers in the age group rise, but in reality these needs may increase more rapidly or less rapidly than the total school population. They will be affected by political, social and economic developments. For example the Armed Services are to be drastically reduced, and this ought to reduce the number of Service children eligible for education grants. On the other hand, officers' children assisted at boarding schools in this country at present outnumber the children of other ranks by four to one, despite the relatively small proportion of commissioned officers in the Services. A successful integration of the public schools could affect this ratio, and thereby keep the numbers at a level higher than the reduction in the forces would suggest. If this country joins the European Economic Community, more people may work abroad and want their children to attend boarding schools at home. A fall in demand for fee-paying places might encourage some schools to accept rapid changes; but an increase in demand might have the opposite effect. Unforeseen changes in housing, the employment situation, labour mobility, the divorce rate, immigration and other factors may all upset our forecasts.

189. The number of boarding school places available at any one time depends not only upon the number of children who are awarded places, but on the length of time they stay in the schools. This will be affected by the changing aspirations of parents and children and associated with the developing

patterns of secondary education. The total number of places would depend upon the type of course assisted pupils followed, the continuance or otherwise of their need for boarding education, and above all upon their age of entry to boarding. For example, assuming a continuing need for boarding, a child entering boarding school at 8 and going on to 'A' levels, would spend about 10 years at boarding schools, compared with as little as 3 years for some children entering at 13 or later.

190. In making total estimates we must not overlook pupils in public and other independent schools who are in need of boarding education but are not assisted from public funds—some of whom might qualify for assistance in the future. Their parents may be employed overseas, yet there may have been no need for the parents or guardians to seek help, or they may have preferred not to do so and have been able to manage without it. Our survey of replies to the questionnaire to the public schools and the sample of other independent recognised efficient schools shows that about 15 per cent of boarding pupils at the time of the enquiry had parents living overseas (excluding foreign nationals). Applying this percentage to the total number of boarding pupils in independent schools recognised as efficient gives a total of 18,000 pupils in need of boarding education because their parents are abroad. The parents of some 10,000 pupils in recognised independent boarding schools are assisted by government departments (see Table 26); but not all of them are abroad at any one time, and the whole 10,000 cannot therefore be included in the 18,000 overseas pupils in recognised independent schools. On the other hand, some pupils within the total of 18,000 are the children of parents working overseas who are helped by local education authorities but not by government departments—we do not know how many. Yet again, the 18,000 undoubtedly includes some children of British subjects who have gone to live more or less permanently overseas, and who might not qualify (see paragraph 168) for assistance with boarding under any new arrangements resulting from our report.

191. When making projections for the future, it cannot be assumed that overseas employment will take a constant proportion of this country's labour force. Also it may not be right to include a fully proportionate increase for overseas pupils when we estimate the additional boarding need for pupils of average and below average ability, and we shall not do so. It seems probable—though we have no conclusive evidence for saying so—that the children of parents in executive and similar positions overseas tend to be above average in attainment, and many of those who are not may be placed privately in schools catering for less able children.

192. It has been represented to us that there are many boarding pupils already in independent schools without assistance who are in need of boarding on grounds other than their parents' absence overseas; but it would be impossible, without excessive probing into personal circumstances, to estimate their numbers. Their needs, therefore, cannot be taken into account, but they should not be forgotten.

193. This is not a field in which precise and detailed forecasts can be made. Estimates producing different conclusions from our own could readily be defended. The Boarding Schools Corporation which we hope to see established would no doubt find it helpful if alternative forecasts were proposed and

publicly debated before it starts work. Integration will be a long process, and we hope that new information or ideas about the extent of boarding need will continue to be fed to those responsible. Meanwhile the following calculations are sufficiently convincing to place the onus of proof on those who think there is no substantial additional boarding need, rather than upon those who believe, like ourselves and many of those who have given evidence to us, that the need is considerable and is likely to increase.

FUTURE NEEDS PROJECTED FROM CURRENT PRACTICE

England and Wales

194. What basis is there for estimating the numbers of children who will need boarding education in the future? We look first at a report published by the Association of Education Committees in 1965 ("Boarding education—a report on the facilities available to local education authorities.") This report collated estimates made by local education authorities in England and Wales in 1964 of the numbers of pupils whom they expected in the future to provide or assist with boarding education in all types of school. It concluded that some 5,000 assisted children would enter boarding schools for the first time each year:

650 of primary age (400 boys, 250 girls)
4,350 of secondary age (2,800 boys, 1,550 girls).

Of the secondary age boys, 2,100 were expected to need courses leading to G.C.E. examinations; such courses were thought unlikely to be suitable for the remaining 700. The equivalent figures for girls were 1,250 and 300. The report went on to list boarding schools of all kinds (maintained, direct grant and independent) which were willing to admit pupils sponsored by local education authorities—the academic level catered for being shown in each case.

195. As the list contained a very wide variety of schools from which local education authorities could choose, we assume that they would not have found insuperable difficulty in placing the great majority, if not all, of the pupils for whom they wanted places. Yet there is good reason to believe that the 1966 figures of assisted places we have mentioned do not represent a bigger annual demand for places by authorities than they perceived in 1964. (For example, the 1966 level of take-up of places would presuppose an average length of course of only $4\frac{1}{2}$ years for each of the 5,000 children in the 1964 estimates—despite the fact that 2,050 of them were considered to have 'A' level expectations.) The probability is rather that the 1966 take-up of places represents an underachievement of the estimates made in 1964. We may, for this reason, be unduly cautious in using the 1966 figures as a baseline; but at least we are most unlikely to exaggerate the needs to be met in the future. We shall therefore take as our basis for forward estimating the known figures of pupils assisted with boarding education in 1966. It is not possible to tell from the 1966 figures how many of the pupils assisted with boarding were of G.C.E. calibre and how many were not; but we shall make the reasonable assumption that the proportions were in approximately the same ratios as in the 1964 estimates made by authorities, If there were difficulties in placing some of the children thought in 1964 to need boarding, these probably arose with the less able rather than the more able children—and this again means that estimates based on the 1966 figures are unlikely to be exaggerated.

196. In our estimates for the future we start, therefore, by taking the total number of children at present assisted with boarding education by local education authorities—22,722 in all. From this total we exclude all those helped additionally by government departments. This is because we want to isolate overseas need as far as possible in view of the considerations in paragraph 191 above. We also exclude an estimated 3,000 children (see paragraph 176) who are attending maintained boarding schools without a need for boarding education. The resulting figures are:

maintained schools   4,651 pupils

direct grant schools   1,391 pupils

independent schools 8,099 pupils.

This makes a total of 14,141 pupils. We estimate that about 1,600 of these children are of primary school age and about 12,500 of secondary school age.

197. We now consider whether 14,100 pupils assisted with boarding by authorities on grounds of need is a reasonable basis for forward estimating. In the authorities' estimates at paragraph 194 above, within the total of 4,350 children of secondary age considered to require boarding, 3,350 places were for pupils expected to be able to take G.C.E. 'O' or 'A' level courses and 1,000 places were for pupils below this level of ability. The implication of these figures is that one child in 41 capable of obtaining at least three 'O' level passes needs boarding education compared with 1 child in 442 below that standard[1]. The social and educational handicaps known to afflict less able children make it very unlikely that this can be the true position.

198. It would be wisest to assume that boarding need is found fairly consistently throughout the ability range. 3,350 places were estimated as being for pupils of G.C.E. calibre. If this is taken as a modest level of ability to pass in 3 or more 'O' level subjects, the 1966 Statistics of Education (Volume 2) shows that 23 per cent of maintained school leavers in 1965-66 had achieved this standard. Let us assume that 25 per cent of pupils, to include a proportion who did not fulfil expectations, came within this category. Among the 12,500 pupils of secondary age assisted in 1966, the proportion of G.C.E. to non-G.C.E. pupils would (in terms of the local education authority ratio of 3,350 to 1,000 in 1964) be 9,600 to 2,900. These 9,600 places can be regarded as having been allocated to children in the top 25 per cent of the ability range. To make equivalent boarding provision for pupils at all levels of ability would produce a requirement of 9,600 + 28,800—a total of 38,400 places, which is 25,900 secondary places more than are taken up at present (see paragraph 196). The A.E.C. Report did not distinguish between different levels of ability in its estimates for primary age pupils, and we have therefore left them out of this calculation; but here, too, there may well be an additional need for places for less able pupils.

---

[1] In 1965–66, there were 578,000 maintained school leavers. Of these:

        136,000 had obtained three or more 'O' level passes

        442,000 had not.

If the 1964 ratio (in the authorities' estimates) of 3,350 boarding places needed annually for pupils capable of 'O' level courses, compared with 1,000 for those below this level were applied to the 1965–66 leavers, the extent to which need was assumed by authorities to exist for the two categories would be:

    (i)   136,000 ÷ 3,350 = 1 place per 41 children

    (ii)   442,000 ÷ 1,000 = 1 place per 442 children

199. Children below the ability level required for a G.C.E. course are, however, less likely to stay on at school than their more able contemporaries. We hope and expect that increasing numbers will take a sixth form course suited to their needs. The remainder at present generally leave two years before their contemporaries who take G.C.E. 'A' level courses. To allow for this factor we reduce the additional need of 25,900 secondary places in the previous paragraph by about a quarter to, say, 19,000, to arrive at a more realistic total figure of about 31,000 secondary boarding places which would be currently required to give pupils at all levels of ability an equal opportunity of boarding education.

200. This total does not, however, allow for the provision of equal opportunities for girls. In their estimates, the authorities allowed 1,550 secondary places for girls compared with 2,800 for boys, and 250 primary places compared with 400 for boys. Within the 1966 figure of 14,100 pupils in need who were assisted by local education authorities (see paragraph 196), our estimate is that 4,300 were girls and 9,800 boys. To provide girls with opportunities of boarding education on the same scale as boys would therefore increase the total number of secondary places required by a fraction of about $\frac{5,500}{14,100}$ if 1966 practice is taken as the base. This would raise the total need to something over 43,000. But to allow for the continuing higher proportion of boys in the school population, we shall reduce this figure to 41,500. The primary school boarding requirement for girls, if increased by a similar calculation, would raise the total equivalent primary boarding need from 1,600 to about 2,000 places. Thus the baseline of 14,100 primary and secondary places in paragraph 197 becomes 43,500 places in all.

201. It may be thought that a projection of 41,500 secondary places is unrealistically high (for example, it may be argued that many parents who would allow a son to go to boarding school would not permit a daughter to do so). We now turn, therefore, to another aspect of local education authority assistance which has been considered by Dr. Lambert[1]. His enquiries of authorities showed that their practice in providing assistance with boarding education differed markedly from one area to another. The variations were greater than could reasonably be accounted for by variations in the needs of different areas, and must therefore have arisen from different interpretations of the criteria of need. For example, among authorities which provided information for Dr. Lambert, the number of pupils assisted with boarding education at the secondary stage in English and Welsh counties varied from 1 in 27 to 1 in 4,736, and in county boroughs from 1 in 66 to no assistance at all. His study of their policies showed that some authorities interpreted boarding need generously, while others appeared to regard it as meriting assistance only in cases of quite exceptional hardship.

202. It cannot be assumed that the less generous authorities always acted unwisely. Need for boarding and the resources for meeting it vary considerably from one area to another. It is plain however, that some authorities have not been willing to accept—or look for—what many people would regard as

---

[1] "The State and Boarding Education": Methuen, 1966.

reasonable evidence of need for boarding education. A conclusion, to which we shall return, is that if better opportunities are to be given to all children in need of boarding, regardless of where they live, decisions should be made by groups of authorities under the guidance of a central agency on which local authorities would be represented. For the purpose of our present estimates, we note the discrepancies of treatment which exist, and—unless the more generous authorities are being wildly extravagant, which seems unlikely— we conclude that, if consistent policies were applied nationally, the real need must be much higher than the 41,500 secondary places we have suggested. How much higher we cannot tell; but we regard this as further evidence that our figure is an underestimate of need.

203. Finally, we shall refer in Chapter 15 to the scales of contribution at present required of parents, which may well have deterred the parents of many children in need of boarding education from seeking it. This suggests again that the number of pupils currently assisted is less than it should be.

Increases in school population

204. We must now consider the effect of expected changes in the population of school children. For this purpose, we assume that the need for boarding education among pupils living in this country (i.e. those whose need does not arise from parents' employment overseas) will increase at the same rate as the school population as a whole. The projected increases in school population (taken from the Statistics of Education, 1966, Volume 1) and the corresponding estimate of the numbers of pupils requiring boarding education are shown in the following table. We have discounted any need for boarding under the age of eight.

	1966	1970	1975	1980
Child population[1] (8–10)	2,019,000	2,279,000	2,526,000	2,612,000
Estimated number of junior pupils in need of boarding	2,000	2,257	2,502	2,587
School population seniors (11–18)	3,402,600	3,509,600	4,475,200	4,879,700
Estimated number of senior pupils in need of boarding	41,500	42,805	54,582	59,516
Total estimated number of pupils in need of boarding	43,500	45,062	57,084	62,103

Pupils from overseas

205. We have already explained how difficult it is to forecast the numbers of pupils who might require boarding education because their parents are abroad. That is why we have excluded them from the projections so far made. We have also excluded the children referred to in paragraphs 190 and 192 who attend boarding schools without assistance from public funds. We cannot estimate

---

[1] The Statistics of Education do not show the projected numbers of children *in school* at ages 8–10; hence we have taken the child population figures. This does not affect our calculations, as almost all children are in school at these ages, and the proportion of those who are not is likely to be fairly constant.

the need from either of these sources in 1980. The reduced armed forces may or may not produce the same level of effective need as at present. There may or may not be more parents employed overseas as civilians. Some pupils who need boarding education and whose parents at present pay for it may come within the scope of our recommendations, and no longer be identifiable as a separate group in 1980—as indeed may the children of parents in public service overseas. We shall therefore make no projection for future population increases for any of these categories. To avoid any risk of overestimating, we shall take into account only the number of pupils at present assisted by government departments, and we shall regard this as a constant figure for the future to cover all the pupils we have just described. The present total of 18,387 children so assisted, added to the figures in the previous paragraph, would bring the total need, rounded down to the nearest thousand, to:

1966	1970	1975	1980
61,000	63,000	75,000	80,000

Dr. Lambert's research

206. Our alternative method of arriving at estimates of boarding need was to invite the Research Unit into Boarding Education at King's College, Cambridge—headed by Dr. Royston Lambert—to study the problem on our behalf. We include in Appendix 9 a paper which presents the interim findings of the Unit. These findings, the methods of research on which they are based and the views expressed are the responsibility of the author and his colleagues. Their general conclusion, which follows enquiries made of parents and teachers in certain selected areas, is that there was in 1966 an effective need (i.e. need combined with desire) for 27,400 boarding places at secondary level and 2,100 places at primary level for pupils who were then attending maintained day schools.

207. These figures, as the interim report makes clear, do not take account of children who are already assisted with boarding education. Before considering forward projections to allow for future increases in the school population as a whole, we must therefore add to Dr. Lambert's figures an appropriate allowance for these children. It would not be right to include all children who are now helped with boarding education. These include, as we have already explained, children assisted by government departments, whose numbers may not increase in the future. They also include about 3,000 children in maintained boarding schools who are not considered to be in need of boarding. A cautious estimate might be based on the 14,100[1] pupils (12,500 secondary, 1,600 primary) arrived at in paragraph 196 above. Adding these figures to Dr. Lambert's, we arrive at totals of 39,900 secondary pupils and 3,700 primary pupils.

---

[1] It may be argued that some of the children surveyed by Dr. Lambert would in the normal course of events receive boarding education at public expense, and therefore that to add the whole of the 14,100 pupils (or their future equivalents) who are now assisted with boarding on grounds of need—even though this is a limited figure in the terms we have described in paragraph 196—would involve some double counting. Against this, it will be noted from a reading of Dr. Lambert's report that no specific allowance has been made in his calculations for pupils who may acquire a need for boarding at ages later than those he has surveyed. Neither of these considerations can be quantified, and we do not think that grave error will occur if we regard them as cancelling each other out.

208. The projections from these figures are as follows:

	1966	1970	1975	1980
Primary				
Dr. Lambert's survey in day schools	2,100	2,370	2,627	2,716
Boarding pupils already assisted on grounds of need (by local education authorities only)	1,600	1,806	2,001	2,069
Secondary				
Dr. Lambert's survey in day schools	27,400	28,262	36,037	39,295
Boarding pupils already assisted on grounds of need (by local education authorities only)	12,500	12,893	16,440	17,926
Total (primary and secondary)	43,600	45,331	57,105	62,006

209. At this stage, as in our own calculations, we add in the present total of 18,387 children who are assisted by government departments—regarding this, as in paragraph 205, as a constant future figure to cover different categories of overseas pupils and pupils at present in boarding schools without assistance from public funds, some of whose successors might be assisted under our recommendations. This brings the totals, based on Dr. Lambert's research, and rounded to the nearest 1,000 to:

1966	1970	1975	1980
62,000	64,000	75,000	80,000

Summary

210. In view of the uncertainties we have mentioned, we do not claim to have arrived at accurate or final figures of effective need for boarding education—that is, a child's need to go to boarding school coupled with the parents' willingness to contribute towards the cost. But what is clear is that, over and above the 35,000 pupils in England and Wales already assisted with boarding education, there will be increasing numbers of children who also have a strong case for assistance. From the existing practice of local education authorities, the total need can be inferred to be at least as many as 80,000 places in 1980. Dr. Lambert's research suggests that there is an effective need which, added to the number of boarding pupils who are already assisted because they need boarding, and projected forward to 1980, would also be about 80,000 places—although the proportions of primary and secondary places would be different from those in our own calculations.

211. If the total of effective need were found eventually to vary by as many as 10,000 places above or below 80,000, this would not affect the policies we shall advocate. There are sufficient children likely to need and want boarding education to justify a study of the part which public and other independent schools might play in meeting this need.

CHAPTER 8

The part independent schools might play

212. We concluded in the previous chapter that there would in 1970 be a need for something like 63,000 boarding school places for pupils in need of boarding, rising to 75,000 in 1975 and 80,000 in 1980. As the time scale of the integration scheme we shall propose extends at least until 1980, if not well beyond, we shall take the 1980 figure as our basis of working and of subsequent costing. How far could the public and other independent schools accommodate this need?

213. There are at present some 35,000 pupils (excluding handicapped pupils) helped from public funds with boarding in all types of school in England and Wales. Deducting 3,000 pupils in maintained schools who board although they do not need to, this leaves 32,000. The potential unmet need in 1980, therefore, if the present total of assisted pupils remained the same, would be about 48,000 (80,000—32,000).

Additional grant-aided provision

214. First, what can the grant-aided sector do to meet this additional need? It would in theory be possible to insist on filling all boarding places in maintained and direct grant schools with pupils in need before contemplating any increase in the take-up of places at independent schools. This, we are convinced, would be educationally unsound. Our evidence about the composition of schools suggests that it is sensible to have in any boarding school a substantial element of pupils who are there by choice unrelated to need. The maintained schools already meet a boarding need for some 8,000 of their 11,244 boarders, and the direct grant grammar schools include about 4,000 assisted pupils among their 9,318 boarders. Thus, even if we accepted, which we do not, that these schools should admit only children in need of boarding, the additional provision already available for such pupils could not amount to more than about 8,000 places in England and Wales. There may be some scope for an increase in the proportion of need pupils in direct grant schools; but we shall be considering these schools in our second report and we do not want to prejudge this. What is clear for our present purpose, however, is that the room for expansion is in practice likely to be limited.

215. The next question is therefore whether maintained boarding school provision can be greatly enlarged. There is no doubt that it can and should be increased; but there are capital investment implications which hold out little hope of this providing a ready answer to the problem. A new residential place in a boarding school costs at present about £1,100, in addition to teaching provision at £450 per place in secondary schools. A school for 500 pupils would cost about £775,000. An additional 50,000 places would cost £77·5 million in initial outlay, or £55 million if the teaching provision is discounted. If places were filled on the basis of two-thirds need to one-third choice, £77·5 million would provide only about 33,000 places for children in need of boarding. At

this point the claims of boarding education must be set against those of other educational developments. Although these are not our direct concern as a Commission, we would not wish to see capital resources devoted to boarding schools in the face of other needs arising, for example from the raising of the school leaving age or the implementation of the Plowden Report. Nevertheless we shall recommend later in this report that some new maintained boarding schools should be built in areas in which the total boarding provision is inadequate.

216. Although it would be unrealistic to expect more than a gradual increase in maintained boarding provision as capital resources permit, we must nevertheless adjust the 48,000 additional places required by 1980 to take account of the further contribution which maintained and direct grant schools may be able to make. New provision in maintained schools for pupils in need of boarding is unlikely to exceed 5,000 places in the next 15 years—and to achieve this would mean building about 7,500 places if authorities followed their usual practice of admitting a minority of pupils without boarding needs. The increase in the number of pupils boarding at maintained schools has hitherto been much slower than this—about 3,000 in the past 15 years. In this report we can only guess at the number of extra pupils with boarding needs the present direct grant schools might admit; but if the proportion of their boarding places so filled rose to a half this would provide about another 1,000 places. These two factors taken together would reduce the gap in 1980 from 48,000 to 42,000 places.

Summary of need

217. There appears, therefore, to be a need for 42,000 additional boarding places in England and Wales which, if the need were to be met in full, would probably have to be provided in independent schools. To summarise, this figure has been arrived at as follows:

1980 PROJECTION OF BOARDING NEED

England and Wales (figures to nearest 1,000)

(i) Total boarding need	80,000
(ii) Places already available for assisted pupils in need of boarding	
Maintained schools	8,000
Direct grant schools	4,000
Independent schools	20,000
Total	32,000
(iii) Residual need (i) - (ii)	48,000
(iv) Possible additional provision in the grant-aided sector by 1980	
Maintained schools	5,000
Direct grant schools	1,000
Total	6,000 places
(v) Residual need in 1980 (iii) - (iv)	42,000

Independent schools—a realistic contribution

218. Is it realistic to suppose that independent schools should be asked to take 42,000 more pupils (mainly secondary pupils—see paragraph 204) assisted from public funds in the next 15 years? These pupils would be additional to the 20,000 assisted pupils already in independent schools, making a total of 62,000. There are only 120,000 boarding pupils at present in all recognised efficient schools; 111,976 of them are in schools with 25 per cent or more boarders (37,471 in preparatory schools or departments, 74,505 in secondary schools or departments), and 98,422 in schools with 50 per cent or more boarders (30,752 in preparatory schools or departments, 67,670 in secondary schools or departments).

219. We cannot contemplate taking up places in schools which are not recognised as efficient. There may in due course no longer be any unrecognised schools, in the light of the Secretary of State's decision to require all boarding schools to be recognised as efficient (see Chapter 19). How far the recognition of all schools will affect the figures in the previous paragraph we cannot anticipate; but the addition of a proportion of the 9,847 boarding places in schools which are at present unrecognised would not be very significant, and we do not propose to take these places into account.

220. There are therefore at present between about 100,000 and 110,000 places in schools which might be considered for integration. No one can be sure how many of these places are in schools which may in the future be suitable for assisted pupils. We return in the next chapter to the important issues this raises. Meanwhile it is clear that we must be cautious in our assumptions.

221. In Chapter 7 we made additions of 19,000 and 10,500 to the boarding places now taken up by local education authorities, as our estimates of the unmet needs of less able pupils and of girls respectively. These figures were subsequently increased by about a half within our projections of additional need resulting from increases in the school population between now and 1980. We believe these needs are real; that is why we allowed them full scope in a series of calculations in which we deliberately excluded a number of other factors about which there was possible doubt. Yet to say that these are real needs is quite a different matter from saying that they can be met realistically within the terms of this report. We are not asked to make recommendations to meet the whole of the country's boarding need, even at the minimum levels arrived at in our calculations; but only "to ensure that the public schools should make their maximum contribution to meeting national educational needs".

222. If the total number of places in independent schools were much greater than it is, we would not hesitate to recommend that the needs of the least able children should be met in full by the adaptation of schools over a suitable period. As it is, we must have regard to the considerations we have already touched upon in our Introduction. The first is that some of the least able boys and girls needing boarding education ought probably to be placed in boarding special schools. They ought not all to be included in our reckoning of children who might attend integrated schools. The second is that places for pupils not taking G.C.E. courses are not yet available in substantial numbers, and it will take a considerable time for all public schools to adjust to C.S.E. courses. Third, there will be reasonable limits beyond which it would not be right to

expect the smaller schools to take a disproportionate number of pupils of very modest ability if they are still to retain strong sixth forms. Fourth, we are convinced that there are some pupils who, because of a very low level of general ability, or due to emotional difficulties—even though their handicap may not be so severe as to justify a place in a special school—would not be able to benefit from boarding education except in schools especially staffed and equipped to meet their needs. We shall say more about this in Chapter 10.

223. We are urging that there should be more assisted boarding places for girls at all levels of ability, provided partly through the development of co-education. But here too—allowing for the fact that the extra provision we propose for children of C.S.E. levels of ability would include additional provision for girls—we do not see that it would be realistic to think in terms of an additional 20,000 to 30,000 places being made available to girls in the next 15 years.

Conclusion

224. We accept, therefore, that there is no yardstick which can give us a firm answer to the question how many boarding places to take up in independent schools. We can only make what we think is a sensible estimate of places in schools which will, we hope, prove suitable—places which could undoubtedly be filled by pupils in need of boarding. There are between 100,000 and 110,000 places in independent schools which might be reckoned as boarding schools, in many of which the boarders are in a minority. We shall make what we think is a reasonable proposal that 45,000 of these places should be taken up by assisted pupils. This number would include (the future equivalent of) the 20,000 boarding pupils already assisted at independent schools. In other words, we propose that by 1980 there should be 25,000 more assisted pupils than at present. It may be possible at some future date to look beyond this target; but meanwhile it is a target which we believe will meet our terms of reference, and it is the one we shall adopt for planning and costing our policy.

Scotland

225. Before going further however, we must take the Scottish figures into account, as they must be included in our estimates of the cost of integration, even if a different scheme is eventually adopted in Scotland. The figures in Chapter 18 show that by 1980 there may be 3,000 pupils in Scotland requiring boarding for whom places will not be available in Scotland. There is no reason to suppose that all independent schools in Scotland, any more than in England and Wales, would be suitable to take part in a scheme of integration, and there may be other special factors to take into account. For present purposes, however, we think a minimum assumption of need (and therefore of cost) is that 2,000 extra places may be required in independent schools in Scotland. This would raise the total need in Great Britain as a whole to 47,000 places which might be sought in independent schools by 1980.

Primary and secondary places

226. Our provisional estimate is that about 38,000 of these 47,000 places should be taken up in secondary schools or departments (including some pupils below the age of 13), and about 9,000 in primary or preparatory

1—E

schools or departments (including some pupils up to the age of 13). This is in terms of the present age structure of the schools, which may itself change as a result of our proposals. Only the experience of the Boarding Schools Corporation will tell whether this is exactly the right balance between primary or preparatory and secondary provision, but it is at this stage as good an estimate as we can make for costing purposes.

CHAPTER 9

Are independent schools the right place?

227. Can the independent schools meet these needs? Can they educate and care for pupils who will be rather different from those they are accustomed to? Will the assisted pupils be happy in these schools? In what ways will the schools have to modify their way of life in the face of the new demands on them? These are questions that we have asked ourselves on our visits to schools. They are also questions to which the research of Dr. Lambert and his colleagues is highly relevant. Some of their findings may be published about the time our own report appears—others rather later—and those who have to consider our recommendations will obviously look at these findings carefully. One central issue raised for our recommendations by Dr. Lambert's work is this: what is the depth of change that will be required in an integrated school, if it is to provide a happy and constructive environment for all its pupils?

228. In the majority of public schools we have visited, changes have already taken place, and are continuously taking place, which have modified their character since a generation ago. There have been changes in the curriculum: in particular, there is far more emphasis on science and technology. Far more attention is paid to public examinations and to the civic universities, to colleges of education and further education. More of the teaching staff, the younger masters and mistresses especially, have been trained for their work. The customs of the schools and the behaviour of the boys and girls in them have changed. The seniors expect greater freedom from rules, and restrictions and prefectorial duties have in some cases been significantly reduced. There are fewer compulsory services in Chapel and in houses. There is less corporal punishment, and personal fagging has been modified and in some cases abolished. There is less emphasis on team games and military exercises, and more on cultural and creative activities. These are only a few of the instances in which the public schools are changing.

229. So change is already occurring. But how deep do these changes go? It is possible for a school to adapt itself in various ways, indeed in very noticeable ways, without basically changing either its goals or its underlying institutional structure—the roles, for instance, played by housemasters or prefects. In fact there is reason to think that even the goals of the schools have changed, above all in the greater emphasis on academic success. This itself can have various effects on the other values and on the organization. In one school we visited, for instance, senior pupils had been released from prefectorial duties so that they could devote more time to their own work and intellectual pursuits. This meant that younger pupils were now taking more responsibility, which itself affected the way the school was run; and the change had produced a genuine shift in values which a senior teacher registered, from a particular point of view, by suggesting that it had made the older pupils "rather more

selfish". From a different point of view, this same change could be described by saying that the values of service, loyalty and cohesion were rather less stifling of individual exploration than they used to be. However it is put, it was clear that something significant was happening. We do not think that the change to a greater academic emphasis and what goes with it is the change most relevant to integration. We mention these facts merely to show (what might otherwise be doubted) that there can be, and have been, changes which are not merely superficial.

230. In many schools, even quite radical changes are contained in a general framework of values and assumptions which relate to the existing types of pupil, and would not necessarily apply to assisted pupils from a different background. If integration is accepted as a principle, not merely customs will have to be re-examined, but the working of the school as a social system. Certain features of the environment which are virtually invisible to those working in it, or which appear as a legitimate and entirely normal reflection of the culture of the pupils and parents, may seem intrusive or pointless or an affront to pupils from a different background. A system of customs and rules, which appear unexceptionable to those who have grown up with them, may well need to be re-examined and submitted to the remorseless question: "What function is this regulation expected to fulfil?" Nothing is more difficult than to cultivate the kind of detachment and reflectiveness that enables one to stand outside an institution in which one is working and ask how it should respond to a new kind of social situation. Yet this is in fact what ought to be done if the public schools are to question whether what they have hitherto regarded as a "natural" way of doing things is entirely appropriate to satisfying the needs of a new type of pupil.

Staffing

231. If the necessary changes are to take place, a great deal will depend on the staff. From studying the experience of public schools which have taken children from the State system, and from conversations we have had with staff in the schools, we believe there are differences in attitudes, behaviour and culture which many of the staff in public schools do not fully comprehend because they have never taught working class children in a day school. Dr. Lambert points out that some of the smaller independent schools and maintained boarding schools already do excellent work with assisted pupils, partly because they have for years welcomed children from maintained day schools who have not experienced the boarding preparatory schools in which, he says, "the attitudes and assumptions of the public schools are learned". We have no doubt that the very many humane and sensitive teachers in public schools will also be well-disposed to deal with the problems. But it is a question, not only of sensitivity, but of experience.

232. There are on the staff of public schools some who have been themselves educated in the State system and understand the day school environment; some, again, who have taught in the maintained system. There should be more. There should ideally be the same interflow of staff in boys' schools as occurs to a much greater extent between girls' public schools and girls' maintained schools. The public school boy who goes into teaching would do well to work first in a maintained school if he intends to teach later in a public school. There will in any case be a continuing turnover of staff in the

schools. For example, in a 1 in 10 random sample of public schools we found that, over a period of four years (1962-66), about a third of the teaching staff in boys' schools and about a half in girls' schools, had been newly appointed. This suggests that there would be considerable scope for making new appointments from other types of school. We recommend in Chapter 11 that replacements at integrating schools should be deliberately chosen to bring in teachers from the kinds of school the assisted pupils come from.

233. Boys' public schools are often staffed solely by men, and girls' schools (less frequently) solely by women. The schools should consider ways of introducing more women on to the staffs of boys' schools and more men on to those of girls' schools. The institution of the Dame at Eton is one method of achieving this in boys' schools which we would commend. If this were done, one element of the sexual divisiveness in the schools would be mitigated. Children need counsel and advice from their elders of both sexes and too often in the public schools they have only one to which to turn.

234. We turn now to some specific areas in which changes are likely to be necessary.

Prefects

There are substantial differences both between day and boarding schools, and between public schools and others, in the prefectorial system. Even though some public schools have modified the powers and duties of prefects, there is in these schools a defined hierarchy of guidance and control, exercised by prefects, monitors and senior pupils in other offices of authority over the rest of the pupils in the school. The personal interest which senior pupils in authority often show in the progress of those in their care is admirable: and there is no doubt that the delegation of responsibilities to pupils enables the staff to give more time and effort to pupils and establish good relationships with them. But pupils from the maintained sector are likely to find this kind of prefectorial control strange. They will be used to being controlled by prefects in matters of school routine, but may be surprised if prefects assume what they would regard as the function of adults.

Punishments

235. Many people picture the public schools as places where corporal punishment is frequently used, often for trivial offences. It certainly was so in the past. But there is good evidence that a marked change has taken place in the last decade, and beating is on the decline. This is in line with the view of the then Secretary of State (in answer to a Parliamentary Question on 19th December 1967) that "the practice of corporal punishment should be dropped from our schools" and his hope that "the local authorities, the governing bodies of schools and the teachers themselves will all use their power and influence to achieve this end". We think all boarding schools, and in particular any public schools which are going to accept assisted pupils, should review most carefully the ways in which they sanction corporal punishment. In day schools such punishment can be checked by parental and public opinion. In boarding schools this is more difficult and it is not easy for boys to complain, for that would be to flout the conventions of the school. Nor, in independent schools, do their parents have recourse to the local education authority, as have parents of children at maintained schools.

236. While we hope that this form of punishment will decline and disappear, there is one feature of it which should now cease—as indeed it has already ceased at a number of public schools. This is the beating of boys by boys. For years the public schools have been criticised for permitting this practice to continue, and we are unconvinced by any of the defences which have been made to us. If, as it is claimed, the practice is dying out, why not abolish it? We agree with the statement made by the headmaster of a famous public school: "It is worse for those who inflict this punishment, and for those who watch it being inflicted, than for the boy who suffers it". We would not be prepared to accept for integration any school where the practice continued.

237. There are other physical punishments which should be reconsidered at the same time. We have been told of punishments such as restriction of diet or of sleep. These are not wise. Nor are they typical. Before assisted pupils are sent to public or other independent boarding schools, the Boarding Schools Corporation ought to satisfy themselves that the scale and type of punishment within a school is sensible.

Fagging

238. Many public schools have now abolished personal fagging. It would be undesirable in an integrated school. There is everything to be said for boys (as well as girls) helping to run the house they are living in and taking on a reasonable share of minor chores, but nothing to be said for boys having to run messages, clean shoes or sweep out studies for the sole benefit of senior boys. Personal fagging, like beating by prefects, is a type of excessive authority which would be deeply resented by the vast majority of children in the maintained sector, and by their parents.

Other changes

239. We may also mention one or two other features of their domestic arrangements which we think that public schools should consider changing. Many schools could provide more privacy, in particular by the partitioning of large dormitories, where practicable, to make them less like barracks. Some schools, both boys' and girls', could accept somewhat freer forms of dress, especially at the weekends. There are still schools at which uniform is not only deliberately eccentric or archaic, but also flaunts class differences. In our view, a school uniform should normally be one which the child can reasonably wear, if he or she wishes, in the holidays. It would not be right for public money to be spent on equipping assisted pupils with an unnecessarily costly uniform, or for an undue amount of extras on clothes. Last among these suggestions, we think that there should be more alternatives to Cadet Force activities, with genuine freedom to choose between them; and also more choice and variety of games.

Parents and their children

240. Children at boarding schools tend to be less cut off from their homes than they were. In these days choice of schools is often conditioned by the car rather than the railway: many parents choose schools they can visit within a day's return journey. An increasing number of schools now allow visits by parents three or more times a term. Pupils at some schools are allowed home at least twice each term. On the other hand, very few schools

let pupils go home every weekend or every second weekend, and this is a practice which might be attractive to many parents and pupils unfamiliar with boarding education. There are arguments against weekly boarding. Many schools hold that the weekend is a time of special value in the school community, providing opportunities for activities in which pupils could not join at home, as well as the spiritual focus of Sunday chapel, central to the life of many denominational schools. They would regard a regular weekly exodus as too disruptive and time consuming. Another argument is that pupils whose parents live abroad or too far away would not be able to go home so frequently and would be made unhappy if the majority did so. But against these arguments must be set the advantages of children who can do so maintaining frequent and close contact with their homes and with life outside the school, and we do not believe the problems are insurmountable. In schools where frequent home visits are allowed, a quite different environment, free from many of the normal rules and restrictions, can be created for those who are left behind. Children who cannot go home to their parents at the weekend are often invited to the homes of their friends, and there take part in family life and the life of the neighbourhood. The regular weekly service can be held on Sunday evening after the pupils have returned from their weekend, and parents can be invited to attend with their children. Each school must make its own decisions about weekly (or other periodic) boarding; but we urge them to be adventurous, and also not to overlook the relief to teaching staff of having more weekends free.

241. In those weekends that are spent at school, and in the evenings, the boarding school can offer its pupils some leisure; indeed, boys and girls at boarding schools may have more chance of leisure than their contemporaries at day schools who have long journeys to make each day. There are boarding schools at which some of this advantage is lost through free time being too regimented. But the best schools use such leisure time most creatively to awaken in their pupils an interest in all sorts of topics and pursuits. There is here, however, a difference which those coming from day schools will feel: these pursuits will be organised in the school and the children will no longer have their weekends to themselves free from the constraints of school life. It is important that, as far as is practicable, children at boarding school should be able to continue to engage in the leisure pursuits which they themselves like and to play the games they are used to.

The individual and the community

242. Behind these more particular issues, there is the central question of what types of character development the public school seeks to encourage; here, most fundamentally, it will have to consider its goals in the face of the new situation. It is many years since E. M. Forster, describing his days at a public school at the end of the last century, criticised them for making boys believe that "firmness and self-complacency between them compose the whole armour of man" and for sending them out into the world "with well-developed bodies, fairly developed minds and undeveloped hearts". The public schools—and the world—have changed since those days, but during the past fifty years the public schools have been repeatedly criticised for quenching natural affection, originality and spontaneity, and for imposing pressure on the individual boy who feels compelled to fit in with the dominant

opinion in his house. Some of these criticisms have been exaggerated, and the schools and their traditions vary a great deal. Some of the criticisms spring from the fact that these are boarding schools. Maintained boarding schools face similar difficulties.

243. Yet when all this is said, the public schools will face a delicate problem if they are to admit large numbers of assisted pupils. Children from one class in society can express themselves in a different way from those in another and it is important to distinguish between a superficial style and fundamental concerns. Serious argument about society, appreciation of its creative arts and scientific achievements, the development of a capacity to learn from the achievements of the past and the desire to create a better future have formed the basis of every good educational system. They should not be confused with the manners which particular classes in society have adopted as a norm. There should be no question of the public schools admitting from the maintained sector only those boys or girls who fit in with their prevailing code of manners and rejecting those whose outward behaviour does not accord with the conventions to which the schools have been accustomed.

The effects of integration

244. Some schools would already like to change in directions which would make integration a success; they have as yet had no incentive to do so. It is above all integration itself, the arrival of assisted pupils, which will provide the opportunity and the motive force for change. If a good number of schools become co-educational, this change will deeply modify the style and ethos of those schools. However, Dr. Lambert's work points to a danger of which we are bound to take note, and which we must urge schools to keep constantly in mind. That a school will change if it admits a half or more of assisted pupils, is obvious. It unhappily does not follow that the resultant change will necessarily be in the best interests of those pupils, or indeed any of the pupils. A school could react to such a new situation in a negative way, by imposing a stricter and less flexible regime than it ran before. A change to co-education, again, may elicit an alarmed response, with segregation and an outbreak of regulations designed to minimise the effects of the change. If we thought that these negative responses were likely to be general, we clearly should not be making our recommendations. They are, however, possible, and imaginative, reflective and sympathetic thought will be needed to guard against them. The schools themselves would not accept that they are incapable of changing in constructive and imaginative ways; neither do we.

245. In urging, as we have done, the need for various sorts of change, we have been drawing attention to vital aspects of the integration process which may well be underestimated or overlooked. We do not want to give an impression that there is little of value in the schools as they are. There is a great deal. Very obvious is the high level of academic achievement in many schools, and the tradition of hard work well done; this scarcely needs emphasis. In the best schools there is also an insistence that pupils should commit themselves wholeheartedly to leisure-time activities of their own choosing, giving of their utmost—whether it be in singing, team games, drama, athletics, painting, debating or chess. In days gone by, such enthusiasm was demanded almost solely for corporate activities such as team games; but today it is widely recognised that what matters is to arouse interest first, and then devotion and hard work, in pursuits which the boy or girl is given time to enjoy.

246. Important above all is the manner in which many teachers in the public schools view their responsibilities to their pupils. This is very impressive.To refer to it can sometimes provoke misunderstanding, for it suggests to some people that here is an implied criticism of other teachers. One of the harmful effects of the division between the independent and the maintained sectors is that those who work in each do not fully understand the other. The staff of public schools do not know how often their colleagues in the maintained day schools have to correct their pupils' work at home, not merely during the week, but over weekends; and how much time some of them devote on Saturdays and in the holidays to school games and other activities. The staff of maintained day schools do not always appreciate how exacting are the functions of housemasters and tutors at a boarding school and how much work they do informally with pupils and parents. In praising the work in one sector we most emphatically do not wish to denigrate the other. But we wish to express our admiration for the open and relaxed relationship between pupils and teachers in the best independent schools, and the willingness of teachers to devote so great a part of their off-duty hours in term-time to their pupils.

247. It is often in these off-duty hours that the informal relations develop between the staff and pupils, which are so notable a feature of the good boarding school. A school ought to encourage its pupils freely to develop their own interests and activities, yet wean them from the trivial and worthless to the serious and valuable. Some public schools are more successful than others in doing this, as some maintained schools succeed better than others; but that a considerable number are successful, aided by the fact that they are boarding schools, seems to us beyond question.

248. When the representatives of the public schools have met us, they have put to us their fears that integration could mean the end of that excellence which the best public schools accept as their aim. This need not be so. What we are proposing is in certain ways a harder task than most of the schools have had till now. While all teaching is difficult, the task of eliciting academic achievement from children with academic ambitions is not the most difficult task a teacher can face; nor is that of encouraging poise and good manners in children with social advantages. Integration offers a wider range of things to be done.

Part Four

Integration

CHAPTER 10

Integration—boarding schools

Introduction

249. This chapter contains the most difficult and contentious part of our task. We attempt to answer the question how the public schools are to be integrated with the public system of education.

250. Any scheme will probably take 15 or 20 years to work out. That is why it must take account of the way in which secondary education is developing in the country at large. It would be futile to make proposals which will be grossly anomalous in twenty years' time. The scheme must bring about integration by sure degrees while at the same time ensuring that r o school is changed at a greater speed than it can endure. The pupils who are going to boarding school—and to an independent boarding school—for the first time must not be sacrificed to the traditions of the school: yet neither must the educational value of the school be diminished by such pupils being accepted there. The way of life in the schools will have to change; but the changes must not be so great as to annihilate their most valuable qualities.

Summary of our proposals

251. We shall argue first that as a guide-line the proportion in any integrated school of pupils who are assisted and have previously attended maintained schools for at least three years, must be at least half the total number of boarding pupils in the school. Second, that as the development of schools in the maintained sector is governed by the policy of comprehensiveness, independent schools which are integrated must conform as far as possible to this policy. On the comprehensive principle we shall make an important reservation in paragraphs 273 to 275 below; but if the public schools are to be integrated at all, they must follow the pattern of education in secondary education in the public sector. There is a wide variety of ways in which individual schools can do so. We set these out in detail in order to show how the independent schools could help to educate different kinds of children.

Numbers of assisted pupils

252. If only a small number of assisted pupils were admitted, they would have virtually no impact upon a school. Some headmasters and headmistresses in talking to us have said that they should not be asked to take more assisted pupils than the school can "absorb". This is not the right way to look at the matter. The influx of assisted pupils in the school, so far from being a storm which the school must weather, should be regarded as a migration which will make the school a better place. If these children are to have the chance to make an impact—if the social spectrum of the public schools is to be widened to the point where they are no longer identifiable with particular classes in society—they must be admitted in substantial numbers.

123

253. That is why we recommend that:

(i) No school should be regarded as having established a numerical basis for successful integration—quite apart from any other necessary changes—until the proportion of boarding pupils who are assisted and who attended maintained schools for at least three years before entering an integrated school is at least a half. This proportion would be in addition to assisted pupils who have not attended maintained schools but are nevertheless in need of boarding. Attendance at maintained schools should normally have been immediately prior to the admission to the public (or other independent) school.

(ii) Until this stage is reached, a school entering an integration scheme should not be regarded as integrated, but as "integrating".

(iii) As soon as possible after the start of a scheme of integration, at least a half of the pupils *admitted* to a school in any year should be assisted pupils. The proportion of assisted pupils in the school as a whole should reach a half within not more than seven years from the first intake of pupils under an approved scheme.

254. Some of us, foreseeing in detail the difficulties which individual schools will face in adjusting to an intake of assisted pupils, would have preferred to leave the proportion of such pupils to the good sense of the school's governing body and headmaster. Others of us would have preferred to see a higher proportion mentioned as the goal, partly because this would ensure a better social mix among the assisted pupils and therefore in the school itself, and partly because they fear that with the limited funds available there is a danger that a number of schools will remain for many years partially integrated and very few schools will be fully integrated. But on balance we are agreed that the phrase "at least half" is a reasonable guide-line to what we have in mind.

255. After the period of build-up of assisted places, at least a half will be the minimum acceptable intake to any integrated school of assisted pupils who have previously attended maintained schools. It may be, however, that there will be further assisted pupils who have not attended maintained schools; this would certainly apply to a significant proportion of those now assisted by government departments. To this extent, the proportion of assisted pupils may, when our proposals have taken full effect, be significantly higher than a half at some schools.

Schools outside integration

256. Although all recognised efficient secondary boarding schools should be regarded as eligible for integration, no school should have a prescriptive right to be brought into the new scheme. Some may be too small, others may have inadequate premises or be otherwise educationally unsuitable. Some might over a period be able to reach the standards required and for this reason we put no terminal date upon negotiations with the independent schools as a whole. The real obstacle to widespread integration may well be financial; we consider this in a later chapter, and make recommendations as to the priorities which we think should be applied.

257. Those independent schools which are not integrated with the maintained sector should, subject to observing standards which we shall recommend the Secretary of State to apply to all independent boarding schools (see Chapter

19), and to a reserve power of fee control which we shall also recommend, continue to develop in whatever way they wish.

258. We do not propose any formal measures for closer association with the maintained sector for those boarding schools not brought within an integrated system. But we recommend that such schools should establish relationships with schools in the same neighbourhood, through games fixtures, joint social occasions, joint use of teaching facilities where appropriate, and should develop links between teaching staffs as well as pupils. There may in the long term be other roads to integration which we cannot at present foresee, but for which developments of this kind would be a useful preparation.

Towards a comprehensive policy

259. The present national policy in secondary education is to postpone academic selection until as late as possible in a child's school life and to apply it normally in the form of self-selection. This means in practice:

(i) the provision of academic opportunities for all children—either by providing them in the schools which they attend from the age of 11, 12 or 13, or by making transfer to another school available to all at some later age.

(ii) no impoverishment of other schools through creaming off their most able pupils.

(iii) as great a social and academic mix as can be achieved in individual schools, subject to restrictions of size and location but not of deliberate policy.

260. Our terms of reference require us to propose ways by which the public schools should conform "increasingly" with these principles. We also have to ensure that the schools "make their maximum contribution to meeting national educational needs".

261. We found this problem the hardest of all which have confronted us. On the one hand we are faced by the plea of the public schools that while they are willing to broaden their entry they cannot easily become fully comprehensive because the vast majority of the schools are too small. They also plead that, if they became fully comprehensive and admitted children from the lowest to the highest range of ability, they would not be exploiting what is in a number of schools their strongest suit, namely a well-staffed and large sixth form. On the other hand it would clearly be unacceptable to schools in the maintained sector if, at the very time when they are moving towards a comprehensive system, the public schools were to be excluded and placed in a special position. In this situation we believe that a compromise must be struck. Those independent boarding schools[1] in the process of integration

---

[1] *Boarding*

By boarding schools we mean, as a working premise, those which have a quarter or more of their pupils in residence. This is an arbitrary definition and we do not propose that all schools with a boarding element of only 25 per cent should necessarily be brought within our recommendations. It would depend upon the size and nature of the school, and the contribution which it might make to meeting boarding "need". Our purpose in fixing the proportion so low is that schools should not *automatically* be excluded from boarding integration because they have at present less than half their pupils as boarders, although it may well be that in practice schools with at least a half of their pupils in residence would be more suitable candidates, and it is on these that the main emphasis will lie. There were in January, 1967, 103 boys', 80 girls' and 3 co-educational public schools which were predominantly boarding schools (i.e. had more than 50 per cent boarders), as well as 70 boys', 76 girls' and 41 co-educational recognised efficient secondary schools which were not public schools.

which are not large enough to be fully comprehensive should nevertheless significantly widen both their curriculum and their examination objectives in order to include a substantial amount of work directed at the Certificate of Secondary Education. This examination has itself great flexibility, both in subject matter and in style of assessment, and is (as an objective in few or many subjects) well within the capacities of pupils across a very wide range of ability. Since it could, within the environment of a boarding school favoured by a good staffing ratio, provide the framework for the education of some three-quarters of the ability range, it follows that the schools we are here describing should expect to admit something like this proportion of the ability range. But they would not be expected to admit assisted pupils for whom meaningful work within the C.S.E. context would be impossible.

262. A minority report signed by three of our colleagues criticises us for excluding "large numbers of pupils . . . as being unable to cope with the courses envisaged". This is not so. Under our proposals the great majority of integrated schools will be expected to take pupils from 70 to 80 per cent of the whole range of ability. Those which are large enough should admit from the whole ability range, just as maintained comprehensive schools admit all children except those who go to special schools. This cannot happen at all boarding schools, because of the small size of so many of them; but even some of the smaller ones should concentrate on provision for the less able rather than the more able. It is true that some of the least able children in need of boarding education may not find a place under our proposals; but they will not be many.

The scope of the reorganisation

263. When people mistakenly say that the public schools are already comprehensive, they usually mean that some of the pupils are of lower measured intelligence than would be found in grammar schools. But few—especially of the boys' schools[1]—in fact admit pupils of below average ability and the great majority, geared as they are to G.C.E. examination, much more closely resemble grammar schools than comprehensive schools. Clearly the schools bring out the latent academic ability of their less able entrants. But as well as showing that the schools are doing this job well, the figures[1] also indicate that there is a proportion of pupils already in the schools for whom something other than a grammar type curriculum would be preferable. (The figures point to the same conclusion for the maintained grammar schools[1], even when allowance is made for early leaving, and there is undoubtedly

---

[1] Mr. Kalton's figures of measured intelligence ("The Public Schools: A factual survey"; page 30) are the only ones we have and we quote them with the reservation that the I.Q. records of less than one-third of all new entrants to the schools in 1962–63 were available to him for his analysis. Only 2 per cent of these entrants had an intelligence quotient of less than 100—i.e. were of less than average intelligence; 27 per cent in boarding/day schools and 20 per cent in wholly boarding schools had a Moray House score below 115; the great majority were within what might broadly be termed the grammar school range.

In the same year (1962–63), according to Mr. Kalton's figures (page 86) only about 10 per cent of boarders leaving H.M.C. schools failed to achieve four 'O' level passes in G.C.E., compared with 33 per cent of boys in maintained grammar schools. Less than 40 per cent left without at least one 'A' level pass (page 88), compared with 62 per cent of boys in maintained grammar schools. (The 1965–66 figure for boys leaving maintained grammar schools without at least one 'A' level had improved to 51 per cent. We have no figures for H.M.C. schools since 1962-63—see Appendix 6—but the indications are that here, too, there has been some improvement since 1962–63).

ground for thinking that not all pupils in grammar schools are best suited by the curriculum and teaching methods). A different type of curriculum would be appropriate for a significant proportion of the pupils who would be assisted under our recommendations, assuming that they will represent a much wider ability range. Something other than a straightforward continuance of the grammar type of curriculum is therefore required, and there is no inconsistency in our making proposals which will enable boarding public schools to play an increasing part in the comprehensive provision of the country as a whole.

264. There is one other way in which small schools can widen their ability range without loss of academic standards: that is by cutting down the age range. In practice this means a tiering system, with different schools catering for different age ranges. This is what is happening in the reorganisation of maintained day schools, with transfers at 13, 14 or 16 according to authorities' predilections, where there are not all-through comprehensive schools. Except in the case of some sixth form colleges, transfer will not normally be based on assessment of ability.

265. Public schools, however, are not keen to have a break which would result in transfers to other schools for the last two or three years of school life. Their doubts may in part reflect an element of distrust of something which is as yet unfamiliar in this country. This form of organisation is not unknown in other countries, at least in day schools—and we believe that in practice a three year school, with a deliberate approach to the needs of older pupils, could be a valuable form of organisation. We have sympathy with the objection that, under arrangements for tiering by age range, a number of schools would lose their sixth form work. No school wants to lose an existing sixth form, and it is fair to add that the problem is not one which the maintained sector has had to face in large measure; under comprehensive reorganisation, nearly all former grammar schools have been able to retain their sixth forms.

266. Nevertheless, a tiering system may be the right answer for some of the schools we are considering. In particular, some of the schools with a boarding preparatory department now admitting at 8 might reorganise this department to cater for pupils of say 11 to 14, leaving the main school to concentrate on the age range 14 upwards. This would make possible a larger annual intake and should result in a broadening and strengthening of the school over the whole secondary age range.

267. It is not necessary for schools to have similar numbers of pupils at each age point. For example, schools which, under a tiering arrangement, became a sixth form "top" within a group of associated schools, need not necessarily cease to provide for all younger pupils. A school could be shaped in its age structure like a mushroom, with an all-through age range, but having a greatly expanded sixth form drawing pupils from other schools.

268. Despite the flexibility which tiering would offer, it is important not to overlook the needs of families who may have more than one child attending boarding school. The parents may prefer to have their children in the same school and this means that some schools with a wide age range should be available; they should be co-educational schools where possible, in order to cater for brothers and sisters.

269. The organisation within individual secondary boarding schools should thus be such as to enable them to admit children over either the whole or part of the age range 11-18. Some might have a regular pattern of dual entry at say 12/13 and 15/16, leading to a larger than average sixth form. Others might decide to concentrate on the age group 11-16, with relatively few pupils staying on after that age, to follow general sixth form courses.

Age of entry

270. If need is the criterion, assisted pupils should ideally be able to enter boarding school at the age when need arises—for example, if orphaned, or when parents move overseas. This presupposes a more flexible age of entry than at present. Some schools already admit at different ages, but their late admissions are only on a small scale and the schools are not geared to admissions on a significant scale above the age of 13. The question is how to build flexibility into the system without causing schools to hold places vacant on the off-chance of "need" occurring. It would be unwise to try to draw up a blueprint to meet the as yet unknown incidence of late entry. Only a fairly long period of build-up will show how big a factor this is. But it may eventually be possible—and would certainly be helpful in the allocation of places —for some schools to be organised to take their *normal* entry at 11, others at 12, 13 or 14, with any older need pupils being admitted to senior forms or sixth form colleges. If schools within a group[1] adopted a tiered system, by allocating pupils of different age bands to different schools within the group, this would solve the problem of varying ages of entry within the group.

Boarding/day provision

271. A medium sized or small boarding school, as has already been said, will have difficulty in restructuring itself on comprehensive lines. There is an important device which would help them to do so. Where they are situated in or on the outskirts of cities and towns, they could form a consortium with maintained schools, sharing teachers and equipment in subjects for which teachers are scarce, or in which only a few pupils from each school might wish to follow a particular course.

272. There is another development which could be even more important. If local education authorities would co-operate, there might be day school additions to existing boarding schools to form comprehensive boarding/day schools. This would normally mean the provision of day school buildings from public funds, adjacent to an existing independent boarding school. There are legal and administrative difficulties in such a scheme. We understand that, under the present law, either there would have to be two separate schools or the single resultant school would have to be a new kind of legal entity. The question is therefore how far public funds could be devoted to capital works at, and continuing maintenance of, what is at present an independent school. Some new legal arrangement, possibly similar to that which enables capital works to be carried out mainly at public expense at voluntary aided schools, would have to be devised. There would remain the question whether all tuition should be free, as it is by law in schools maintained by local education authorities. We do not see that these should be insuperable

---

[1] See Chapter 11 for references to group arrangements.

problems, or that there is any reason why a hybrid school of this kind should not be just as successful as are many existing boarding/day public schools.

The exception to the comprehensive principle

273. We said above that at this stage we could envisage only partially accepting the comprehensive principle and that we must make an important reservation. Ideally the full range of ability should be represented within a public school. But only in the very largest schools would it be possible to include the whole ability range without detriment to the education and well-being of any of the children. In schools of less than six or seven forms of entry[1] pupils at both ends of the spectrum of ability could not have their needs adequately met under any form of organisation which could be devised.

274. We also doubt whether the least able of the pupils for whom a boarding school might on social grounds be regarded at first sight as an answer to their needs would in fact be happy in, or would benefit from being at, most of the schools in our terms of reference. We are here thinking only of that minority of pupils who would be incapable of coping successfully within a school accepting the C.S.E. examination as an integral and important part of its work. Such a minority, as we have said in paragraph 261, would be contained within the least able quarter of any year group of secondary school age.

275. If such children were sent to a boarding school of average size, they would be a tiny minority within the whole range of assisted and fee-paying pupils. They could not fail to sense their educational inadequacy; they would be deprived of the ways in which in a day school they could compensate for it, for instance with friends outside the school. In a day school, school has an end in the evenings and over the weekends. In a boarding school it never ends until the holidays. It is true that they might find the special sympathy and understanding which public school staffs have so often shown in enabling children who do not take kindly to books to enjoy boarding. But they would have a more difficult time with their contemporaries. Real unhappiness would, we believe, occur if a small group of very much less able children were admitted to a closely knit community—with a life to be lived outside the classroom—in which the great majority of contemporaries were significantly more able, including some perhaps at the opposite extreme of ability. Such children might find it difficult to escape from continual reminders of their academic limitations in other fields of community life.

Emotionally deprived children

276. There is another category of children whose placing in integrated schools will need special care—those with emotional difficulties. We are not referring to children considered by a local education authority to be maladjusted and in need of special educational treatment. Equally, we do not mean the normally well adjusted child who, leaving a day school for a boarding school environment for the first time, will need to adjust and may in the process have minor and temporary emotional troubles. Between these two categories there may be a number of children with very real difficulties who need especially sympathetic care. Definition of this group cannot be precise but teachers and social workers will know the kind of children we have in mind. A boarding

---

[1] This is the lower limit suggested in Circular 10/65.

school will not always be the best environment for their educational and social development. But, where it is considered to be (and this already applies to a number of fee-paying pupils), if a school is to do full justice to the majority of its pupils it should not be expected to take more than a limited number of children who may make excessive demands on the teaching staff and—particularly in a boarding school—on their fellow pupils.

277. We regret having to recommend making such exceptions. Some of these are the children of *Half Our Future* who so often come at the bottom of educational priorities. Something must be done for them. The public schools which have been so adamant in saying that they could not possibly envisage teaching such children should pause for thought and ask themselves whether as a sector of secondary education they should not contribute to this work. Some other independent schools already do; and their contribution to boarding need is of great value; indeed we would give this priority over many other schemes of integration. We would welcome proposals from schools which are prepared to see their task not in terms of high academic achievement but of meeting the equally important needs of less able children. Such schools would take some of their pupils to 'O' level—and there would have to be recognised and easy arrangements for those who were successful to transfer to other schools for sixth form work. But children who could not cope with the C.S.E. would not in such a school be made to feel miserably inadequate. Again, schools which are willing and able to cater specially for a higher proportion than is normal of disturbed children should be encouraged to do so. How many public schools will respond to this challenge?

THE DIFFERENT PATTERNS OF INTEGRATION

The majority of schools

278. The majority of independent schools would be expected therefore to admit any assisted pupil who would be capable of taking a course at a level of ability approximating to that required for C.S.E. Only if this is done will it be possible for a substantial majority of all children needing boarding education to be regarded as eligible for State-assisted places in these schools. It follows that the schools should be equipped for all types of work from C.S.E. to G.C.E. 'A' level[1].

279. What size of boarding school would be able to offer good sixth form education and also admit pupils with the C.S.E. as their goal? It is not much use looking at the size of comprehensive schools for guidance because:

  (i) in many boarding schools the pupils are in smaller class groups, and this means that a wider range of ability can be admitted within a smaller sized annual intake of pupils.

---

[1] There are two riders to add at this point (i) The first is that, although we are speaking in terms of C.S.E. and G.C.E. work, we recognise that much thought is likely to be given to the desirability of these examinations and their future development or possible replacement. We do not want our proposals to be read only in terms of the 1968 situation. We are referring to levels of ability which are at present identifiable roughly in the way we have described, but which at some future date—and integration will be a lengthy process—may call for some quite different designation. (ii) The second is that we recognise the difficulties of prognosis of ability in C.S.E. terms for children at the age of admission to a secondary boarding school, particularly if they have suffered deprivation. Children should normally be given the benefit of any doubt which arises on educational grounds.

(ii) if the majority of public schools do not admit pupils over the *whole* ability range, this will enable them to provide an adequate range of courses within a much smaller annual intake of pupils than is possible in a comprehensive school.

It should be possible to meet the needs of children in this spread of ability within the compass of five forms of entry or even less. Schools may vary widely in their class sizes. But to take an example, assuming an average class size of 25, five forms of entry would mean an annual intake of about 125 children. A five year school (from 13 to 18) would have a total of some 600 pupils (with a sixth form of over 200) if the great majority stayed the full course. A three year school covering the same ability range would be adequate with 375 or so pupils. The equivalent sizes of schools with four forms of entry might be 475 and 300 pupils (i.e. for five and three year courses respectively). With the smaller teaching groups which many schools have, similar forms of organisation would be practicable with smaller total numbers. Yet it is bound to be the larger schools which can offer the most educational flexibility.

280. What of the teaching requirements? Both boys' and girls' schools already take pupils below the normal grammar school level of ability. We have commented that boys' schools tend to set their sights on 'A' level achievement for all pupils. This will still be essential for many pupils, but not for all. Sixth forms may be expected to have general as well as 'A' level 'sets'. In the girls' schools this already applies, and to this extent they are better poised for the developments we have outlined; their weakness, as we have suggested, tends to be in the opposite direction, of not providing sufficient 'A' level opportunities. In both boys' and girls' schools, however, and particularly in the boys', there will have to be a deliberate, well thought out and imaginative extension of the curriculum to meet the needs of C.S.E. students, if the aims of integration are to be achieved. This is a challenge which many of the heads we have met are already contemplating in respect of their less able pupils. We are sure that they will not find it insurmountable. It will, of course, take time to build up knowledge of the requirements of pupils at C.S.E. level, and there should be opportunities for schools to second staff for courses and to recruit some staff with experience of this kind of work as retirements occur (see paragraph 232). Special care will be required in the organisation, staffing and equipment of schools to ensure that the interests of the less academic children are as well catered for as those of the more able children.

Sixth form provision

281. Academic opportunities for all pupils are important. So, however, is strong sixth form education. This is something which the best public schools have developed so admirably and which they have for long been willing to offer to suitable pupils from the maintained schools. When the school leaving age is raised and the sixth form curriculum is itself reformed, a great strain will be placed on the country's capacity to provide an education of the highest quality for the 15-19 year olds at school. That is why we want to advocate the establishment of some sixth form colleges.

282. The sixth form college is universally held to be consistent with the principles of comprehensive reform within the maintained sector. There has as yet been little opportunity to study the working in this country of such an institution but the next ten years are almost certain to witness a growth in the

number and reputation of such colleges. A school which successfully negotiated recognition as an integrated college would concentrate its attention
exclusively upon the needs of older pupils, who would not be admitted below
the age of 15, to follow a course directed at university entry. These are the
kinds of pupils who would qualify for admission to a sixth form college:

(i) pupils with recognised boarding need who have attended integrated
schools at which 'A' level (or equivalent) opportunities do not exist, or at
which appropriate specialist courses (e.g. in Russian or Further Mathematics) are not available.

(ii) pupils from day schools who need boarding at sixth form level, for any
of the reasons we have suggested in Chapter 6, including the need for
education in subjects not available by daily attendance at school or
college of further education.

283. The sixth form in general, and the academic sixth form in particular, is
in the difficult situation of having to bridge the gap between a system of
schooling which is comprehensive up to the age of 16 and a system of higher
education which is sharply selective from the age of 18. It is therefore entirely
proper that the existence of some special sixth forms of high quality should be
defended. We believe that no legal or administrative obstacle should be placed
in the path of any school which decides to cease to admit younger boys or
girls and to expand its sixth form—particularly if it were willing to admit
pupils of both sexes to study in that sixth form.

"Mushroom" organisation

284. Yet it would not be proper to press such a development until and unless
the schools and their governing bodies come to desire it. For this reason we
favour the "mushroom" type of development already mentioned in paragraph
267. What is this development? Suppose the total population of the school in
question to be 600, and the age range to be 13-18, with a two year sixth form
course. The composition of the entry at different ages and the balance between
the size of the sixth form and of the rest of the school can be varied. In the
examples given in the following diagram the sixth forms of A and B have
300 and 360 pupils respectively.

285. The evidence from the public schools shows clearly enough that they are
not attracted by the idea of a sixth form college and there may be no takers
for this option. They stand firmly on their traditional principle of educating
boys or girls from 13-18. But their opinions or policy may change. Some
schools would certainly like to extend their sixth forms and provide places
for pupils with boarding need who might come from other integrated but
smaller schools. A smaller number of schools might, as sixth form colleges—
with or without a "stem" of younger pupils—find an opportunity of opening
a sixth form of the very highest quality to pupils from the maintained and
independent sectors alike. Everyone knows that there exist in this country
independent schools with an impressive record of sixth form achievement
and with an international reputation. We hope that some of them will choose
to be integrated in this way.

286. A minority of us[1] believe that, if this were done, assisted pupils might
be recruited on the basis of outstanding promise, without regard to boarding

---

[1] Lord Annan, Dr. Bliss, Mr. Dancy, Dr. Judge. See also note of reservation by Dr. Bliss
and Mr. Dancy at the end of this Chapter.

Diagram 8

EXAMPLES OF 'MUSHROOM' ORGANISATION OF SCHOOLS

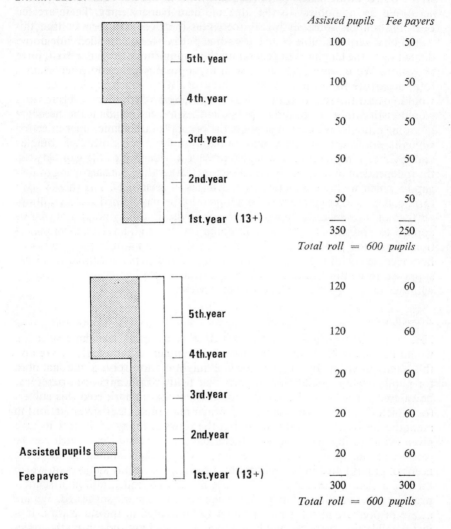

	Assisted pupils	Fee payers
5th. year	100	50
4th. year	100	50
3rd. year	50	50
2nd. year	50	50
1st. year (13+)	50	50
	350	250

Total roll = 600 pupils

	Assisted pupils	Fee payers
5th. year	120	60
4th. year	120	60
3rd. year	20	60
2nd. year	20	60
1st. year (13+)	20	60
	300	300

Total roll = 600 pupils

need. They hold that a genuine concern with equality of opportunity justifies what might at first sight be represented as a departure from the strict form of the comprehensive principle extended beyond the statutory school leaving age. They share the majority view that it is in the recognition and satisfaction of boarding need that public schools will make their major contribution to the national educational service. At the same time they believe that the existence of some sixth forms dedicated to the pursuit of academic excellence would set the highest standards in the national educational system of which they would be an integral part. They do not believe—since these sixth forms would be either self-contained residential colleges or attached to boarding schools—that this development would in any way harm the growing and confident sixth forms of local comprehensive schools.

287. The majority of us do not, however, agree that schools should be integrated on the basis of opening their sixth forms to pupils from the maintained sector on an academically selective principle and *without regard to boarding need*. We do not object to the idea of there being among the integrated boarding schools some sixth form colleges; it indeed seems to us that this would be a very desirable course for some public schools to take. Nor do we dissent from the emphasis in general on the importance of superior sixth form provision. We disagree, however, with a proposal which would represent a total departure from the principle of boarding need which in all other cases would govern the selection of assisted pupils, and which alone, in our view, would justify the expenditure of public money to send pupils to independent boarding schools. We cannot support the process of academic super-selection which it would entail; that would be undesirable in principle, and complex and invidious in practice. It would represent a widening of the gap between the independent and the maintained sectors (rather than the narrowing of that gap to which we are committed by our terms of reference). The role of sixth form colleges, where these may be adopted in the maintained sector, will not be that of academically super-selective schools. If this concept were to be applied to "mushroom" schools, it would involve high-level academic selection of assisted pupils *at age 13*, since the sixth form would presumably be homogeneous with regard to high ability, and the pupils recruited at 13 are supposed to continue into it. This seems to us to conflict even more sharply with our terms of reference and our own views.

Academies

288. A possible exception to the principle of avoiding academic selection would be the establishment of a very small number of "academies". We give this name provisionally to schools which might exist to serve a national need for pupils having special gifts in particular fields which might not otherwise be catered for adequately. We do not claim to have considered this subject (on which there are many views, and which requires further investigation) in an authoritative manner. But we reflect the views of many of those who have given evidence in suggesting that there may be some subjects which can be catered for adequately only in "academies", specially staffed to meet the needs of pupils gifted in certain specific directions. The only subjects on which there is a clear consensus about this are music and ballet, although schools providing teaching *in* a foreign language have also been suggested. We are aware of pressure also for mathematics to be treated in the same way. It is just possible that there are children having a special aptitude in mathematics who should be taught in specialised academies, but we think this is a matter for further study. Meanwhile, we confine ourselves to recommending that there might be one or two academies for music and possibly one for ballet, which would admit children down to an early age. Their establishment would require very special study and preparation.

Schools for gifted children

289. It would be possible to contemplate making boarding provision nationally available to children with quite exceptional academic talents who, for one reason or another, may be unable to cope satisfactorily with a normal school curriculum. We are not convinced that there is a category of such children

who can be readily identified, although we understand that there are children (perhaps up to 0·5 per cent of the age-group) of exceptionally high intelligence (say 140+ I.Q.) who can create a problem for ordinary schools and do not always receive an education which extends them sufficiently. It is by no means certain that, if such children could be brought together in a single school or a small group of schools, this would be the best way of safeguarding their emotional as well as intellectual growth. As the Plowden Report mentioned, there are other ways of attempting to meet their needs. For example, highly intelligent children can be brought to a centre from day schools for one day a week for lessons with those who are similarly gifted. Alternatively (or in addition) their needs may be met by imaginative teaching in the normal school environment, including individual programmes of work, facilities for private study, with full access to all available reading matter. Segregation into schools for the specially gifted, which has been the subject of experiment in the United States, is not necessarily the right answer.

290. Our conclusion is that there *may* be a case for boarding schools wholly for gifted children, but that this has not yet been adequately demonstrated to be the best way of meeting their needs. Nor is it by any means certain that a school of this kind would be appropriate at the secondary age range only; if it is appropriate at all, there might be an equal need at an earlier age. We do not, therefore, rule out the possibility that one or more public schools may wish to carry out a controlled experiment in education solely for the gifted. If such a proposal were made in the context of integration, we would think it right that approval should be given only after very careful consideration, and subject to conditions governing the selection of pupils and the allocation of places which would ensure that the school met a need for quite exceptional children who would be in real difficulty in any other type of school—a situation in which fee paying would be irrelevant, and in which all pupils should be those having this kind of need, and should all be assisted. It should not become a device for providing education in separate schools for clever children who could manage without difficulty in other schools. But above all, as the Plowden Report recommended, there is a need for research in the matter of gifted children, and we hope it will not be long delayed.

Patterns of organisation—summary

291. The developing pattern of integration would therefore comprise:
  (i) Schools large enough to be fully comprehensive.
  (ii) Schools which would provide for a wide range of ability over the whole or part of the secondary age range. Some in this category might cater for children in the ability band comprising C.S.E. up to 'A' level—others for the band G.C.E. 'O' level and below. There should be opportunities for transfer between the two types of school, particularly at sixth form level.
  (iii) A limited number of sixth form colleges.
  (iv) Possibly academies for music and ballet.
  (v) Possibly an experiment in schools for the gifted.

NOTE OF RESERVATION

Being two of the minority referred to in paragraph 286, we believe firmly in "the existence of some sixth forms dedicated to the pursuit of academic excellence". But we see no good reason why this pursuit should be forbidden before the age of 15. There is a handful of boarding schools where it is the prime objective of pupils from the age of thirteen, and we see nothing whatever to be gained by putting a stop to their work. We agree that almost all the schools within the Commission's terms of reference could without loss extend their ability range to include pupils for whom C.S.E. is more appropriate than G.C.E. But to insist that all of them should do so would be to level down with a vengeance.

We do not believe that the retention of a very few such schools would in any way handicap the burgeoning comprehensive schools. Nor do we accept the assertion in paragraph 287 that it would be in conflict with our terms of reference. Those terms require us "to move towards a *progressively wider* range of academic attainment among public school pupils, so that the public school *sector* may *increasingly* conform with the national policy for the maintained sector" (our italics). Careful attention to the text shows that nothing in it requires every individual school forthwith to accept less able pupils than in the past. In any case, it should not be assumed that, while public schools are fluid and changeable, "national policy for the maintained sector" will remain exactly what it is now. If educational opinion were steadily to move towards support of 100 per cent comprehensive education up to the age of 16, these few pockets of resistance would soon perish of atrophy: but if it moves the other way we shall all have cause to be grateful for the survival of this temporarily disfavoured minority.

Kathleen Bliss
John Dancy

CHAPTER 11

Integration—further considerations

292. The options we propose for the schools were explained in the previous chapter. This chapter makes further proposals which should be considered by schools contemplating integration.

Federal schemes

293. Some schools would find it easier to choose one of these options if they were part of a federal scheme. Boarding schools might be grouped because they are situated close to each other, or share a common foundation or common educational or religious policies. Each school within the group might provide for a different age range or for a somewhat different band of abilities along the lines we have described. Some groups might find it easier to cater for a wider range of abilities and provide opportunities for the most advanced academic work if they established a sixth form college within the group, provided it included a school sufficiently large and distinguished for this purpose.

294. We have held useful discussions with representatives of the Woodard Corporation and a Working Party of the Friends' Education Council. Both bodies have shown an interest in approaching integration as a group, and statements from them are reproduced in Appendix 11. The Society of Head-masters of Independent Schools have also recently started a clearing house to assist local education authorities, and have assured us that they would like to make similar arrangements under any acceptable national scheme. These, and other groups which might be formed, may be able and willing to work directly with the Boarding Schools Corporation and with consortia of local education authorities to help to select pupils and place them in suitable schools within the group. We see great value in their doing so. If schools with common interests are able to negotiate their future development as a group rather than individually, the way will be open for the group to decide, in consultation with the responsible placing bodies, on the educational role which each school in the group should play. Negotiations between the Boarding Schools Corporation and individual schools could be kept to a minimum.

295. Or one can envisage a consortium of independent and maintained schools and colleges of further education in the same area working together, each school or college playing a complementary role. Scarce teaching facilities and equipment, particularly at sixth form level, could be shared. Such schemes need not wait on changes in intake and organisation which we propose. In such a group the boarding school would also be able to admit from the day schools pupils who might need to board, if, for instance, their parents were moved suddenly from the district.

"Aided" status

296. The Working Party of the Friends' Education Council would like to see integration develop through a form of association with the State analogous

137

with what is known in the maintained system as aided status. An aided school is one whose current expenditure is met by the local education authority (including all staff salaries, equipment, teaching materials and internal decorations and repairs). The trustees of the school are responsible for external repairs and capital works, and are entitled to a grant from the Department of Education and Science of four fifths of the cost of approved works. The premises of the school remain the property of the trustees. Two thirds of the managers or governors are appointed by the trustees (of the foundation) and one third by the local education authority. This status, developed over the period following the Education Act, 1902 and culminating in its present form in the Education Act, 1967 has proved a workable compromise between full independence and control by the local education authority—and has been acceptable, subject to periodic debate about the levels of capital grant, to the voluntary bodies responsible for the schools. The governors are required to conduct schools in accordance with regulations made by the Secretary of State; but they retain the right to appoint staff (subject to agreement by the authority as to the suitability of the head teacher's educational qualifications) and to ensure that religious observance and instruction are in accordance with the doctrines of the founders.

297. The kind of aided status suggested by the Friends (who, among their schools, already have experience of co-education and with children of widely differing abilities) is one which would subsitute a central government body for the local education authority as being responsible for the maintenance of the schools. In other words, the Exchequer would not only assist the schools by capital grant, but also maintain them. In return, the schools would make all places freely available, on a basis of admission to be agreed. They would no longer be independent schools, but maintained boarding schools governed by voluntary bodies. There are already a number of aided schools with boarding pupils which are maintained by local education authorities. The reason why some Friends would prefer maintenance by central government is that they regard an integrated boarding system as something which should be centrally administered and not subject to the possibly varying policies of the local education authorities in whose areas their schools are situated. This does not imply criticism of the boarding policy of any individual authority; rather it is in line with our own emphasis, expressed in earlier chapters, on the need for a national policy, to be implemented nationally. But it may be that if the number of local authorities were to be reduced following the recommendations of the present Royal Commission, the Friends' objection to aided status of the present kind would lose some of its force. Meanwhile, we recognise that this is a far-reaching proposal, and we urge serious consideration of a new type of aided status for suitable schools which are prepared to forgo their independent status.

Girls' schools

298. The difficulty of making proposals for the girls' schools has been set out in Chapter 4. There are some schools with high academic standards which we would welcome within any scheme of integration. A few admit girls regularly at the sixth form stage, which would be an asset for girls "acquiring" a need for boarding education at this stage. The majority are less distinguished academically, and do not retain a high proportion of their pupils for sixth

form work. But the fact that most girls' boarding schools are not dedicated to academic success to the same extent as the boys' schools means that they should have less difficulty in providing education for less able girls. On the other hand an integrated school should cater for both less able and clever girls. If it is not big enough to do both, what answer can be found? Adequate provision for both academic courses and C.S.E. courses would not normally be practicable in a school with less than about 300 pupils, and there are only 38 girls' boarding schools above this size (including day pupils and some pupils of primary age) in England and Wales.

299. If it were possible to regard provision for boarding need as a separate consideration from academic opportunity, many of the smaller schools would have a great deal to offer. Their small size may itself be a desirable asset in meeting the needs of girls who are obliged by circumstances to seek boarding education. The question is how far the satisfaction of boarding need can in fact be considered in isolation from the capacity to cater adequately in academic terms for girls wishing to go on to higher education. It is true that many of the girls who now leave the schools before taking 'A' levels go to day schools or colleges of further education for 'A' level work, and that their public school may have given them an excellent basis for this. Nevertheless we must be guided to some extent, in considering the placing of "need" pupils, by the capacity of schools to take girls to 'A' level work *within* the boarding environment of the school—both by having courses available and by meeting the social needs of the older girls—thus giving them every encouragement to stay on. These are the directions in which development is necessary. Add to them the need to become increasingly comprehensive—that is, to provide adequately for less able as well as more able girls—and the dilemma becomes apparent. Only the bigger schools can hope to fulfil all these roles. Large scale building programmes to expand existing schools are not an immediately practicable possibility, whether from private or public funds. The schools must be considered, for the immediate purposes of boarding integration, at their existing size.

300. Close association with neighbouring day schools, wherever this is physically possible, would make possible a sharing of teaching resources and thus broaden the academic potentialities of the school. Where the range of curriculum of the smaller girls' schools can be strengthened by that kind of association, this may well remove any academic or curricular obstacles to integration, and enable the boarding provision to be used with less misgiving about the academic opportunities for assisted pupils—and it is in this direction that we would see the greatest hope for the small schools. A school may be too small to be considered as an immediate candidate for integration. We do not want to be too specific about the size; each school should be considered on its merits. But if a small school is able to provide evidence of a sufficient broadening of the academic options open to pupils over a wide range of ability, we would urge that it should be brought within the scope of integration as soon as possible. A grouping of schools, each providing for a different tier of age groups, may be particularly relevant to the problem of the smaller girls' schools. Meanwhile, as an exceptional and limited measure, if the boarding needs of girls for whom places were not available at schools approved for integration made it necessary to take up places at non-integrating schools, assistance might be given for this purpose until such time as there were

sufficient places available in integrated schools. In such a case, it should be made a condition that a pupil seeking advanced work should be transferred to an appropriate integrated school (possibly a sixth form college) at a suitable stage—assuming that she is in continuing need of boarding education.

Co-education

301. As we have discussed this matter, we have come more and more to the conclusion that if girls are to have equal opportunities with boys in the integrated sector, they can get it only through co-education. Some boys' schools ought to become co-educational. Some girls' schools ought to expand, but the capital costs of expansion would be higher than those of the co-educational reorganisation of the larger boys' schools. We believe that many parents would welcome co-education either for its own sake, or so that brothers and sisters may attend the same school where this would be more convenient than attending separate schools. We do not accept that because there are only three co-educational schools among the schools in our main terms of reference[1], this represents the proportion of parents preferring co-education. The development of schools which nearly always cater for one sex only reflects the intentions of their founders, and the conventions of their day. It takes no account of current parental attitudes and contrasts sharply with the maintained schools from which most assisted pupils will come.

302. Many of the objections levelled at co-educational schools—for example, the different academic interests of boys and girls, and the disparity in their career aims—are not related specifically to boarding education. In the maintained secondary sector some 60 per cent of pupils are already in co-educational schools, and we do not know of any evidence that co-education is unsuccessful. Arguments against co-education, to be valid, would therefore have to bear directly on the boarding rather than the academic situation. Here too we have no evidence that co-education has any serious drawbacks. It may be the case that it should, for preference, begin either at the primary age or after puberty; but we see no case for hard and fast rules about this. The fear of sexual relationships, although not always stated, underlies a good deal of resistance to boarding co-education. These dangers are in our view much exaggerated. Many heads and teachers whom we have met would welcome a lead on this matter, and if governing bodies propose that their schools should become co-educational, we hope that such proposals will be welcomed and will receive financial support for the necessary extension or adaptation of buildings. Many schools could become co-educational without increasing their total size; but in small schools this may be necessary if wasteful staffing is to be avoided. More subjects must be taught in a co-educational school, and teaching groups may become too small unless the school grows in size.

Boarding at primary age

303. Time has not allowed us in this first report to consider the integration of preparatory schools. Some of us believe that, even when a clear case of boarding need is established, it would generally be better to seek other ways

---

[1] See footnote to paragraph 64.

of meeting the needs of younger children. But even if most younger children in need continue to go to day school, thanks to the help of foster parents and others, there will still be a number of children of primary school age, and many more up to the age of 13, who must board. The matter should therefore be properly considered: if not by us in a later report, then by the Boarding Schools Corporation. We think that the outline scheme of integration we have proposed for secondary schools will offer guidance for the integration of preparatory schools, many of which are keen to take part in any acceptable scheme. It will often be best to place young children in the preparatory departments (or associated preparatory schools) of secondary schools in which they might continue their education. This would not preclude the use of other preparatory schools for the placing of children not old enough for public schools, and indeed the figures in Part Three suggest that a substantial number of places may be required in these schools. We would prefer to look to schools at which the numerical and other criteria for integration would over a period be satisfied than to schools at which assisted pupils were always in a minority. We would also wish to give first priority to co-educational preparatory schools.

304. Integration of the public schools will cause difficulties for some preparatory schools. There will be fewer places available at the public schools for their pupils. But integration will take time and preparatory schools not playing a part in it will have the chance to re-plan their future. They could, for example, extend their age-range or go co-educational. They should in any case, in their own interests, as well as those of their pupils, arrange matters so that children can transfer as easily to maintained as to independent schools.

Schools already "integrating"

305. Some schools are providing already for substantial numbers of pupils assisted either by local education authorities or under charitable schemes. If the number of publicly or charitably assisted pupils at a school is already high enough for it to satisfy the *numerical* requirements of integration, it should be regarded as eligible for early recognition as "provisionally integrated"— subject to recommendations which might subsequently be made by the Boarding Schools Corporation about its future development. The financial basis of assistance at such schools, if from charitable funds, would not necessarily have to be changed; it would not be sensible, for example, to make assisted pupils a charge on public funds where charities already existed for the purpose.

Curricular developments and experiments

306. We would like a few independent boarding schools (as well as maintained boarding schools, although these are not our direct concern) to be given facilities for trying out and testing new ideas in education—as some already do. This must be left to the initiative of schools staffs, who might care to work in conjunction with a University Department of Education or a College of Education. Special support might be given to such schools by the Schools Council for the Curriculum and Examinations. Such work should not go on solely in schools for more able pupils. It may be even more important for it to be done among less able children.

Holidays

307. None of the schools on our main list enables children to remain at school during holidays. Parents abroad generally arrange either for their children to visit them during holidays or to stay with friends or relations in this country. Children should spend their holidays away from school, and if there are assisted pupils in need of boarding who cannot go home or have suitable holiday arrangements made by their parents, the local authority Children's Department or other child care organisations should be invited to help. But they may not be able to do so, and one of the developments arising in the course of integration may be that schools should take it in turns to remain open during holidays to meet this need.

Immigrant children

308. We have assumed throughout our recommendations that there will be no differentiation between pupils on grounds of race, creed or colour. There is no need to stress the social divisiveness of the gulf between coloured immigrants and the community as a whole. If one of our aims is to remove divisiveness, no school should reject an assisted pupil because he is the child of an immigrant to this country. Nor do we believe they would wish to do so. Many of the public schools already take coloured children from homes overseas, and their experience shows that this policy could with advantage be extended to coloured pupils from this country, including those of non-Christian faith.

Foreign pupils

309. Nothing we have said about the future composition or organisation of the schools is intended to affect the valuable part they have played in admitting a number of fee-paying children from other countries. There is everything to be said for encouraging this feature of public school life.

Common entrance

310. In the context of boarding need and the varying ages of admissions to which we have referred, as well as the wider range of ability of entrants, there would be no place for an examination of the Common Entrance type for assisted pupils; knowledge of previous school records, and possibly an intelligence test, would give heads the basic information they required. We return in the next chapter to the placing of assisted pupils. So far as fee-paying pupils are concerned, it would be for the schools to decide whether to retain an entrance examination. We know that the present Common Entrance examination is under radical scrutiny by the public schools, and that they have already shown signs of moving away from the old-style achievement test with an emphasis on Latin to a more flexible type of test. We hope that, if an entrance examination remains for fee-paying pupils, it will be as flexible as possible in the interests of the children's primary education.

Inspection

311. Those who are going to be responsible for guiding children to suitable schools must have plenty of information about the schools: not only about their academic standards and material conditions, but about their suitability as boarding communities for different kinds of pupil. This work can fall only

on H.M. Inspectors, and the additional demands on their services may be substantial. A new kind of approach to the inspection of boarding schools may also be required—based on frequent informal visits. The Inspectorate will have to concern themselves with the internal life of the school, the relations between staff and pupils and between the pupils themselves, as well as with academic performance and the physical state of premises. They will have to judge how far the ethos of a particular school has been or can be adapted to meet the needs of assisted pupils.

Exchange of teaching staff

312. There is one development which would be of benefit to both the public and maintained school sectors, either as part of a process of integration or independently of it. This is a regular annual interchange of teaching staff. Such interchange already takes place between this country and the Commonwealth and the United States. We referred in Chapter 3 to the lack of experience of the maintained sector by boys' public school staffs, the great majority of whom have not taught in any other type of school. This applies much less to girls' schools, which, much to their credit, already recruit many teachers from the maintained sector. We recommend, as a start, an annual interchange of a hundred masters between boys' public schools and maintained schools. The administrative and domestic problems should not be great, particularly for single men, and we feel that nothing but good could result from such a scheme. If there were financial difficulties about the organisation of the scheme, some Trust might be willing to meet the overhead expenses as part of what we think could be a valuable educational experiment. Any complications arising from different salary structures would be avoided by the secondment of staff on their existing salary scales; the scheme should not be held up pending any closer alignment of salaries which may develop between the two sectors.

Governing bodies

313. Finally we ask: how should the schools in future be governed? Clearly, as independent schools they must have independent bodies of governors, responsible for financial control and educational policy. But equally clearly, if a high proportion of their pupils is assisted from public funds, the governing body should include representatives of public authorities.

314. Many public schools are already compelled by their trust deeds to have among their governors representatives of outside bodies. We think that it would be reasonable if one third of the governing body at any integrated school were non-foundation governors under a scheme to be approved by the Boarding Schools Corporation.[1] We set out in Appendix 10 an outline of a possible future constitution of governing bodies and their functions, more as an illustration of the spirit in which this matter should be approached than for literal interpretation at every integrating school.

The relation of governing bodies to heads of schools

315. One of the admirable features of the public schools is the extent to which their governing bodies delegate authority to headmasters and head-

---

[1] In the case of direct grant schools, either one third of the governors are appointed by the local education authority (or authorities) concerned—or alternatively a majority of the governors are representative of a wider range of public interests.

1—F

mistresses. They have much more discretion in the day-to-day running of the school than have most heads of maintained schools. One of the effects of integration could be the extension of this practice to maintained schools. This need not detract from the overriding powers of local education authorities, nor from the powers of the governing bodies of maintained schools. Indeed, if the present Royal Commission were to recommend that there should be a smaller number of local authorities, this would probably lead to a wider delegation of powers to the governing bodies of maintained schools, and in turn, the governing bodies of these schools would find it apposite to delegate more authority to the heads.

The integration of boarding schools with substantial numbers of day pupils

316. We have dealt in this report solely with boarding schools, and in our view the Boarding Schools Corporation ought first to consider the integration of schools which have no day pupils or very few. Some boarding schools (if we include schools with 25 per cent or more of boarders) will have substantial numbers of day pupils, and the integration of such schools could lead to an anomaly. The problem could arise of a school in which, although the number of assisted pupils who were boarding was greater than the number of fee-paying boarders, the assisted pupils remained in a minority because all the day boys were fee-payers. We shall try to meet this situation in our second report, recommending meanwhile that the Boarding Schools Corporation should look first to the integration of schools with higher proportions of boarding pupils.

CHAPTER 12

The placing of pupils

317. How are children to be chosen for assisted places? Who is to consult their parents or guardians about their wishes? Who is to decide which school would be most suitable for a particular child? Who is to negotiate with the schools? Can a head refuse to admit a child?

318. These problems are more complicated than may at first sight appear. There will be children in need of boarding whose parents regard boarding schools as an alien environment, and much careful work will be needed if parents, and those upon whom they rely for advice, are to understand the advantages which a good school can offer to children in need of boarding education. Someone will also have to judge whether a particular child would benefit more by boarding education than by other methods of meeting his or her needs.

319. We do not believe that a single central clearing house could carry out the whole of this task, nor would we welcome the kind of impersonal bureaucratic control which this might entail. A comparison, as we have said, of the needs of an orphan with those of a child from an overcrowded home, if a choice has to be made between the two, is one which can only be made by those with full personal knowledge of the circumstances. Whatever the arrangements, they must ensure that those who know best the children, their schools and their homes are responsible for deciding which children should be assisted with boarding education.

The Boarding Schools Corporation

320. At the centre of these arrangements we propose that a body to which we have already referred, called the Boarding Schools Corporation, should be set up. In our view there must be a national body responsible for the whole integration policy and for identifying need and guiding children to suitable schools. The lack of such a body was a major factor in the undoing of the Fleming scheme. We envisage it as an independent body established by Act of Parliament and responsible to the Secretary of State for Education and Science. It would be for the Secretary of State for Scotland to decide, in the light of our recommendations (and our comments in Chapter 18) whether to use the same body or a different one in Scotland. The Corporation would be the central point of contact between government and local authorities and the independent boarding schools which entered the integrated sector. We deal later with its functions and the sources from which the Corporation would draw its income.

Identifying need: applications for boarding

321. It would not be the task of the Boarding Schools Corporation to decide whether a child should be considered for a boarding place. That would be the

task of those who are in far closer touch with the child—above all, the parents. Primary and secondary school staffs, medical practitioners, members and officers of Children's Committees and of local health and welfare services, and possibly the parents' employers would frequently be in a good position to identify children's need for boarding and to assist parents in setting out the reasons for it in an application. They might even do this themselves, with the parents' permission and on their behalf. It would in many cases be for them to take the initiative in suggesting boarding either to parents or to the local education authority. Nothing further should be done without the parents' or guardians' agreement and willing co-operation. There are analogies for this kind of informal approach to children's boarding education in the special schools field. The experience which has been built up in dealing with the parents of handicapped children could be valuable to authorities in explaining boarding education to parents who are unfamiliar with it. When need has been identified either indirectly in this way, or by a direct approach from parents, the next step should be to apply for boarding education. This need not be an application for a place in a particular school, for the reasons given below. Some kind of standard application would be necessary for purposes of comparison; but there should be as little formality as possible. All applications should be accompanied by reports from the heads of the schools currently attended and, if appropriate, from the health or welfare services.

Consortia of local education authorities

322. No application should be blocked by the local education authority; all should be forwarded to one of the consortia of authorities which we recommend should be established in each of the regions in England into which local education authorities are normally grouped, and in Wales. Different arrangements might be appropriate for Scotland. No application, however apparently frivolous, should be prevented from reaching the consortium. If the responsibility for placing children in a boarding school is to be regional rather than local, parents should be assured that their applications have been considered regionally.

323. The consortium of local education authorities within a region would have functions delegated to it by the Boarding Schools Corporation on the one hand and by the local education authorities in the region on the other. It would have to decide whether a child should qualify for an assisted boarding school place and to decide in which school the child should be placed. We think this balance of central and local responsibility is right. A national policy for boarding education must entail a central agency i.e. the Boarding Schools Corporation, assessing each year the relative volume of demand in the different parts of the country. At the same time it is important to underline the responsibility of local education authorities for the education of children living in their areas. The work of the consortia should therefore be a joint responsibility. Administrative responsibility might well be in the hands of a major local education authority in the region. Policy guidance would come from the Corporation, which would also be represented at meetings. There would be representatives of each authority in the region, a Chairman appointed by the authorities, and co-opted members would include heads of maintained schools and of independent boarding schools admitting children from the region, serving in rotation.

Volume of work

324. There would, after the initial period, be a lot of work to do. If we regard integration as entailing over the years the take-up of 45,000 independent boarding school places in England and Wales, 9,000 children would have to be placed each year if they were all going to boarding school for five years. In addition, we hope the consortia would be placing children in maintained and direct grant boarding schools. Boarding need cannot be timed to arise at the age of transfer to secondary schools; neither can we be sure that all the pupils would stay to the age of eighteen; and if this is so the number of places available annually, could amount to, say, 12,000 or more. If applications outnumbered vacancies, as there is reason to suppose that in time they will, the average volume of applications to be handled by each consortium might be at least 1,500, and possibly 2,000 a year when the scheme reached full operation (although the fact that some applications—see paragraphs 335 to 337—might be handled centrally by the Corporation would tend to reduce these figures).

Procedure

325. It would not be practicable, nor necessary, for the consortium or its panels to interview applicants and their children except in circumstances of special difficulty. The right stage for interviewing would be when parents and children visit the schools. If applications have been prepared adequately under the guidance of local education authorities, a consortium, working through selection panels as necessary, should be able to assess and compare the needs of children reliably without interview. It may be desirable, in the interests of speed and efficiency as the volume of work increases, for an initial scrutiny, classification and matching of applications with vacancies to be carried out centrally by the Boarding Schools Corporation, using the latest techniques. The experience of the Universities Central Council on Admissions should be a useful guide. This would greatly ease the task of consortia in sorting out applications; but it would not relieve them of the responsibility for making final decisions about the acceptance and placing of children from their areas. The circumstances of individual children and their need for places in particular schools or types of school, will be of paramount importance, and the consortia should take account of parents' preference for specific schools, even though this might not always be possible to satisfy. Regular meetings would be necessary in order to enable applications to be handled promptly, and to place pupils in urgent need of boarding education each term.

Placing in schools

326. It would normally be clear from the application, supported by comments from the head teacher and local education authority, what kind of school place the child required; for example, whether the parents preferred single sex or co-education, weekly or whole-time boarding, a school of a particular religious denomination, a school with certain characteristics, one catering for special aptitudes, or indeed a specifically named school.

327. The public schools, and indeed all boarding schools are so unevenly distributed throughout the country that a share of places will have to be allotted to different areas if all parts of England and Wales are to have a fair

share of boarding places. Children will find it easier to settle in if they find others in the school coming from the same part of the country. The schools should, therefore, form close and continuing relationships with the authorities responsible for selecting and sending the children. This will be possible only if each school serves a limited number of areas. In allocating places to regions, the Corporation would have regard not only to variety but also to travelling distance. Schools with relatively easy access from the North of England would, for example, probably be asked to admit assisted pupils primarily from this region. Some schools in the South might be expected to draw children from the Midlands, East Anglia and the South West. It is this sort of planning which the Boarding Schools Corporation will have to carry out as places become available in schools approved for integration. Assisted children in boarding schools should be helped to preserve a sense of identity with their home area, especially when distance from home makes weekly boarding impossible. It is not a matter of all the assisted children in a school being drawn from the same locality, but of their being drawn from a small number of different localities.

328. Even with the best distribution scheme that can be devised, not all parts of the country can be served by schools which will be within sufficiently easy travelling distance to allow weekly or other periodic boarding or very frequent parental visits. That is why we believe that more maintained boarding schools should be built in under-provided areas; we return to this in paragraph 457.

329. It is inherent in our proposals that available boarding places, whether in independent, direct grant or maintained schools, should be regarded as part of a common pool for placing children in need of boarding. They will not be so regarded unless local education authorities which maintain boarding schools, and the governing bodies of direct grant boarding schools, use the Corporation and the consortia as the agencies for allocating any spare places in these schools—or still better, for the allocation of a substantial proportion of their places, as part of the national provision.

Choice of school

330. Each consortium should inform parents through local education authorities of the range of schools available to pupils—with a brief description of the facilities available at each school. Parents would be entitled to express a preference between schools but they would not be obliged to do so. There will be many parents who will know little of the boarding schools and will put down as their choice the name of the school which is most familiar: and thus there might be massive applications for one or two schools and others, no less and perhaps more suitable, would be under-subscribed. It would be better to put the name of a particular school to a parent after considering his application. It should be open to a parent to object to the school suggested and to be offered places at other suitable schools from the list; but we do not want to encourage a "pecking order" of social or intellectual hierarchy at integrated schools, and it is important that what parents primarily apply for should be suitable boarding education—possibly of a particular kind, but not necessarily at a particular school, nor at an independent school as such. It is fundamental to our view of integration that direct grant and maintained boarding places should be regarded as the equivalent of independent school places.

331. When the consortium has suggested a specific school—or an alternative
—the parents (or guardians) should in all cases visit the school with the child
to meet the head and the housemaster or housemistress, to be shown the
school and in particular where the child would live. Parents should be helped
to meet the cost of this visit where necessary. Such a visit is crucial. Children
should never feel that they are being "sent away" to a totally strange place.

332. There would be a two-way process of acceptance following a school
visit. No parent should be obliged to accept a place; parents could not, however, at public expense flit on visits from school to school before making their
decision. Only where there were good grounds for not accepting a place in the
school—as there might well be—should further visits be assisted from public
funds.

333. A head would also be entitled to reject a pupil, if he or she considered
that the needs of the child could not be met by the school; but they should not
reject children in order to preserve academic or social selection at their
schools. It is in order to help heads to see the work of the consortia, and to
become familiar with the areas from which they would draw pupils, that we
have suggested their serving in rotation on the regional consortia. The
consortia must get to know the schools, and the heads the work of the consortia; that should assure reasonable give and take in the matter of placing.

334. There would thus be four parties to the placing of a child in a school.
First, the Boarding Schools Corporation would offer guidance to regional
consortia on the criteria for selection and placing. Second, the consortia of
local education authorities would consider applications in the way we have
described. Third, the parents (and pupils) would decide whether to follow up
the suggestion made, or an alternative. Finally, the heads and housemasters
and housemistresses would decide whether they could accept or give places to
the children who came forward. At first sight this looks cumbersome. But it
would not prove so in practice. It is little more than already happens, under
other headings, when children are placed in boarding schools by local
education authorities, or when fee-paying parents choose places with the help
of educational agencies.

Pupils from overseas

335. Regional consortia are probably not the best organisations to deal with
applications from pupils overseas. These might be dealt with direct by the
Boarding Schools Corporation. Where a child is already overseas with his
parents, they would apply to the Boarding Schools Corporation who would
have reserved a number of places in the schools for overseas pupils. Parents
should be encouraged to visit the schools when on leave in this country.
There is no reason why the Corporation should not also help fee-paying
parents from overseas to find suitable places if—but only if—they wanted
guidance (for which they would pay a fee).

Sixth form placings

336. The Corporation would also be the best body to advise and offer places
to the relatively small number of pupils applying for places in sixth forms. In
addition to pupils already at integrated schools, who may need to change their
school to follow a course of study available only in a sixth form college (or a

school with a "mushroom" top), there would be pupils from day schools with a need for boarding at the sixth form level, for any of the reasons given in Chapter 6. If application was made on the ground that the pupil could not get the education he needed in a day school or college of further education, the head of his school should set out to the Corporation (through the local education authority) the reasons why the pupil required a residential place at public expense.

Academies

337. We assume that the very small number of places in "academies" and in any schools for gifted children which might be started as an experiment would also be handled centrally by the Corporation; but we do not think it necessary at this stage to offer guidance on the procedures to be followed.

Cost of the consortia—their development

338. We realise that the setting up of regional consortia of local education authorities may be regarded as unnecessary and extravagant. We think they will be necessary, once there is a substantial volume of placing work, in order to give children more equal opportunities of boarding education irrespective of where they live, and also in order to make for close relationships between integrated schools and a small number of placing agencies. We do not, however, rule out the possibility that consortia of authorities would be unnecessary if local government were to be reorganised into a relatively small number of authorities much larger than most of the present ones. In this case, it would be for the Government to decide whether each authority should handle its own placing work. In any event, we do not envisage the establishment of consortia until integration is well in train. Up to that time, the Boarding Schools Corporation should be capable of handling most if not of all the placing work (much of which would be in respect of pupils from overseas) in consultation with local education authorities. After that, we would expect the consortia to evolve, but not necessarily at the same time in all regions.

339. So far as the cost is concerned, about 35,000 children are already in boarding schools in which they have been placed with help from public funds. Some 20,000 of them are in independent schools, and this number would increase to about 45,000 under our proposals. Boarding school placement already involves authorities in a good deal of administrative work, and the total volume of work would not be doubled, even under a full scheme of integration, if direct grant and maintained boarding school placement is taken into account. The difference is that most of it would be eventually carried out by the consortia instead of by individual local education authorities. There should be no duplication of work between the consortia and the authorities. Indeed, there is reason to hope that the increased volume of work could be carried out more economically at one point in each region than in a number of different local offices—subject to the small amount of new work for authorities in forwarding applications. We shall consider administrative costs as a whole in Chapter 15.

CHAPTER 13

Denominational schools and integration

340. The religious affiliations of the 284 public schools are as follows:

Table 28[1]

	Church of England[3]	Roman Catholic	F.C. and C. of S.[4]	Quaker	Jewish	Christian Science	Inter-denominational[2]	No Denomination	Total
Mainly boarding									
Boys	79	9	7	2	1	—	2	9	109
Girls	54	4	8	1	—	—	3	12	82
Mixed	—	—	—	2	—	—	—	1	3
Mainly day									
Boys	16	2	—	—	—	—	2	9	29
Girls	31	4	2	1	—	1	6	16	61
Mixed	—	—	—	—	—	—	—	—	—
Total	180	19	17	6	1	1	13	47	284

Source: Commission's questionnaires to schools, subject to the notes below.

Notes: 1 Denominational character has been determined in the following way: first, if the school's instrument of foundation prescribes a denominational character, this denomination is taken; secondly, if it cannot be determined in this way, the denomination is taken as that of the school's weekday services (about one third of the schools being day or mainly day schools).

2 In view of the above definition, the category "Inter-denominational" has been used for those schools which specifically provide more than one kind of denominational worship.

3 Church of England includes the Church in Wales and the Episcopal Church in Scotland.

4 F.C. and C. of S. = Free Church and Church of Scotland.

341. The religious affiliation of schools takes a number of different forms. Some schools are associated with a religious organisation. Friends' schools, for example, are owned by territorial groupings of the Society and receive financial support in the form of bursaries for pupils from Meetings and from the Friends' Education Council. Methodist schools are, with a few exceptions, connected with the Education Committee of the Church through a Board of Management. Most of the Roman Catholic public schools are run by religious orders. But whereas, within the maintained sector, Roman Catholic and Church of England voluntary aided schools are linked with central or diocesan ecclesiastical authority, the Roman Catholic and Church of England public schools are not.

342. Church of England schools are far the most numerous. Most of them are Church of England in accordance with their trust deeds, the rest are so by long usage. Some trust deeds specify an evangelical or a catholic emphasis in worship and teaching; others do not. The Woodard schools founded in the 19th century are an organized group of Anglican schools: but most Church of England schools are not connected with any other school in an organized way.

343. None of our recommendations affects the existing denominational liberty of independent schools, the arrangements for worship, the religious instruction in the curriculum, or the freedom to choose staff, on which the ethos of a school so greatly depends. We recognise the role of the chaplain in worship, teaching and pastoral work as one of great importance to the schools. Some people may imagine that these schools, being specifically religious foundations, are in sharper contrast with maintained schools in matters of religion than is in fact the case. The direct grant and voluntary aided schools conduct a daily act of collective worship and give religious instruction in accordance either with their trust deed or with the practice already being observed in the school before it became a voluntary aided school. Their right to do so is safeguarded by the Education Act, 1944.

344. We suggested in Chapter 11 various ways in which schools might work in groups, and clearly one way to form a group would be for schools of a particular religious persuasion to come together. Their governing bodies could negotiate among themselves and with the Boarding Schools Corporation on the method of dividing educational responsibilities within the group. We have already referred to the Friends', Methodist and Woodard Schools, and we would hope the Roman Catholic schools and some new groups among Church of England schools might find ways of working together.

345. The public schools will obviously wish to admit in the first instance assisted pupils from maintained schools of their own denomination. But whereas 83 per cent of public schools are denominational foundations and 17 per cent are not, the proportions among maintained secondary schools (including "controlled" schools) are almost exactly reversed. This will create problems for the Boarding Schools Corporation, which will have to ensure that adequate opportunities are provided in integrated schools for children of all Christian denominations, of other religions and of no religion. If some schools insist that in their particular circumstances they cannot accept any but pupils of their own denominations, then some others will have to be invited to take a higher share of pupils from other denominations—and even of other faiths or none. We would therefore urge the public schools to look beyond the schools of their own denomination in the maintained sector, and also to consider whether and how they could adapt their present religious practices without betraying what is to them of value, in order to allay the anxieties of those parents of assisted pupils who not only know little of boarding schools but are also suspicious of them because they associate them with religious conformity. The practices of each school in regard to worship and required attendance, the type of religious teaching, the attitude to confirmation, exercise of pastoral care and chaplain's functions should be described for the benefit of parents and of those responsible for matching schools and assisted pupils.

346. Many schools are already making or considering changes in religious practice: there is experiment in teaching, more variety in forms of worship on weekdays and also on Sundays, more choice and some element of voluntary attendance. In Church of England schools it is emphasised that confirmation is a matter of personal choice and it is accepted that smaller numbers will be confirmed as a result. Integration may bring to some schools weekly boarders and consequent further changes in the pattern of Sunday. The 1944 Act

provides that parents of children in maintained boarding schools may withdraw children from Sunday worship and, if they wish, send them to local places of worship. Many public schools already permit or encourage attendance at local churches.

347. As we have said, worship and religious teaching in direct grant and voluntary aided schools are safeguarded by statutory provisions. But these statutory provisions embody a conscience clause allowing parents to withdraw their children from both. Parents who apply for assisted places at integrated public schools may legitimately expect the same sort of opportunities for the withdrawal of their children from religious instruction and worship. Some boarding schools already permit withdrawal in special cases. We believe that this opportunity should be extended to the parents of all pupils in an integrated school. Experience in the maintained schools suggests that very few pupils would make use of a conscience clause, and that the great majority would attend religious instruction or worship. The conscience clause, however, is a freedom which needs to be preserved for the minority whom it would affect.

348. Looking beyond the rights of parents, we believe that many schools are ready to consider whether and at what ages the choice should become one for the pupil to make for himself or herself. In our view, there is a good case for asking schools to allow, for example to sixth formers, some right of choice in the matter of attendance at school worship. In enunciating this general principle as one which we think should apply to both assisted and fee-paying pupils, we must make clear our view that decisions about its implementation ought to be left to the schools, including decisions about the age at which pupils should be permitted to make these choices for themselves. We would add that, if there is to be opting in or out of religious worship or instruction by pupils, it should be arranged in such a way that pupils are not able frivolously to change their minds. The choice should not be the result of a passing whim, or a device, for example, to gain more time for other activities.

Part Five

Finance ; Administration ; Legislation

CHAPTER 14

The finances of the schools: support from public funds

349. In this chapter we consider how far independent schools and parents using them are supported directly or indirectly from public funds. Full or part payment of fees for pupils is a large element in this support. 20,000 boarding pupils are assisted at independent schools by local education authorities and/or central government in England and Wales (see Chapter 7). Day pupils are also assisted, as the following table shows.

Table 29

Numbers of day pupils at independent schools assisted by local education authorities in England and Wales

	Independent recognised efficient schools			Independent non-recognised schools		
	Boys	*Girls*	*Total*	*Boys*	*Girls*	*Total*
Fully assisted	9,668	9,496	19,164	129	40	169
Partly assisted	955	1,423	2,378	7	14	21
Total	10,623	10,919	21,542	136	54	190

Source: Special questionnaire to local education authorities.

350. Thus a total of some 42,000 pupils (day and boarding pupils combined) are assisted from public funds to attend independent schools, out of the total of about 435,000 pupils attending these schools. Local education authorities at present spend some £5·5 million a year on independent school fees, and a high proportion (probably £3·9 million) of the £5·5 million a year which is disbursed in education grants to government employees is also used for this purpose. These two figures represent about nine per cent of the total annual income of all independent schools.

351. We are not concerned primarily, however, with assistance towards fees, which is payment for services provided, and which will grow if our recommendations are accepted. There are less tangible, but nevertheless substantial benefits which independent schools can receive, either through fiscal and similar concessions to the schools themselves, or where parents make use of some general tax relief in order to help them pay school fees.

Benefits of charitable status

352. At the end of 1967, out of a total of about 1,500 independent recognised efficient schools in England and Wales, nearly 900 were charities—including, we understand, all public schools. Of 1,650 non-recognised schools, less than 200 were charities. Charitable status confers fiscal and other privileges.

157

Tax reliefs

353. Charities enjoy a general exemption from tax on their income other than business profits. Thus a school which is a charity is entitled to exemption from tax on its income, including any profits made from the running of the school. The exemption also extends to payments made under deeds of covenant, on which it can claim repayment of income tax at the standard rate paid by the covenantor.

354. The amount of tax the schools would have to pay on their income from fees if they were not charities is impossible to assess. The fees are a receipt of the schools' trade; and if the schools were not charities they would be liable to tax on their net profit, after deducting expenses. It may be that, if they were not exempt from tax on their profits, they could arrange matters so that there was virtually no profit. The covenanted income which the schools receive can be considered separately because this attracts positive concessions in the form of tax repayments which the schools would not receive unless they were charities. Mr. Glennerster's estimate (Appendix 12) is that the value of tax relief deriving from covenants to independent schools in 1965-66 amounted to about £0·85 million. An example of the effect of covenanted income was provided by the Industrial Fund, which raised money for laboratories and similar provision between 1955 and 1959. As a result, some £3 million was given to schools, and of this figure about £1·2 million was accounted for by repayments of tax by the Exchequer.

Rate reliefs

355. Those schools which are charities pay a half of the normal rate to local authorities. The amounts vary; a major public school may be relieved of between £5,000 and £10,000 a year. Most schools would be relieved of much less. Mr. Glennerster's estimate is that the rate relief to all independent schools in 1965-66 was just over £1 million, of which the public schools accounted for £0·55 million. This would average about £5 per pupil at public schools.

Selective Employment Tax

356. Charities are also entitled to repayment of Selective Employment Tax, which, according to Mr. Glennerster's estimate, relieved the fees of schools which were charities of a total of £2·52 million in 1965-66. At public schools, the average relief is probably of the order of £11 per pupil. This would tend to be higher at boarding schools and lower at day schools, in relation to the number of staff employed[1].

Endowments

357. Endowments accumulated by some schools can also benefit the parents of pupils attending them. Income from these endowments has sometimes been earmarked by the donors for particular purposes, such as new buildings, scholarships or prizes, and is sometimes available for the general purposes of the school, which may use it to help meet the general running costs and thereby reduce fees. Endowment income of a school which is a charity is not liable

---

[1] In his Budget speech on 19th March, 1968, the Chancellor of the Exchequer announced a 50 per cent increase in the rate of Selective Employment Tax.

to tax. It is either exempted from tax at source and received in full by the charity, or if it is paid under deduction of tax at the standard rate, as in the case of income paid under deed of covenant, the charity can claim repayment of the tax deducted. The schools which have endowment income have been fortunate in their benefactors, and pupils are able to attend the most generously endowed schools at a fee much below that which would enable the schools to provide the same services without endowments.

358. Table 11 in Appendix 12 sets out the percentages of income derived from sources other than the payment of fees in 1965-66. It shows that, of 104 boys' boarding schools which answered Mr. Glennerster's questionnaire, five had income from these sources amounting to more than 25 per cent of their total income, two between 20 and 25 per cent, twenty-two between 10 and 20 per cent and fifty-six between 5 and 10 per cent. Of the 77 girls' boarding schools, eleven received between 10 and 20 per cent, and thirty-seven between 5 and 10 per cent of their income otherwise than through fees. The probability is that, at the most generously endowed boys' schools, the annual fees might be some 20 per cent higher on average if it were not for income from sources other than fees.

359. Pupils may also benefit from scholarships or bursaries provided from general or special endowment funds. Many of these awards are not related to parental income, but to academic merit. They are seldom large enough to bring in pupils of an income group appreciably lower than would normally be represented in the school. Their purpose is not to meet needs but to attract the best pupils. Although changes have recently been made in the scholarship examinations at certain well-known schools, most awards can only be competed for successfully by pupils who have specialised early in the examination subjects at preparatory schools familiar with the requirements. Thus, although the intention of some benefactors may have been to provide opportunities for poor boys, free or assisted places provided through endowment income are seldom open to pupils regardless of means. We reproduce in Appendix 4 the original objects of foundations of a number of boys' schools, some of which illustrate how far the present practice of the schools has departed from the original intentions of their benefactors. It has been argued that the public schools have as much right as the universities to do as they like with their endowments, but there is a fundamental difference. Entry to the universities is not barred to candidates whose parents cannot afford to meet the cost. A policy of integration would revive and reinterpret in modern form the intentions of the donors of many benefactions which no longer benefit the kind of children they were originally designed to help. We return to the use of endowment funds at integrated schools in Chapter 16.

360. There are in Britain well over 100,000 charities. The proper scope of charitable status was one of the matters considered by the Nathan Committee[1], and the Committee decided that education should continue to be regarded as a charitable purpose. We recognise the serious implications if we were to recommend that, of all the institutions at present receiving the fiscal benefits of charitable status, the only ones to be denied them in the future should be a fairly limited number of schools—whatever may be our views on the truly charitable nature of their work. Some of us feel, however, that the purposes of

---

[1] Committee on the Law and Practice relating to Charitable Trusts. Cmd. 8710, 1952.

many schools having charitable status seem to be something other than charitable on any ordinary interpretation of the word. It is difficult to see a truly charitable purpose in relieving parents who can pay school fees of £500 a year or more of part of the economic cost of their children's education. It is right that parents should be free to pay school fees if they wish; but, not right that they should, without good reason, be relieved by the Exchequer or local authorities of part of the true cost of what they are buying. At the very least, the public should be aware of the contribution it is making.

Conclusion—charitable benefits

361. Should action be taken to remove the fiscal and other benefits which schools enjoy as charities? To remove these concessions would, we appreciate, have the incidental effect of raising the fee which public authorities would pay for assisted pupils at integrated schools. But this would in practice be of no financial detriment to local authorities (taken as a whole) or to the Exchequer, which would indirectly recoup more than their additional outlay through the cessation of rates and tax reliefs to all charitable schools.

362. In favour of action is the argument that we have here a plain anomaly, due to the complexities of the English law of charities, by which benefits are enjoyed by institutions which are, for the most part, only in a technical sense performing a charitable function. The typical public school is, after all, an institution providing a service, on the basis of private choice and for substantial fees, to people able and willing to pay those fees. It is not easy to defend provisions by which such institutions (and, indirectly their fee-payers) receive, via charitable reliefs, what is in effect a subsidy from the tax-payer and the rate-payer. As the researches of Mr. Glennerster have shown (see Appendix 12), the sums involved are not enormous in themselves, but they are large enough to be concerned about; and at the level of principle, a strong case against the existing provisions exists.

363. On the other hand, it can be pointed out that among public schools there are some whose activities are, in a non-technical sense, genuinely charitable; and that it would be hard to penalise these. This is true; but it can be replied, first, that one is bound to give weight to the general situation over the majority of the sector, and second, that such schools are particularly likely to be willing and suitable for integration, and would suffer no loss from a change.

364. More generally, however, it may be argued that the very reforms we are proposing will make the privileges of charitable status less objectionable. The existence of the reliefs represents a public interest in the schools, the policy of integration will increase that interest, and it is at least unnecessary to abolish the reliefs at the precise moment when such a policy is being proposed and (as we hope) going to be put into action. Hence it might reasonably be suggested that no action be taken at this point on charitable reliefs, but that if the progress of integration were unsatisfactory, the question should be reconsidered.

365. This suggestion is one that we have seriously considered. It has, however, serious disadvantages. If little integration were to occur, and reliefs were then subsequently withdrawn, this would be inequitable to such schools as had been integrated. If it were proposed that integrated schools should retain the reliefs, while others should forfeit them, there is the difficulty that there might well be

schools which, while willing to be integrated, were found unsuitable, and there would again be inequity. In general, it seems that proposals for partial, or qualified, or conditional withdrawal of relief are likely to produce greater inequity between schools, and certainly greater complications, than either leaving the position as it is, or totally withdrawing these reliefs.

366. Granted that these are the two alternatives, the majority of us think that the weight of the arguments against what are in effect indirect subsidies from public funds is such as to indicate which course is to be preferred. Accordingly, we recommend that the fiscal and other benefits which follow from charitable status should be withdrawn from all independent schools which at the time of the appropriate legislation receive the greater part of their income from sources other than the payment of fees by public authorities or by charities. The reason for drawing such a line of division is to safeguard the charitable privileges of schools which are used mainly by handicapped children (or other children in need) with assistance from public or charitable funds. We realise that the distinction between different schools may need closer definition; but we think that what we have said makes our intention clear and that ways can be found to implement it.

367. A minority of those signing the report feel that, anomalous though the situation may be, the Commission is not competent to pronounce on it, and that the matter should be further considered by the Government.

Personal fiscal benefits

368. We are not impressed by the argument sometimes heard that parents paying school fees are paying twice for their children's education—once through fees and again through rates and taxes for the maintained schools which they are not using. Every taxpayer and ratepayer contributes towards public services, whether he or she uses them or not. Fee-paying parents are, in this respect, in no different situation from single people or married couples without children.

369. In addition to the advantages which may accrue to a parent through indirect subventions of schools from public funds of the kind we have outlined, there are ways of meeting the cost of an independent school education which do not involve the parents in annual payment of the full fees out of their existing capital or current income. This is a difficult area to consider, because the kinds of fiscal concessions we describe may to some extent be available to people buying services other than private education and it is not possible for us to attribute definite sums accruing through personal tax relief as being spent on education. Nevertheless, we feel it would be wrong not to mention concessions and devices which in greater or lesser degree affect the whole community as taxpayers and which undoubtedly play a part in subsidising independent education. As the Confederation for the Advancement of State Education say in their evidence to us:

"Whereas in the public sector all educational expenditure is closely controlled, both nationally and locally, there can be no similar control exercised by the community over the individual decisions of parents which result in the payment of these rebates. This appears to us to be an indefensible use of public moneys when all parts of the State educational system are severely restricted by lack of resources".

370. Newspapers regularly carry advertisements by insurance and similar firms offering parents the opportunity of paying school fees by means of advance payments which will assure the payment at a future date of fees much higher than the sums the parents are required to contribute to the scheme. In some cases the arrangement is to take out an endowment assurance policy, which does not differ in principle from any other kind of endowment policy. An example given by a firm of consultants estimates that a payment of £4,300 made in respect of a child aged five will secure full payment of fees amounting to £4,300 at preparatory and public schools, together with a cash return, after schooling has ended, of £3,820. The same quotation says that income tax relief and surtax benefits can as much as double the estimated cash return.

371. Other arrangements are based on the payment of a capital sum, by the parents or anyone else wishing to benefit their children. The income from such capital payments attracts tax relief (with no restrictions on the incomes of the families who benefit from it) if the capital is made over either to a person paying tax at lower rates than the donor, or to a charitable trust— which may be either a school or a trust operating on behalf of a school or group of schools. If capital is made over in the form of a "composition fee payment" in respect of school fees, there is a considerable gain in value if the sum is deposited some years before school fees become payable. This is due partly to the normal accretion through interest earned and partly to relief from payment of tax on the interest.

372. Deeds of covenant, under which a taxpayer transfers part of his income over a period of years to some other person or persons, are another method of helping to meet education costs. A covenanted annuity in favour of a minor by someone other than his parent can carry tax advantages. The tax benefit of such an annuity stems from the fact that the annuity bears income tax at the minor's tax rate, not at that of the covenantor. The covenantor could, until 1965, claim not only income tax but also surtax relief on the payments made; but covenants made after April, 1965 do not qualify for surtax relief. We understand from the Board of Inland Revenue that in 1964-65 the total number of annuities to minors was about 60,000, involving income of some £10 million on which income tax of about £3 million was repaid. The advantages of such annuities are limited by the fact that, under existing law, (i) if the child's own income exceeds £115, the parent can no longer claim a full tax allowance for the child and (ii) if the child's annuity income exceeds about £520 a year the excess will be subject to the standard rate of income tax. The maximum tax advantage from a covenanted annuity for a child whose parents are paying income tax at the standard rate is, therefore, we understand, about £99 a year.

373. Minors may also be the beneficiaries of capital settlements, under which assets have been transferred outright to trustees, who apply the income for their benefit. The Board of Inland Revenue are unable to make any estimate of the extent to which minors benefit under capital settlements.

374. In their second report, the Royal Commission on the Taxation of Profits and Income (1954) considered whether the income of minor children, or at least their investment income, should be aggregated with that of their parents for tax purposes. The Commission was divided on this matter. In a reservation to the report, a minority of members suggested that unearned

income in excess of £25 of unmarried minors should be aggregated with that of their parents. We have asked the Inland Revenue what would be the yield to the Exchequer of introducing this change. Although no accurate figure is available, estimated figures suggest that, on the basis of ignoring the first £25 of minors' unearned income, the annual yield would be of the order of £20 million; if all unearned income were taken into account, the yield would be about £25 million. We appreciate that a measure of this kind would affect the tax treatment of covenanted income used to pay school fees only as a by-product of a much wider change. Nevertheless, the sums are considerable, and if any substantial proportion of them is used to pay independent school fees, this is a matter of legitimate public interest in the terms of our report.

Conclusion—personal taxation

375. As these broad issues of fiscal policy affecting personal taxation are not directly within our terms of reference, we do not feel it right to make any specific recommendations about them. We cannot prove, without an exhaustive enquiry, that any particular sums accruing through personal tax reliefs are being used to support the independent school system at public expense. But it is undeniably the case that some support—and many of us feel that it may be considerable—is being given in this way. What action should be taken will be for Parliament to decide.[1]

---

[1] The Chancellor of the Exchequer has now announced, in his Budget speech of 19th March, 1968, his intention to aggregate the investment income of minors with their parents' income for tax purposes—to have effect from 1969–70.

CHAPTER 15

Assistance to parents: cost per place

Should there be a parental contribution?

376. We are asked to ensure that the public schools should progressively be opened to boys and girls irrespective of their parents' income. It is essential to the success of our scheme that the parents of pupils who need boarding education should not be deterred by the cost. Nevertheless it would be wrong in our view (except under the arrangements which exist for special educational treatment, or where education cannot otherwise be provided) to devote public funds to boarding education regardless of parental means. There is in any case some saving in home expenditure where children go away to school. Also, we think that with the limited funds which will be available, it is only sensible that they should be directed to those parents who most need help. Finally, the evidence we received overwhelmingly accepted that some parental contribution should be made according to means.

Tuition

377. Under their present arrangements for placing children at independent schools, authorities are not obliged to pay the tuition fees and in many cases parents are required to contribute towards a combined tuition and boarding fee. We have considered this matter most carefully, bearing in mind that a number of pupils qualifying for assisted places will be the children of parents with high incomes who could if necessary afford to pay the whole or part of the tuition fee as well as the boarding fee. We have come to the conclusion that the parents of all pupils qualifying for assistance should be assisted with the ccst of tuition, irrespective of means, but should contribute towards other costs in accordance with their ability to pay. There are a number of reasons which have led us to this view:

   (i) A considerable body of evidence we have received, including that of some of the associations of local authorities, supports the view that tuition should be free.

  (ii) We are aiming at a situation in which boarding need should be met on equal terms at independent, direct grant and maintained boarding schools. If tuition fees were to be charged at independent boarding schools, they ought, by the same criterion of possibly high parental incomes, also to be charged at maintained boarding schools. This would be not only against the law as it now stands, but would in our view be an unreasonable provision to embody in new legislation. The form of boarding in many maintained schools is that of a hostel attached to a day school. If pupils in wholly boarding schools were to pay tuition fees then so should pupils in hostels attached to day schools. This would create an indefensible anomaly between day pupils and hostel based pupils attending the same school.

(iii) One of the major categories of assisted pupil is likely to be the child of a parent serving overseas. Such parents might reasonably claim that, had they been in this country, they would have sent their child to a maintained school. In any case, working overseas ought not to deprive them of the opportunity of free tuition for their children which they would have had at home.

(iv) If, as we believe, there are unsatisfied and urgent needs for boarding education, there is no justification for discriminating against pupils on grounds of means, whether great or small. If a child is so physically or mentally handicapped as to require a place in a boarding special school, he is entitled to a free place (including free boarding provision) whatever the parents' income. The need we are considering in this report may be less extreme than that of a severely handicapped child, but if we accept that boarding education—another kind of special educational treatment —is needed, then it is right to accept a public liability at any rate for tuition fees.

378. In short our aim is to build an integrated sector of education increasingly close to the maintained sector. To charge tuition fees to assisted pupils would run counter to an essential feature of the maintained sector, namely that tuition must by law be free. To erect between the two sectors a barrier of tuition fee payments for assisted pupils would be out of keeping with the spirit of our recommendations. But, having said this, we would find difficulty in supporting, for all assisted pupils, a title to free tuition at a cost above the level prevailing at any given time in maintained schools. For this reason, we propose that there should be a notional standard tuition fee at integrated boarding schools, which would be the minimum level of assistance to which every parent of an assisted pupil would be entitled. It would not be related to the tuition fee at any particular school.

379. The fairest arrangement would be to equate this notional tuition fee with the standard recoupment payments made by a local education authority when pupils from their area are educated by another authority. These are calculated on the average costs (including administration and loan charges) of educating children in maintained schools and are reviewed periodically. They are, for the financial year 1967-68, £89 per annum for pupils in primary schools, £164 for pupils under 16 in secondary schools and £289 for pupils aged 16 and over. We think it may be unduly complicated to apply these separate charges (according to age) in the integrated sector. The alternative would be to work out a single notional tuition fee for all pupils attending secondary boarding schools, and another one for pupils attending primary or preparatory schools or departments, based on the recoupment charges at any given time. This would also have the advantage of according more closely with current practice in the public schools, which do not usually charge different fees for pupils aged 16 and over, or in the case of preparatory schools for pupils aged 12 and over.

The residual fee

380. There should be no direct connection between the fee level at individual schools and the choice of school which an assisted pupil might attend. Besides a standard tuition fee paid from public funds, there should also be a

standard residual fee for each child attending an integrated boarding school at public expense. The sums paid by the parents of assisted children would depend on the family's resources, not on the fees charged by the school attended. Only then could the choice of school be determined by the pupil's needs and his parents' wishes, rather than by reference to the cost of places at different schools within the integrated sector. The standard residual fee would be worked out by the Boarding Schools Corporation and would be arrived at by dividing the total cost of assisted places at all integrated schools by the number of places, and deducting from it the notional tuition fee. It is towards this residual cost that parents would contribute according to their means.

381. Parental contributions should not deter parents earning average or less than average wages from accepting boarding places for their children. Many parents, whatever their children's needs, have been accustomed to regard all education as a service which should be provided free of charge. If children who need boarding education are not to be deprived of it by their parents' reluctance to contribute, the assessments will have to err on the side of generosity, at least in the early years and at the lower income levels.

Present arrangements—central government

382. Before considering what the level of parental contribution should be, we review the existing arrangements for assisting boarding pupils from public funds. Some pupils are assisted by the government departments which employ their parents, others by local education authorities, and some by both (see Chapter 7).

383. In the case of central government, assistance takes the form of a standard allowance rather than a sum varying according to means. Thus, for servicemen, the allowances in 1967-68 were £250 per annum for the first child, £300 for the second child and £355 for the third and any subsequent children. Only the net expenditure on tuition and boarding fees is paid if this is less than the allowance. The allowance is payable if a serviceman is serving overseas (in which case it is not taxable), or when he is stationed in this country if it is certified that he is unlikely to remain in his present place of duty for more than four years from the date of the certificate.

384. Payments are made at the same rates to home civil servants who are posted abroad and accompanied by their wives. They are not payable to employees in this country unless they are in work which involves frequent overseas posting and unless the Department concerned expects them to be posted overseas within the next three years. The allowance is taxable if it is paid while the civil servant is in this country but not if he is serving overseas.

385. More generous allowances are paid to members of the Diplomatic Service. For the academic year 1967-68 the allowances for staff serving overseas were:

Boys	1st child	2nd and subsequent children
At public school	£478 p.a.	£582 p.a.
At preparatory school	£430 p.a.	£526 p.a.
Girls		
At public school	£459 p.a.	£563 p.a.
At preparatory school	£413 p.a.	£509 p.a.

These sums are not taxable. Allowances are paid for up to five years to staff who have returned to this country, in which case they are taxable but are increased to the following amounts to allow for this:

Boys	*1st and subsequent children*
At public school	£702 p.a.
At preparatory school	£632 p.a.
Girls	
At public school	£674 p.a.
At preparatory school	£607 p.a.

If the school fees are less than the overseas allowances, staff overseas receive only the actual fee; those in this country receive the actual fee with an increase to allow for the tax deduction.

Present arrangements—local education authorities

386. Under present arrangements local education authorities are free to determine their own income scales for parental contributions towards the cost of pupils who attend independent boarding schools with the authority's assistance—with the exception that, under Section 6 of the Education Act, 1953, the authority must meet the full cost if education cannot otherwise be provided. The majority have been using scales which are the same as or similar to that recommended by the 1960 Working Party (the Martin Committee). The present scale provides for contributions to be made towards tuition as well as boarding, at the rate of one fifth of the parents' assessable income after the first £450 has been deducted. As families with assessable income after the first £450 would typically have gross incomes of about £650, this means that parents start contributing to fees when their incomes exceed £12 10s. 0d. a week. A family with an assessable annual income of £1,000 (gross about £1,200 p.a. or £23 per week) would pay a contribution of £110 towards boarding school fees. A contribution of this order must have a significant deterrent effect on many parents in the middle and lower income ranges: about a half of households with children have incomes ranging from £10 to £25 per week. Thus many pupils who might have particularly benefited from boarding education have probably, under this scale, remained as day pupils in unsatisfactory circumstances.

Impending changes

387. A working party of the local authority associations has recently reviewed this scale and has recommended that contributions should in future begin after the first £675 of assessed income has been deducted. Assuming an allowance of £200 p.a. to be deducted from gross income to arrive at the assessable income, families would thus start contributing when their gross incomes reached about £17 per week. The family with an assessable income of £1,000 would contribute £65 p.a. This is a considerable advance on the earlier scale and brings the starting point of the scale much closer to that at present prescribed by the Department of Education and Science for university awards.

Comparison with university awards

388. Table 30 compares the income scales (i) recommended by the 1960 Working Party (the Martin Committee) (ii) recommended by the recent

working party of local authority associations (iii) prescribed for university awards.

Table 30

Scales of parental contributions

Assessed Income	Martin Committee Allowances (1960)	Local Authorities Working Party Recommendations (1968)	University Awards Scale (1965)
450	—	—	—
475	5	—	—
500	10	—	—
525	15	—	—
550	20	—	—
575	25	—	—
600	30	—	—
625	35	—	—
650	40	—	—
675	45	—	—
700	50	5	8
800	70	25	16
900	90	45	24
1,000	110	65	32
1,100	130	85	40
1,200	150	105	48
1,300	170	125	56
1,400	190	145	64
1,500	210	165	74
1,600	230	185	84
1,700	250	205	94
1,800	270	225	104
1,900	290	245	114
2,000	310	265	124
2,100	330	285	134
2,200	350	305	144
2,300		325	154
2,400		345	164
2,500		365	174
3,000		465	224
3,500		565	274
4,000		665	324

Note:
There are minor variations in calculating the assessable income under these scales. For example, the Martin Committee recommended that the net annual value of a house owned by the parents should be added to gross income. It also proposed a range of allowances for dependants according to age from £100 for children under 12 to £170 for dependants over 18 years, whereas the university award scale allows £200 for any dependant. The university scale provides for a number of other allowances to be set against income which are not covered by the Martin Committee recommendations.

389. At the lower levels of income we can see no good reason why the parents of a child who needs boarding education should be asked to pay more than those whose son or daughter qualifies for higher education. But at higher levels there is a difference which we consider it right to take into account in our recommendations. The great majority of university students are grant-

aided, whereas up to a half of pupils, even at a fully integrated school, may still be paying full fees. We shall try to avoid what might otherwise appear to be a severe inequity between the treatment of fee-paying and assisted pupils who might have parents in similar income brackets—the second category benefiting from very substantial assistance on the basis of boarding need, the first receiving no direct assistance (although indirect benefits may accrue to them from the fiscal concessions touched upon in Chapter 14). We shall propose a scale which will assist relatively less generously the better off parents of assisted pupils, bearing in mind that they will in all cases qualify for the notional tuition fee.

390. We appreciate that many fee-paying parents make considerable sacrifices to pay for their children's education, and that some of those who can only just afford it may be paying more than would be expected of parents of assisted pupils in a similar income bracket under any of the scales we have quoted. The outlay of parents who have placed a particularly high value on this form of education, however, is not necessarily the right yardstick for assessing contributions for assisted pupils. The parents must contribute as much they can reasonably afford; but it would not be right to expect the sacrifice to be too great. The children's interests must come first, and the scale of contributions should not be such as to deter a willing, though not necessarily enthusiastic, parent from accepting a place for his child. The effect of a relatively generous scale of assistance, despite our proposal to taper it off at the higher income levels, may be that there will be fee-paying parents who are financially worse off than the parents of some pupils receiving assistance. This highlights the importance, which we have stressed elsewhere, of adhering strictly to need for boarding as the criterion for assistance. Assistance will be expensive, and the need must be real.

391. To take an example, if a parent earning £2,500 a year has a child boarding at a public school, he will normally pay at least £400 in fees and some extra incidental costs. If the child qualified on need grounds and we adopted the university awards scale, parents with a gross income of £2,500 would probably contribute about £150. There would thus be a considerable material gain in having a child accepted as an assisted pupil. Nevertheless a child of parents at this income level may be in very real need of boarding education. We shall try to draw the right balance between economy in the use of public funds and protection of the rights of children in need of boarding education whose parents may be unwilling to make a substantial contribution.

Reviews

392. Only when an integration scheme has been running for some years will it become clear which children are coming forward, what their parents' incomes are, and how willing the parents are to contribute. Whatever scale is initially adopted, it should be reviewed at intervals by the Boarding Schools Corporation. Decisions about the scale will be decisions about policy, in that they could help to determine the social composition of the schools. In such circumstances, we think it would be right, where priority of need could not be determined on other grounds, to favour the children of poorer parents, even though this would have the effect either of limiting the number of places to be assisted within the Corporation's budget or of increasing the cost of integration.

A recommended scale

393. We recommend, in 1967-68 terms, a scale which would be identical with the present university awards scale[1] in its lower reaches, but in which the contributions would increase more steeply at the upper end. Contributions would be at 8 per cent on that part of assessable income between £700 and £1,400 a year, at 10 per cent between £1,400 and £2,000, and at 15 per cent on that part over £2,000. The contribution would in each case be towards the residual fee as defined in paragraph 380. This scale is as follows:

Table 31

Assessed income £	Parental contribution £
700	8
800	16
900	24
1,000	32
1,100	40
1,200	48
1,300	56
1,400	64
1,500	74
1,600	84
1,700	94
1,800	104
1,900	114
2,000	124
2,500	199
3,000	274
3,500	349
4,000	424
5,000	574
6,000	724
et seq.	*et seq.*

394. The reason for extending the scale of contributions in this table beyond the limits of the residual fee for an individual school place is to illustrate the rates of payment which would be expected of parents having two or more children in integrated schools as assisted pupils. However many children a parent might have as assisted pupils, his total contribution would not exceed that shown in the scale as being appropriate to his income. For example, a parent with one assisted child and an assessed income of £6,000 would pay the full residual fee. If he had more than one assisted child he would pay his maximum contribution of £724 only when the total of residual fees equalled or exceeded this figure. A parent with an assessed income of £1,500 would pay £74 whether he had one or more children as assisted pupils.

395. It will be important to take account of the situation in which some children in a family are assisted pupils while others might qualify for university

---

[1] We understand that changes in the scale of parental contributions in respect of university awards will be introduced in September, 1968. This will not affect the relationship with the university awards scale on which our proposed scale is based; but it means that the figures we suggest will have to be revised before integration is set in train. If, as we understand, the outcome will be a slightly higher *average* contribution from parents, this would tend to reduce the cost of integration.

awards. Parents should not be expected to contribute under each of the respective income scales without regard to payments made under the other. In these circumstances, a single contribution should be assessed and allocated between the grant awarding bodies. The method by which this might be done is more properly for negotiation between the Boarding Schools Corporation and the Department of Education and Science than for detailed consideration in this report.

Assessment of income

396. The amounts of gross income and of the allowances to be set against it to arrive at the assessed income should, subject to review by the Boarding Schools Corporation, be calculated on a basis similar to that for university awards, with one exception. Details of the present awards arrangements are set out in Appendix 13. The exception is that we would think it right not to set against parents' gross income allowances in respect of school fees for other children in the family.

Additional grants

397. At the lowest income levels, below the point at which parental contributions begin, it may be essential for extra assistance to be given if a child is to be enabled to take his full place in the school community. To avoid hardship among parents in these income groups, we suggest an initial outfitting grant and annual grants for clothing, travelling expenses and pocket money. There might also be a "tapering" provision to avoid an abrupt severing of special assistance at the point where parental contributions begin. The size of these grants should be decided by the Boarding Schools Corporation, which should also be enabled to make provision to meet circumstances of exceptional individual hardship—and might sometimes authorise heads of schools to make small disbursements to meet emergencies.

398. Even above the lowest income level, it may be that some parents may find themselves faced with high additional costs over and above the standard contribution. For example it may be necessary for children to attend boarding schools at a distance from their homes which would make the travelling costs of school visits for parents or home visits for children a significant item. Arrangements should be made to ensure that additional expenses should be taken into account in assessing income scale contributions. This might best be covered by allowing a reduction in income scale contributions (in respect of any expenditure considered by the Boarding Schools Corporation to be reasonable) to the extent to which additional expenses exceed an amount to be decided by the Corporation.

Compulsory additional charges

399. A number of schools impose additional charges over and above their standard fee. These vary from school to school but include such items as the cost of books and stationery, medical fees, laundry charges, library subscriptions, and contributions to games funds. In general we do not consider that there should be any compulsory charges over and above a consolidated fee. The fee should cover all the necessary activities of the school. Any additional charges should be for genuinely optional extras.

400. An example of the sort of thing we have in mind is the provision of books required for the school curriculum. We understand that, even in the present situation, some public school pupils are less well equipped with books than they should be, and that schools frequently have to make special arrangements for the loan of books to those who cannot afford them. Although children should be encouraged to buy books, it seems to us wrong in principle that schools should not provide essential books (possibly on loan) and charge the cost to the fees. We hope that, by degrees, this may become the generally accepted practice for all pupils—it would be wrong to single out assisted pupils.

The average fee

401. What then will be the average cost per pupil to the Boarding Schools Corporation of assistance on this scale? The first step in the calculation is to determine the average fee for a boarder (i.e. tuition and boarding) in an independent recognised efficient school. To add the fees for all the boarding schools and divide by the number of schools would produce a misleading result because it takes no account of the varying numbers of pupils and fee levels at different schools. We have therefore taken a more accurate average by multiplying the number of boarders at each school by the annual fee charged at January 1967 and then dividing the aggregated total by the number of boarders. In this way we arrive at an average tuition plus boarding fee of £465 for places in secondary schools and departments and £380 for places in primary and preparatory schools and departments—that is, in all schools which are recognised as efficient[1].

Capital expenditure

402. It might be expected that the capital expenditure of an independent school on new buildings, equipment and improvements would be reflected in the fees, and to a large extent it is. Fees can and usually do cover amortisation and interest paid in respect of new buildings, improvements and repairs, as well as interest on mortgages and bank loans in respect of staff houses and overdrafts. Often, however, the fixed assets of the schools are undervalued and depreciation is not allowed for sufficiently, the balance being made up from gifts, bequests or existing endowments. To this extent the fees may be un-economic. This is not a factor to be taken into account in estimating the cost of fees paid by the Corporation for assisted pupils, which should be the same as those for fee-paying pupils; but if it were the case that voluntary contributions from parents, old boys or girls and other donors were reduced following integration—as we hope they would not be—there might have to be compensatory increases in due course in the fees for all pupils.

403. Additional capital works may be required at some schools specifically for the purpose of integration. Also, a number of new maintained boarding schools may be built as an adjunct of integration, with the capital costs pooled

---

[1] As these are average figures for *all* fees, they embody a weighting towards the higher fees charged on the average by boys' schools. If girls assisted in the future represent a higher proportion of assisted pupils than the present proportion of girls' school to boys' school places—as we hope they will—the average cost per pupil might be slightly lower, depending upon the fee levels of the additional places taken up for girls. This is not likely however to be a significant costing factor.

in the same way as the other costs of integration; we refer to this more fully in the next chapter. An addition of £5 to the cost of each assisted pupil would provide for expenditure averaging between £100,000 and £235,000 a year (as the number of assisted pupils rises from 20,000 to 47,000) in repayment of loans for these purposes.

Extra costs

404. Besides the basic fee, allowance must be made for the compulsory and unavoidable charges which we have suggested should in future form part of the consolidated fee. In the light of Mr. Glennerster's research (see Appendix 12) we have allowed an average of £15 for these charges.

405. Also, in assessing the cost to be met by the Boarding Schools Corporation, in addition to the fees paid to the schools, it is necessary to allow for additional assistance to parents, of the kind described in paragraphs 397 and 398 above. An average of a further £5 per pupil should provide adequately for these items, particularly in the early years, when there may be a heavy weighting of parents above the lowest income levels.

Administration

406. Finally, we must allow for administrative costs. It is difficult to assess in advance the cost of the consortia arrangements proposed for local education authorities, which would to a large extent supersede their existing arrangements for placing children in boarding schools and relieve them of expenditure on this service. There will undoubtedly be some additional cost as and when the consortia are established in order to deal with a larger number of applications. It will be for consideration whether this should be met partly by the Boarding Schools Corporation. The Corporation itself would incur expenditure before the consortia were set up—in negotiating with schools about their role in the integrated sector, and in making forward arrangements for the first intakes of assisted pupils. Its work would then (as we explain in Chapter 17) turn increasingly towards the placing of pupils from overseas, placings in sixth form colleges (and academies, if any), financial arrangements with schools and parents, and the allocation of places in schools to consortia of local education authorities. The Corporation would, in addition to its policy function, act as a clearing house and an accounting centre. It would combine some of the functions of, as it were, a University Grants Committee with those of a Universities Central Council on Admissions. The cost in the negotiating phase could not be related to an average cost per assisted pupil, as the pupils would not at this early stage be in the schools; but once the scheme was under way, this would be the right thing to do. Thereafter the administrative cost per pupil should fall as the number of pupils increased.

407. The Corporation would have to be adequately, though not extravagantly, staffed—we offer suggestions about this in Chapter 17—and it should also be equipped to use up-to-date techniques in its placing and accounting work. Its expenditure would depend very much upon levels of staffing and salary scales to be determined by the Secretary of State; but the net cost should also take into account savings on the present administrative costs of assisting pupils whose parents are employed by government departments. Our estimate is that the net cost of administering the Corporation's work would be of the

order of £0·25 million a year.[1] This would represent about £5 per pupil under a full integration scheme involving 47,000 pupils; in other words about one per cent of the average total cost (including parental contribution) per pupil. It would probably be as high as £10 per pupil until the number of assisted pupils reached 25,000 (i.e. 5,000 above the present level); but should then begin to go down. It would be for consideration whether any "surplus" income after this stage should go to meet the costs of the consortia, which would at this point begin to rise significantly because of the additional volume of placing work. But this is for later decision. For present purposes we shall attribute a notional sum of £8 as the average annual cost of administration per assisted pupil during the next fifteen years.

Gross cost per pupil

408. These additions bring the average annual cost per pupil, at 1967 cost levels, to £498 for secondary places and £413 for primary or preparatory places.

Net cost per pupil

409. To arrive at the net cost per pupil the parental contribution must be deducted. In the case of university awards the average parental contribution is about £90. Our scale is similar except that parents earning over £2,000 p.a. will pay at higher rates. On the other hand parents of school children will tend generally to be somewhat younger than the parents of undergraduates and may on average earn rather less. We would expect these two factors largely to cancel out, and we therefore anticipate a similar average contribution of about £90, which would reflect an average assessed income of £1,650. This may appear to be a high figure in relation to boarding need, but it has regard to the considerable proportion of parents with higher incomes whose children would qualify for assisted places because of overseas postings. Indeed it may be an under-estimate of parental contributions in the early years, i.e. until substantial numbers of children of parents with average and below average incomes enter the schools.

410. Our estimate is, therefore, that the full costs of integration can be met within an average charge to public funds (in 1967 terms) of £408 per pupil attending a secondary boarding school and £323 per pupil attending a primary or preparatory boarding school.

---

[1] By comparison, we understand that the levels of administrative cost of some other educational bodies are:

University Grants Committee	(1967–68)	£289,000 (excluding premises etc.)
U.C.C.A.	(1965–66)	£205,000 (inclusive)
Schools Council	(1968–69)	£420,000 (inclusive)
Social Science Research Council	(1967–68)	£157,000 (inclusive)

CHAPTER 16

The cost of integrating independent boarding schools

The gross cost

411. In Chapter 8, we concluded that a total of 47,000 assisted boarding places would be required in independent schools (about 9,000 in preparatory schools or departments and 38,000 in secondary schools) in fifteen years' time.

412. In Chapter 15 we estimated the average annual cost to public funds as being £323 for each preparatory pupil and £408 for each secondary pupil, including an allowance for administrative and other subsidiary costs—at 1967 cost levels. The total cost of assisting 47,000 pupils would thus be £18·4 million (9,000 × £323 + 38,000 × £408).

Savings

413. When the scheme is fully in operation, all assisted pupils at independent schools will be at integrated schools. We can therefore deduct from this first estimate of the cost of integration the full amount of assistance now given by local education authorities and government departments to pupils (other than handicapped pupils) attending independent boarding schools. The amount spent by local education authorities in England and Wales for the academic year 1965-66 was:

	£
Recognised efficient schools	2,159,000
Non-recognised schools	76,000
Total	2,235,000

(*Source:* an enquiry made of local education authorities gave figures for the Spring Term 1966, which we have multiplied by three).

414. The majority of authorities give assistance in accordance with scales which are similar to that recommended in the Martin Report (see Table 30). New scales recently recommended by the working party of local authority associations (see paragraph 387) would increase the total assistance given by local education authorities. Allowing for the fact that increased scales of assistance by some authorities are already reflected in the figures in the previous paragraph, we estimate that something like £0·25 million extra will be spent by authorities as a whole if these scales are adopted by all authorities. This would bring the expenditure of local education authorities on the children at present assisted to about £2·5 million.

415. The equivalent assistance in Scotland (see paragraph 500) is that given by both the Scottish Education Department and education authorities. 127 pupils were assisted in 1965-66, and the cost can be disregarded in our calculations.

416. It is not possible to say precisely what is the expenditure by government departments on pupils attending independent schools, within the total expenditure by Departments of £5·5 million on boarding school allowances (see paragraph 350). However, about two thirds of the children assisted by Departments go to independent schools. Taking into account the fact that the fees at some maintained schools are less than the full allowance (they do not include a tuition fee), we estimate that £3·9 million is paid in allowances for children at independent boarding schools.

417. Government departments and nationalised industries will need to review their policies in the light of the new procedures we recommend. There would be no case for duplication of grants from public funds for the same educational purpose, and there is much to be said for a common basis of assessment and a common source of grants for all children requiring boarding education for whatever reason, regardless of parental employment. As integration will be a consequence of Government policy and will be financed mainly at public expense, there would be no logic in the Government's pursuing this policy and at the same time paying grants to its own employees to enable their children to attend schools outside the integrated sector. It is evident that the number of places required will, over a period, bring a large number of schools, covering a wide variety of provision, within this sector, and that the range of places available will be sufficient to give parents an ample choice. We see no unfairness or inconsistency therefore, in expecting pupils assisted from public funds to take up places in maintained, direct grant or integrated independent schools. We regard it as a cardinal point of policy that parents should not be assisted from public funds, after a date to be decided, if they prefer their children to enter independent schools not approved for integration.

418. For the purpose of estimating the costs of integration, therefore, we have assumed that no grants or allowances will be paid by public employers either in substitution for or supplementation of payments made by the Boarding Schools Corporation for children attending schools in England, Wales or Scotland.

419. The cost offsets so far mentioned (amounting to £6·4 million a year) would in effect be a redistribution of present expenditure. But there may also be savings. For example, it is possible that the demand for boarding places in service schools overseas will be reduced as a consequence of integration.

420. Another possible saving, which we cannot quantify, will depend upon the future choice of school for pupils who may no longer be able to take up places at integrated schools because of the influx of assisted pupils. If they all enter the maintained sector as day pupils, they will more or less balance the assisted pupils coming from maintained schools. If they do not take up so many places in maintained schools (for example, if the independent sector expands) there will be a small saving of local education authority expenditure.

421. If the fiscal and other financial privileges of charitable status were removed from a large number of independent schools, as we recommend in Chapter 14, there could be savings to public funds of up to about £4 million a year.[1] A proportion of this saving would be repaid to integrating schools

---

[1] This saving would depend upon the number of schools considered not to be serving a truly charitable purpose. The total saving could be higher in the future, in view of the increase of 50 per cent in the rate of Selective Employment Tax announced in the Budget speech on 19th March, 1968.

through the higher fees paid for assisted pupils, and we cannot, therefore, estimate exactly what the net saving would be; but it would probably be between £2 million and £3 million a year. It would be for the Government to decide whether this saving should be regarded as offsetting the costs of integration. The same would apply to any savings which might accrue if action were taken to aggregate the whole or part of the income of minors with that of their parents for tax purposes.[1]

422. It has been suggested to us that economies could be made in the running costs of some schools. It is certainly true that there are very wide variations in the range of fees charged by schools (from under £300 to over £600 for boarders in public schools alone); but this itself should not be taken as evidence of extravagance. The commitments vary widely, particularly in the matter of upkeep of (sometimes ancient) premises, and variations will continue to be justifiable according to individual circumstances. In any case it would be unreasonable to expect changes in expenditure patterns in too short a period: there will have to be adequate time for adjustment. We regard it as unrealistic, meanwhile, to allow for any reductions in fees for the purposes of these calculations.

The net additional cost

423. Disregarding possible savings at 418 to 421 above, £6·4 million represents the minimum figure we are entitled to set against the cost of assistance to pupils attending independent boarding schools under our proposals, thus reducing it from £18·4 million to £12 million. This net additional figure would represent 0·7 per cent of total educational expenditure in Great Britain, and 1·3 per cent of expenditure on primary and secondary education.

Number of schools affected

424. The average number of boarding pupils on the roll of recognised efficient secondary boarding schools[2] (including secondary departments of schools catering for both primary and secondary pupils) was 175 in January 1967. To calculate how many of the 460 secondary schools concerned would be affected by the admission of 38,000 pupils on the basis we have outlined is by no means straightforward, and a precise figure cannot be given. Some integrated schools may have scarcely more than a half of assisted pupils in the early stages—others may have significantly more than a half; if, for example, this is necessary to ensure that those assisted pupils who have previously attended maintained schools are not in a minority. We want all suitable schools, small as well as large, to have the opportunity of integration and the acceptance of smaller schools, particularly for girls, will swell the total number of schools. Yet the large schools will have a proportionately bigger intake, and this will help to raise the average number of assisted pupils per school. If as a working premise, and allowing some weighting for the larger schools, we assume that the average number of assisted boarding pupils on the roll of integrated schools would be 110, the admission of 38,000 assisted pupils could lead to the integration of some 350 secondary schools—that is, about three out of every four boarding schools in the recognised efficient

---

[1] Action has now in fact been proposed—in the March, 1968 Budget—to aggregate the investment income of minors with their parents' income for tax purposes.

[2] i.e. with more than 25 per cent of the pupils boarding.

sector. We do not suggest how many preparatory schools should be integrated to admit the substantial proportion of the 9,000 pupils of primary or preparatory age (within the total of 47,000 assisted pupils) who could not be accommodated in junior departments of secondary schools. As we have said, a policy for integrating preparatory schools will have to be looked at separately either by ourselves in a later report or by the Corporation; but if a similar integration policy were applied, the numbers of schools invited to take part would be substantial because most preparatory schools are small.[1]

Priorities—an interim scheme

425. Although £12 million represents a small proportion of total educational expenditure, it is a large sum of money and we are conscious of the many other commitments to educational expenditure which the Government must bear in mind now and in the future. To implement our proposals on the scale we have outlined is the only way we can see of meeting as fully as possible the objectives of our terms of reference; but the economic situation may make it difficult to do this in the foreseeable future without restricting other developments which should have even higher priority. If money for integration is to be limited, it should be used to the best effect.

426. Even if the total number of assisted pupils is severely limited through cost, they must not be distributed in small groups over a great many schools. If integration is to succeed, the proportion of assisted pupils who have previously attended maintained schools should comprise at least a half of the school roll as quickly as possible. If the economy can afford only a partial measure of integration in the early stages, it follows that this should be done by limiting the number of schools to be integrated in the first instance. This could pose a difficult problem of selection of schools and we consider that the fairest and educationally most beneficial method would be to integrate first a cross-section of schools, giving equal priority within certain categories.

427. In England and Wales,[2] the largest boarding schools, and in particular those with the biggest sixth forms, may be among those which can offer the best opportunity for bold and imaginative schemes of integration. Their size would enable them to arrange an intake of pupils at various ages, and to provide for a broader social and academic "spread" than smaller schools; and at the same time to retain real sixth form strength. We would not wish to restrict the choice to schools above a particular size; their suitability is more important. For example, there are 36 boys' boarding schools with more than 500 pupils (including day boys); but there would be room in an interim scheme also for many suitable schools below this size.

428. There are very few girls' schools of comparable size, and it would be necessary to bring in a number of smaller schools. There are only 38 boarding schools with 300 or more pupils, including day pupils, and the integration of all of them would still leave an acute imbalance between the provision for boys and girls. The integration of smaller schools, under suitable arrange-

---

[1] The average number of boarders in preparatory schools mainly for boarding pupils was 72 in January 1967.

[2] We do not deal in the following paragraphs with priorities in Scotland where there may be different views on the developing pattern of integration. For the same reason we do not include a Scottish element of cost in the interim cost figures in paragraph 435 below, although the cost in Scotland is included in the cost of full integration given above.

ments, as well as a steady development of co-education, would help to set this right.

429. There are only three co-educational schools in our terms of reference;[1] we should not only like to see all of them integrated, but also to include all other recognised efficient co-educational schools with 300 or more pupils,[2] making a total of 10 schools in all and about 3,000 co-educational boarding places.

430. As we have said, there may be a number of smaller schools to which the Corporation would give priority equally with the large schools. Some may indeed be more suitable for assisted pupils than the larger schools. Some are in areas which are short of boarding places and it will be important to try to correct the regional imbalance of boarding provision by integrating such schools at an early stage.

431. Local education authorities providing new school places in their area may, as we have suggested in paragraph 272, be able to build an extension for day pupils as part of an existing independent school in such a way that the resulting new school may take its place in the authority's plan for comprehensive reorganisation. This could apply particularly to schools in or near expanding residential areas. Such a school would, because of its wide academic range, be suitable for many pupils in need of boarding. In these cases integration could only proceed at a pace that matched the authority's building programme, but when it became possible it should be given high priority.

432. A number of schools have already made progress towards varying styles of integration, either by taking a significant proportion of pupils assisted by local education authorities or by using trust funds to pay for pupils who need boarding education but who could not otherwise have it. As it is our intention that publicly assisted pupils should, after a transitional period, attend only integrated schools, it is clearly important that schools which may already be meeting a substantial part of the Commission's objectives should have the opportunity to play their full role in integration. Their experience is very much to be valued and we would recommend an equal priority for any not already included in the categories above.

433. Finally a number of schools, including some not in the above categories, have close ties with other schools in a particular denominational or other grouping. We have mentioned the Friends and Woodard groups, which include schools within and others outside these categories. If the schools in such a group preferred to produce a joint scheme for integration, which would enable each school to play a full part while continuing in a special relationship with the other schools in the group, we would very much welcome this, and would hope that the Corporation would give early support to such schemes.

434. We do not intend that these categories should be exclusive. It should be open to any independent school to apply for integration, and to be considered on its merits, even though the funds available may not enable the Corporation to take up the offer immediately.

---

[1] See footnote to paragraph 64.
[2] One of these schools became a public school during 1967.

Interim scheme—cost

435. We would regard the minimum interim objective, if funds were available for something less than the major integration we have recommended above, as providing for at least 32,000 pupils (say, 25,000 attending secondary schools and 7,000 attending preparatory schools or departments). This would cost £12·5 million gross, less the offset of £6·4 million explained above, making a net additional cost of £6·1 million. This might in practice be an over-estimate of the cost. In a limited scheme, children of parents serving overseas would inevitably comprise a higher proportion of all assisted pupils than in a full scheme, and it is a reasonable supposition that the average parental contribution would be higher than the £90 we estimated in paragraph 409.

436. Such an interim scheme would probably bring some 170 secondary schools[1] within the field of integration, on the basis of an average number of 150 assisted pupils in each school. This average is higher than that used in paragraph 424 above. One reason is that the larger schools to be integrated in the early stages would probably account for a higher proportion of assisted pupils in an interim scheme than they would in the full integration scheme. Also, the children of parents working overseas might fill a significant proportion of places. A number of them have not previously attended maintained schools. Fewer schools would therefore be integrated in order to enable pupils who had attended maintained schools to fill at least a half of the places. If the interim scheme included many small schools, however, significantly more than 170 schools in all would be involved, as well as a considerable number of preparatory schools if similar policies were applied to them.

437. We would regard this as an interim scheme only. If the number of pupils at independent schools already helped from public funds remained constant at about 20,000, there would be scope for admitting not more than 12,000 extra pupils into the schools. But the 32,000 pupils would be attending far fewer schools than the present 20,000 pupils, who are spread over at least a thousand schools (including preparatory schools). Sufficient schools would be involved, with a high proportion of assisted pupils in them, to set the integration process irrevocably in train. The interim scheme would also provide a useful build-up period in which the true extent of the effective need for boarding in independent schools could be assessed in practice as well as on paper. We hope that in practice an interim scheme would merge steadily into a full integration scheme, which, as we have shown, would eventually bring in virtually all suitable secondary schools.

Sources of income

438. How would that part of the cost which is not contributed by the parents be met? The existing position is that local education authorities meet individually the boarding costs of assisted pupils belonging to their area, subject to parental contributions, on the basis we have described in Chapter 15. Expenditure by authorities on pupils who do not belong to the area of any authority (including pupils whose parents are abroad or who move after an assisted pupil has started at boarding school) is "pooled"; that is, the aggregate expenditure is divided between authorities according to the school population in their area. The Exchequer makes a contribution to the total

---

[1] including secondary departments, see paragraph 424

expenditure of each local education authority through rate support grant, amounting nationally to about 55 per cent of the relevant expenditure.

439. Experience since the Fleming Report suggests most strongly that, insofar as the Committee's proposals for assisting pupils at independent schools have not been fulfilled, this has been due largely to the lack of a centrally organised and financed bursary scheme. It is understandable that individual local education authorities, left with the onus of deciding whether to assist pupils with boarding, have in many cases preferred to do other things with their money. Despite the widespread support which we hope our integration scheme will command, we believe that its success would be seriously jeopardised if it were subject to acceptance, rejection or varying interpretations by 162 different authorities in England and Wales and 35 in Scotland. The day school problem may be different and we shall return to it in our second report. But for boarding schools, we have no doubt that a central organ having administrative and financial responsibility will be required. This has led us to the view that the proposed Boarding Schools Corporation should have not only oversight of the selection arrangements we have outlined in Chapter 12 but also responsibility for all public financial transactions with integrated boarding schools.

440. It would be wrong in principle for the whole cost of a national service of boarding school education to be borne by the Exchequer. Children at present attend boarding schools with local education authority assistance where it is necessary or desirable for them to do so. Under the revised criteria of boarding need which we are suggesting, more children would attend boarding schools with assistance; but this is a difference of degree rather than kind, and should not affect the financial responsibility of local education authorities. It is necessary to find a formula that shares the burden equitably between central and local government. We think the right principle is that the cost of boarding integration should be divided between the Exchequer and local education authorities in the same proportion as applies at any given time to educational expenditure as a whole. But there should not be a redistribution of present boarding school costs which would place upon local education authorities costs now borne by the Exchequer, and in working out any new financial formula account should be taken of savings which would accrue to government departments following the cessation of education allowances to employees.

441. There are various possible ways in which local authorities could, with assistance from the Exchequer through rate support grant, meet that part of the cost not met by parents. The first method would be for authorities to pay individually for each pupil in their area attending an integrated school. This is in effect the present arrangement, and has the advantages of directness and simplicity, but we do not recommend it. It would not overcome one of the present difficulties, which is that authorities appear to apply widely differing criteria in handling applications for boarding education. Also there is the complication that a high proportion of assisted pupils would be the children of parents serving overseas, who may have no domicile in this country, and whose fees could not always be attributed to an individual authority. If this scheme were adopted, therefore, there would have to be a pooling scheme of the existing kind working alongside it for children from overseas who would be selected and placed directly by the Boarding Schools Corporation.

Pooling of expenditure

442. Having rejected this method of payment, we go on to consider two others, either of which we would find acceptable, and between which we think the Government, in consultation with the local authority associations, should make their choice. Each would involve the pooling of expenditure by local education authorities, with assistance from the Exchequer through rate support grant. Although pooling involves in a sense some derogation of the right of individual authorities to decide how their money should be spent and how the children in their area are to be educated (although in this case they would be represented on the consortia), we do not see any alternative if the aims of an integration policy are to be achieved. Much of our evidence has supported the view that pooling is essential. There are precedents; for example, in expenditure on teacher training. Although we appreciate that an extension of pooling is not to be lightly undertaken, we see no workable alternative and we believe that authorities will, through the consortium arrangements as well as through representation on the Boarding Schools Corporation itself, be able to exert the right degree of influence over their own affairs. The first possibility, therefore, is to use the normal pooling procedures, with a suitable adjustment (for which special provision may have to be made) to allow for any reduction in central government expenditure as a result of a reduction or cessation of education grants to employees.

A variant of pooling

443. There is a possible variant of the normal pooling procedure which we commend for consideration by the Government before a final decision is taken. Different parts of England and Wales at present vary widely in the extent to which children in their areas attend independent schools, thereby relieving local education authorities and the Exchequer of the cost of their education. In some areas the proportion is insignificant and there is little or no saving to authorities because a few children do not attend their schools. But in other areas the saving is significant, both in terms of physical provision and of teachers' salaries. This factor is already taken into account in assessing each authority's share of rate support grant, but we would see advantage in arrangements which went further than this. Just as authorities at present make payments if pupils attend schools maintained by other local education authorities, so they might contribute to a pool in proportion to the number of pupils in an authority's area attending independent schools without assistance from the authority. Such a contribution would only be appropriate in respect of children of compulsory school age. It is up to this age that authorities are indisputably responsible for the education of children in their area. After compulsory school age most children in all parts of the country have left school, although there is a welcome increase in the number staying on voluntarily or attending colleges of further education. It would thus be impracticable to require contributions in respect of all children no longer receiving education at their expense after compulsory school age; and it follows that it would be unreasonable to do so in respect of those continuing to receive private education. The exemption of children over compulsory school age would provide some measure of relief to the authorities having the largest number of children attending independent schools at their parents' expense (and thus contributing most to such a pool) because the independent sector

(in particular the recognised efficient sector) has a higher proportion of pupils staying on till 17 or 18 than the maintained sector, as is shown by the tables in Chapter 2.

444. The special contribution would bear on local education authorities regardless of whether an authority would have had to make extra provision if the pupils concerned had attended maintained instead of independent schools. Such are the variations of local provision that it is not possible to generalise about the point at which an additional number of children coming on to an authority's roll at different ages would cause extra provision to be made. In any case, this is not taken into account when payments are made for children attending another authority's schools, and we do not think it would be relevant here. The important fact is that there are some 435,000 children of all ages at present attending independent schools in England and Wales, and they could not be absorbed into the maintained system without substantial additional cost to authorities as a whole and to the Exchequer.

445. There may be objections to this method of payment. It would inevitably affect some authorities more than others. Contributions would be related to the number of parents in an area choosing at any one time not to send their children to maintained schools—a factor beyond an authority's control. Also, authorities would be required to contribute in respect of fee-paying children attending integrated schools as well as other independent schools, although it would be in the interests of integration that a number should attend integrated schools. Nevertheless, the community as a whole will have to be responsible for that part of the cost of integration which is not borne by parents, and we are anxious that this should be done in the most equitable way. We urge that this method of sharing the cost should be given careful consideration alongside the more usual pooling arrangements.

Income of the Corporation

446. Whatever method of payment by local education authorities is adopted, we envisage that payments (attracting rate support grant) should be made to the Boarding Schools Corporation. The Corporation would be responsible for all financial transactions with the schools. It would also be responsible for assessing and collecting parental contributions.

447. The total income of the Corporation would be determined by the Government, in consultation with local authority associations and in the light of estimates of expenditure. We would urge that an assurance of income over a reasonable future period should be given, in view of the complexity of the arrangements to be made with individual schools, including the forward reservation of places. It is vital that there should not be empty places in the schools, and that governing bodies should have ample notice of the number of places to be made available to fee-paying pupils. The Corporation would, though with limited functions, be the equivalent of a large local education authority having a great many pupils in its care, and it should have no less assurance of continued income at a reasonable level than a local education authority.

Approval of fees at integrating schools

448. In view of the heavy cost involved, it follows that the Boarding Schools Corporation should have the power to approve the level of fees at each

1—G*

integrated school. This has already been done by the Department for many years in the direct grant sector, so far as we know without detriment to their work. We do not think it would be tenable that independent bodies of governors should be free to fix fees without the consent of the major user of the schools. Those using the schools already approve fees in the negative sense of deciding whether or not they can afford to pay; but if the Corporation enters into long term commitments with integrated schools, as is implicit in our proposals, it cannot fall back upon this sanction, and a more positive control will be necessary. In approving fee levels, the Corporation should have regard to all the individual circumstances of each school, and should not seek uniformity. As schools do not normally carry a surplus on their budget which would enable losses to be borne, ample notice of decisions about fees would be of vital importance to their well-being, and it would be essential for applications for increases in fees to be handled promptly.

449. The main element in the fees of any school is represented by salaries paid to teaching staff, and regard should be paid to the number of teachers employed and to their levels of reward—having in mind always the additional burdens of service in a boarding school. Boarding schools need generous staffing, but they should not be staffed beyond levels which the developing experience of the Corporation, coupled with the advice of H.M. Inspectors—who will, we hope, be closely associated with the work of the Corporation—would suggest as reasonable. To control fee levels would seem a better way of ensuring reasonable staffing standards than to attempt to impose a "quota" of teachers at each school. Here again, the experience of direct grant schools is relevant. They appear to be adequately staffed under just such a system of fee control. It would in theory be possible to regard the Corporation as a local education authority for purposes of teacher quota, and to allocate to the Corporation a quota of qualified teachers, not to be exceeded at integrated schools taken as a whole. We do not recommend the adoption of such a scheme. It would be impracticable, particularly in the early years, to calculate and administer a quota for the Corporation's schools as a group when their numbers will be increasing continually. Moreover, we intend that the proposed control of fees by the Corporation should prevent over-generous staffing.

Approval of fees at non-integrating schools

450. If financial stringency should limit the number of schools which can be integrated in the near future, there is the possibility that some schools not selected for integration might deliberately set out to cater for parents who can afford very high fees, attracting them by lavish material provision and an extravagantly high staffing ratio. This would tend to create a new form of divisiveness. We therefore recommend that the Secretary of State should also make the fees at independent boarding schools not selected for integration subject to a reserve power of approval by the Boarding Schools Corporation. This power should be used only where the fee level rose significantly above the fees of any integrated school.

Capital expenditure

451. Control of fees by the Corporation means that it will have to have detailed knowledge of the financial affairs of each integrating school, on

which to base its approval of fee increases. It also means that special regard will have to be paid to the methods of financing future capital development. We do not anticipate that the Boarding Schools Corporation should meet any capital expenditure directly; but that this should be borne by the schools from capital funds or by means of loans. There would have to be provision for appropriate fee increases to cover loan charges and to this extent capital developments would be supported from public funds through the fees paid for assisted pupils as well as privately through other fee income. We think that an arrangement whereby long term loans might be made to integrating schools similar to those made to voluntary schools under Section 105 of the Education Act, 1944, could be of great help in the raising of capital, and we commend this to the Secretary of State for consideration.

452. Linked with the Corporation's approval of fees at integrated schools would have to be an understanding that substantial commitments of expenditure could not be entered into without the prior approval of the Corporation. We recommend that approval should be required for any capital project estimated to cost more than a total amount to be decided by the Corporation. We also recommend that major capital works should be subject to approval of plans and of building costs, either by the Corporation or by the Department, and that the Corporation should be allowed an annual capital investment quota for the integrated sector. The definition of what constitutes a major project (i.e. in terms of cost) should be the same as that applied to maintained schools at the relevant time.

Endowment funds

453. The figures we quoted for boys' schools in Chapter 14 showed that endowment income is at a few schools substantial, at others marginal, but at most schools insignificant. Where it is substantial, the scheme of integration to be approved by the Boarding Schools Corporation should make provision (in consultation with the Secretary of State) for the uses to which it is put. We recommend that the following principles should be observed:—

(i) where funds are earmarked for capital development, they should be used for this purpose for the benefit of the whole school, supplemented as appropriate by the raising of loans to be amortised through fees, and subject to the approval by the Corporation of all capital developments;

(ii) where funds are provided for the annual relief of pupils' fees (whether through scholarships or bursaries) their future distribution should be examined and approved by the Boarding Schools Corporation. We would expect all pupils to be equally eligible for awards from these funds. Where an award is made to an assisted pupil we consider that, subject to disregarding the first (say) £50, the amount of the award should be offset against the charge otherwise to be paid by the Boarding Schools Corporation[1]. Where an award is made to pupils not assisted from public funds, the amount should be assessed according to a parental income scale not more generous than that for assisted pupils—the first (say) £50 being disregarded;

(iii) where endowment income is not assigned by trust to any specific purpose, we would expect it to be used (by agreement between the Governors and

---

[1] This would mean some reduction in the cost of integration, but we have not regarded it as sufficiently important to take into account in our earlier calculations.

the Corporation) for general purposes of integration. These might include benefits for assisted pupils which would not necessarily be met by the payment of their fees—for example, help towards school visits abroad, or other ways of reducing inequalities of opportunity during school life which may still exist between fee-paying and assisted pupils. Many public schools were founded with the original object of helping poor boys or girls to receive an education, and the use of endowment funds in this way may in such cases be entirely consonant with the founders' wishes.

Transitional arrangements

454. Most local education authorities are already paying fees for some children at independent boarding schools. These arrangements cover a wider range of schools than are likely to be integrated in the foreseeable future. The guiding principles during the transitional period, i.e. until all assisted pupils can be placed in integrated schools, should be that:

(i) no child should be required to leave a school at which he is already being educated wholly or partly at an authority's expense;

(ii) subject to this transitional provision for children already in schools, after a date to be decided authorities should no longer take up boarding places at independent schools which have not been accepted for integration, except (to meet exceptional circumstances) with the agreement of the Boarding Schools Corporation;

(iii) as from the same date, grants from government departments and nationalised industries for boarding education (if they have not ceased altogether) should not be paid in respect of children attending schools in Great Britain which have not been accepted for integration, except (to meet exceptional circumstances) by agreement with the Boarding Schools Corporation;

(iv) the Corporation should not accept responsibility for the payment of fees at independent schools not approved for integration, subject to the reservations in the following paragraph.

455. There are two categories of children whose costs at a school might be met by the Boarding Schools Corporation although they would not be attending an integrated school. The first would be where a child was already attending another school as a fee-paying boarder when, due to a change in home circumstances, he or she acquired a need for boarding acceptable to the Corporation. In such a case, it would be within the discretion of the Corporation to consider whether, in order to avoid a break in education, the child should be allowed to remain as an assisted pupil at the present school, or should transfer to an integrated school. The second case would relate specifically to girls. We have set out in Chapter 11 and elsewhere the difficulty of integrating sufficient girls' schools to meet the potential need, and said that, as an exceptional and limited measure, places might be taken up by the Corporation at other schools until there were sufficient places available in integrated schools.

456. Arrangements for placing handicapped children in independent boarding schools should continue to be the responsibility of individual local education authorities, and should not be affected either by these arrangements or by any of our other recommendations.

Maintained boarding schools

457. It has been suggested to us that there may be parts of Great Britain which would not participate fully in an integration scheme, at any rate in the early stages—areas in which, because of distance from suitable boarding schools, or of unfamiliarity with boarding education, parents and authorities alike would feel that the scheme was not really for them. We hope that this picture may change in two ways over the years:

(i) by careful allocation of places (e.g. with a view to avoiding excessive travelling), the Boarding Schools Corporation may encourage parents of children who need boarding education to accept places in integrated schools;

(ii) by setting an example of successful placing of children in need of boarding, the Corporation may encourage authorities in such areas (in conjunction with the Secretaries of State, who control the allocation of capital resources) to provide more maintained boarding schools in these areas if there is a clear need for this. We would regard it as one of the duties of the Corporation to bring to the notice of the Secretary of State evidence of lack of regional provision for boarding need (in independent, direct grant and maintained schools combined) with their recommendations as to the type and scale of provision which should be made.

458. There might in particular be a strong case for providing two or possibly three new boarding schools—or day schools with very substantial boarding provision—in the north of England. Such provision would be an important adjunct of the whole integration policy, and we would not think it right that authorities in the areas concerned should have to meet the whole capital cost, in a situation in which more fortunately situated authorities could make full use of integrated independent schools without capital commitment. The cost should, therefore, be met under arrangements similar to those outlined in paragraph 451. The providing authorities would raise loans (possibly through the Corporation) for the initial capital outlay; the loan charges would form an element in the fee charged by these schools, and insofar as places were taken up by assisted pupils paid for by the Corporation the cost would in effect be pooled.

459. This recommendation is consistent with the view we have expressed in earlier chapters, that boarding provision in maintained and direct grant schools should be regarded as equivalent to, and obtainable on the same financial terms as boarding places in integrated independent schools. We would urge authorities to place at the disposal of the Boarding Schools Corporation a proportion of the places in maintained boarding schools, and the governors of direct grant schools to do the same. It would follow that the same scales of parental contribution for pupils considered by a regional consortium to be in need of boarding should apply at maintained and direct grant schools as at integrated independent schools. If these scales would be more generous than those implemented by a number of authorities at present, this would add marginally to the cost of integration; but we see real advantage in assisted places at maintained and direct grant boarding schools being financed through the same pooling arrangements as at independent schools.

460. It would continue to be the responsibility of local education authorities to make their own decisions about, and arrangements for, any remission of

boarding costs for parents of children desiring but not in need of boarding education at a maintained or direct grant school, subject, in the case of direct grant schools, to the recommendations in our next report.

CHAPTER 17

The next steps; legislation; timing.

461. There will be four readily discernible stages of the integration of independent boarding schools:

  (i) The publication of this report, which will be followed by public debate about our recommendations, leading to their acceptance, modification or rejection by the Government.

 (ii) If the Government accepts a policy of integration, legislation will be required along the lines we discuss below.

(iii) There will follow a stage of crucial importance to the schools concerned—that of negotiations to determine what part each school should play in an integrated system of boarding education.

(iv) When the future role of individual schools has been determined, there will be the continuing work of administering and financing the integrated sector, guiding its future development and placing assisted pupils in suitable schools.

462. Assuming that the Government accepts our recommendations in whole or in part, we now examine the tasks to be carried out at (iii) and (iv) above; these may help to determine the form legislation should take. The first stage will be that of negotiating with individual schools or groups of schools plans for their future development within an integrated system. Even our interim scheme would involve about 170 secondary schools. Negotiations will thus take a considerable time. But as places will be taken up at some schools before others have had their development plans approved, the negotiating, placing and financial work will inevitably overlap. We shall first examine, therefore, whether they might be undertaken by the same body.

The Boarding Schools Corporation—functions

463. We have ascribed the oversight of integration policy to the Boarding Schools Corporation. The Corporation should be responsible to the Secretary of State for Education and Science (and possibly the Secretary of State for Scotland) for the development of a new integrated sector of boarding education, drawing for this purpose upon places made available in independent, direct grant and maintained schools alike.

  Its tasks would be to:

  (i) continue to assess the need for boarding places of different kinds.

 (ii) ascertain and make known the availability of boarding school places for assisted pupils in independent, direct grant and maintained schools.

(iii) allocate places to consortia of local education authorities.

(iv) negotiate with schools and authorities about the number of assisted places to be made available in the future.

 (v) carry out an initial central processing, if appropriate, of applications for places.

(vi) exercise oversight of the arrangements made by consortia of local education authorities for receiving applications and placing assisted pupils.

(vii) consider applications for boarding places from British nationals working overseas, and arrangements for placing their children, either directly or through consortia of authorities. (An agency service might be provided for the placing of children of British subjects living permanently overseas or for foreign nationals living overseas, on payment of a fee).

(viii) make arrangements for placing pupils in sixth form colleges and "academies" which may be established.

(ix) approve fees to be charged by schools.

(x) pay to schools the fees of assisted pupils.

(xi) assess parental contributions towards fees. It would be for consideration whether parents should make payments direct to the Corporation or through local education authorities.

(xii) negotiate with schools about the disbursement of endowment income.

(xiii) approve, in consultation with the Secretary of State and local education authorities, capital developments—whether for boarding or day pupils —at integrated boarding schools.

(xiv) sponsor (though not undertake) research into problems arising in the course of integration.

(xv) prepare annual estimates and accounts and an annual report on the progress of integration.

(xvi) consider appeals from schools or parents against decisions by regional consortia of local education authorities.

A single body

464. The question is whether the work of the body responsible for negotiating agreements with schools would be so different from the continuing work of the Boarding Schools Corporation as to warrant the appointment, for a period of say five years, of a negotiating body quite separate from the Corporation. Our view is that, although the functions are separate and distinct, they are sufficiently closely aligned for us to recommend that there should be one body only—namely the Boarding Schools Corporation. There should be some administrative economy in this. Also, there would be very real advantages in having the two functions—*ad hoc* negotiations and the continuing financial and administrative work—dealt with under the same control. There would be two distinct phases of the Corporation's work; the emphasis would gradually veer from a great deal of negotiation and relatively little placing work to a large volume of placing and little fresh negotiation. Members of the Corporation and its staff would, in the negotiating phase, gain useful experience of the problems of integration. Their knowledge of the progress of negotiations would greatly ease the difficult task of forward planning in preparation for placing pupils in schools. Above all, there would be the asset of there being seen to be one body responsible for all aspects of integration.

Development plans

465. The first act of the Corporation would be to invite development plans from schools, to be submitted within a period of (say) one year. The Corporation should have the power to require schools to supply any necessary information. We know that there are already a number of schools and groups

of schools which are giving much thought to constructive proposals, and there would undoubtedly be a substantial task of negotiation to be undertaken almost from the date of appointment of the Corporation. We envisage the most intensive negotiating phase as lasting about three years, during which time most schools suitable for integration—at any rate in the first phase—would have had schemes approved. There should always be the opportunity for further schools to be considered, however, and this is another reason for giving the Corporation, as a permanent body, the power to approve schemes.

466. Negotiations would mean visiting schools, holding meetings with governing bodies (and with local education authorities as appropriate) and reaching agreement about development plans; then approving schools for integration. Matters affecting the composition of governing bodies (see paragraph 314) or the use of endowment funds (see paragraph 453) would have to be worked out also in consultation with the Secretary of State (in his role of Charity Commissioner).

The Corporation—members and staff

467. The membership and staffing of the Corporation would require very careful consideration. We envisage that there would be a full-time paid Chairman and other members who would be unpaid. Although they should include representatives of the interests of local education authorities and associations of independent schools, as well as of the child care services (see paragraph 160) we would think it preferable that they should not be nominated by these bodies, but be appointed on a personal basis by the Secretary of State. The Chairman should be a person of considerable distinction, and should be remunerated accordingly. He or she would be assisted by a full-time director or secretary (not a member of the Corporation) and administrative and professional staff.

468. The professional staff should include a group of experienced H.M. Inspectors associated closely with integration. We have stressed elsewhere the need for careful inspection as the Corporation's main source of advice about the schools. A lawyer, an accountant, and possibly an architect should be employed. On the administrative side, the permanent staff might be recruited partly from the local education authority service. It would be important throughout to try to recruit staff with a real interest in the work of the Corporation; a proportion might serve for a limited period of secondment from other posts, and others might make their career in the service of the Corporation. Some at least should have knowledge of the handling by modern techniques of accounting and statistical work.

Panels

469. During the negotiating phase there would be a need for two or possibly three *ad hoc* panels of negotiators, working part-time (on a sessional fee basis), each with its own Chairman under the direction of the Corporation. The negotiations might in some cases be long and arduous, and a single panel might not conclude agreements with more than say 25 schools in a year. The panel appointments, particularly those of the Chairmen, should be such as to attract people of standing in the educational world, possibly on secondment

from their existing posts. They should not be regarded as posts for retired men and women, although some excellent retired people might in fact help to fill them. We hope they would attract also some younger men and women who might subsequently transfer to permanent appointments on the staff of the Corporation. The task will be one for people with understanding of and sympathy for the aims of integration and of sufficient standing to negotiate with distinguished bodies of governors. We do not underestimate the difficulty of recruiting suitable men and women.

AN EDUCATION ACT

Powers affecting integrated (or integrating) schools

470. There should be an Education (Independent Schools) Act to set integration in train. Its most important provision would be to establish a Boarding Schools Corporation, with the power to approve schemes for the future development of independent boarding schools and with the necessary funds to carry out the integration policy.

471. The Corporation should have power to use funds allocated to it for the purpose of developing a closer association between independent boarding schools (and direct grant boarding schools if appropriate) and the maintained sector of education. The Corporation would be accountable to Parliament through the Secretary of State. In order to negotiate effectively with schools in the first instance, and subsequently to carry out the tasks listed in paragraph 463 above, the Corporation should be enabled to:

(i) require named schools to submit information needed by the Corporation within a stated period.

(ii) make payments to schools in respect of the fees of pupils admitted under arrangements made by the Corporation.

(iii) approve the level of fees to be charged at schools which have entered into a scheme of integration.

(iv) approve (in consultation with the Secretary of State) proposals for major capital works and the raising of loans in connection with capital works.

(v) require parents of assisted pupils to contribute prescribed amounts towards the cost of boarding education.

(vi) invite bodies other than the foundation to appoint one third of the governors of each school approved for integration.

472. The Act should require each school to make available, and the Corporation to pay for, a number of places for assisted pupils to be specified in the scheme approved for the school. If such places fell vacant and the Governors could not fill them with fee-paying pupils, there should be a liability upon the Corporation to make good any resulting financial deficit. The scheme should provide for a variation in the number of assisted places either by agreement or after a prescribed period of notice.

473. We considered in paragraph 272 arrangements by which local education authorities might build day annexes at independent schools. We set out there the legal and administrative difficulties which would prevent this being done under present legislation. We thought it should be possible to devise a new kind of status for such schools. This should enable the local education authority to provide premises and to make suitable arrangements for the

administration of the school by a board of governors on which the authority would be strongly represented. We would like the Act to enable this to be done.

474. We suggested in paragraph 297 that schools willing to be integrated with the maintained sector to the extent of becoming part of it might be enabled to enter into a new form of aided status, being aided by central government rather than by a local education authority. The Act should enable this to be done if further consideration by the Secretary of State shows it to be a desirable and practicable way forward.

475. The right of a local education authority to place pupils at the authority's expense in independent schools not approved for integration should be safeguarded, pending a date after which all pupils assisted in the terms of this report would be assisted under financial arrangements made by the Corporation. Also, as from an appropriate date, education allowances should no longer be paid by government departments to their employees; here, too, the financial arrangements would thereafter be the responsibility of the Corporation. It would be for the Government to consider whether there should be an exemption for employees who entered service before a certain date. These may be matters for administrative rather than legislative action.

476. The Act should exempt from any of its requirements arrangements made for the placing of handicapped children considered by local education authorities to be in need of special educational treatment.

Powers affecting other independent schools

477. The Act should give the Boarding Schools Corporation the power to approve the level of fees to be charged at any independent boarding school which has not entered into a scheme of integration. This power should be invoked only in the special circumstances set out in paragraph 450.

Reserve powers

478. As we said at the beginning of this chapter, when our proposals have been publicly debated, it will be for Parliament to decide whether the publc schools are to become an integral part of the nation's educational system. If Parliament so decides, it will be the Secretary of State's responsibility to implement this policy. Negotiations will then proceed with the schools. The Boarding Schools Corporation, and the national system of boarding education it will be called upon to create, must both command the confidence of the schools. We would not have made the proposals contained in this report if we were not convinced that a consensus is attainable. But there are bound to be differences of opinion about the timing, the priorities and other detailed aspects of the scheme. Some schools invited to participate may be reluctant to do so; others may be anxious to enter the scheme sooner than the Corporation's priorities permit; and others may wish to enter the scheme in a different role from the one offered to them. We believe that bodies such as the G.B.A., the G.B.G.S.A. and the H.M.C. may be able to play an important role in encouraging their members to enter schemes of integration, and we would regard their co-operation as invaluable to the success of the new policy. Nevertheless, final decisions about such questions can only be taken by the Secretary of State, and we recommend that he should ask Parliament to give him the powers he needs to compel integration after every effort of negotiation and persuasion has been exhausted.

Other legislation

479. The Government would need to take powers either under this Act or otherwise to remove from independent schools the fiscal and other privileges of charitable status to which we have referred in Chapter 14.

Appeals

480. There should be provision for appeals by parents or schools against decisions made by consortia of local education authorities or by the Boarding Schools Corporation (for example in matters of acceptance or rejection of a school for integration, the placing of pupils, approval of fees, raising of loans). Appeals against decisions of consortia should be to the Corporation, and against decisions of the Corporation to the Secretary of State.

The Commission's role

481. The present Commission's role as an advisory body will extend to the making of a second report on day independent and direct grant schools, and possibly (subject to the wishes of the Secretary of State) to a third report on schemes of integration, including the integration of preparatory schools. We see some advantage—although it would result from a coincidence of timing rather than a policy decision—in there being a period of overlap between the Commission before its work comes to an end, and the newly appointed Corporation, in order that there may if necessary be a reference back of questions arising from the interpretation of this report.

Timing of integration

482. This report will appear in 1968. Government decisions and their timing will be influenced by reaction in Parliament and outside, and perhaps not least by the state of the national economy. Effective action will require a new Education Act. It is not for us to judge in which year it would be realistic to expect a Bill to be presented to Parliament. For purposes of timing, therefore, we can only take as a datum point Year X, the year in which legislation is enacted and the Boarding Schools Corporation appointed.

483. Panels negotiating on behalf of the Corporation would, we hope, be able to recommend within three years approval of sufficient secondary schools (not less than 150) to set in train an effective interim scheme—that is, by Year X + 4, having allowed a year for the submission and consideration of proposals. Whether there would be a pause at this stage before enlarging this into a full integration scheme would depend partly upon the Corporation's view of the need for places in the light of social and educational developments in the next few years, and perhaps above all on the financial situation. If asked to do so, the panels could probably reach agreement with a further 200 or so schools (which would be mainly small ones) during the following two years, in which case the stage would be set for progress towards full integration by Year X + 6. If preparatory schools were to be integrated according to similar procedures, the negotiations and approvals would follow a similar timetable, without the need for further legislation.

484. Schools approved for integration would not have to wait until Year X + 4 or Year X + 6 respectively before admitting assisted pupils. As soon as possible, the Corporation would begin to put forward assisted pupils for at least half of the places for new entrants. Assuming, for illustrative purposes only, that a school without any existing pupils who qualified for assistance were to admit 55 per cent of assisted pupils to a seven year course, the build-up would be on the following lines:

Percentage of assisted pupils in each year of course

	1st year	2nd year	3rd year	4th year	5th year	6th year	7th year	Total (approx.)
Year of approval	Nil	Nil	Nil	Nil	Nil	Nil	Nil	Nil
Approval + 1 year	55	Nil	Nil	Nil	Nil	Nil	Nil	8
„ + 2 years	55	55	Nil	Nil	Nil	Nil	Nil	16
„ + 3 years	55	55	55	Nil	Nil	Nil	Nil	24
„ + 4 years	55	55	55	55	Nil	Nil	Nil	31
„ + 5 years	55	55	55	55	55	Nil	Nil	39
„ + 6 years	55	55	55	55	55	55	Nil	47
„ + 7 years	55	55	55	55	55	55	55	55

This is an example which would not necessarily apply directly to any integrating school. But it illustrates how the numerical qualification for full integration could be achieved at a secondary school about seven years after the date of approval of a scheme.

485. Allowing for a reasonable spread of dates of approval of schemes at different schools, an interim scheme should become fully operative by Year X + 12, and a full integration scheme (if it followed immediately on the interim scheme) by Year X + 14—allowing in each case a year between the approval of a scheme and the first intake of pupils. At many schools, with courses shorter than seven years, with intakes at various ages, and with assisted pupils already on the roll, these targets would be achieved in a shorter time. On the other hand, we do not underestimate the difficulties of adjustment to C.S.E. courses and the appointment where necessary of staff experienced in this field—nor the time which may be needed for the kinds of change we discussed in Chapter 9 to be put in hand before approval could be given. This is why we are thinking in terms of a process taking 15 years or longer to complete.

486. It is not possible to determine accurately the rate at which the cost to public funds would build up during this period. We have given in Chapter 16 total costs for the interim and full schemes (at 1967 cost levels). The probability is that, starting from an assumed base of about 20,000 children who are now assisted and would in future be placed in integrating schools, the build-up would begin slowly, accelerate rapidly during the second of three quinquennia, and thereafter rise slowly to the full cost as schools whose approval had been delayed for one reason or another took more assisted pupils during the third quinquennium. Following is an approximate indication of the rate at which the costs of the two schemes would build up.

Interim scheme

	Year X	Year X + 5	Year X + 10	Year X + 12
Number of assisted pupils	20,000[1]	23,000[2]	30,000[2]	32,000[2]
Total cost (£m)	6·4	8·8	11·6	12·5
Net additional cost (£m)	Nil	2·4	5·2	6·1

[1] Assisted under present arrangements.

[2] Assisted under new arrangements.

Full scheme

	Year X	Year X + 5	Year X + 10	Year X + 14
Number of assisted pupils	20,000[1]	25,000[2]	40,000[2]	47,000[2]
Total cost (£m)	6·4	9·6	15·6	18·4
Net additional cost (£m)	Nil	3·2	9·2	12·0

[1] Assisted under present arrangements.

[2] Assisted under new arrangements.

Part Six

Scotland ; Wales

CHAPTER 18

Scotland; Wales

487. The State system of education in Scotland has a different historical and statutory basis from that of England and Wales. In order to consider the application of our proposals to Scotland in their proper administrative and educational context, we shall try first therefore, to identify the main distinguishing features of Scottish educational law and practice.

488. Independent schools in Scotland are a much smaller element in the educational provision of that country than independent schools in England and Wales. There are in Scotland only 134 independent schools, with some 18,000 pupils, compared with 2,999 education authority schools and some 880,000 pupils. Excluding pupils receiving special education, 2 per cent of all pupils in Scotland were at January, 1967, attending independent schools, compared with 5·5 per cent of pupils in England and Wales.

Legislation

489. The main fabric of the present educational system in Scotland was provided by the Education (Scotland) Act 1918. This Act was for Scotland an educational landmark as substantial as the 1944 Act for England and Wales. Among other things, it replaced a multitude of local school boards with a more compact system of education authorities, mainly on a county basis, made provision for free secondary as well as primary education, and settled the question of the denominational schools. The basic statute now is a consolidated measure, the Education (Scotland) Act 1962, with which the Education Act, 1944, as amended, may be compared. The Scottish Act of 1962 defines a public school as any school under the management of an education authority; the expression "maintained school" is not to be found in the legislation; and Scottish educationists and to some extent laymen, in referring to what are public schools within our terms of reference, are likely to use the designation "private" or "independent".

Transfer age and examination system

490. In Scotland primary education in the State sector, starting at age 5, continues for seven years, not six. This has implications for the structure of secondary education and for the examination system. Transfer to secondary education has for many years taken place at the age of 12 plus rather than 11 plus. In the correspondingly shorter secondary course there is less specialisation. The chief examination objective for the most academically able children is the Scottish Certificate of Education on the Higher grade, which is accepted as the basic qualification for entrance to Scottish universities. Although the standard of attainment in individual subjects is lower than in the G.C.E. 'A' level, a broader range of subjects is taken, and this absence of early specialisation is considered to have educational advantages. Higher grade of the S.C.E.

is usually taken at the age of 17 in the fifth year of secondary education, though it may also be taken in the sixth year. We understand that with a view to developing more purposeful study by sixth year pupils the S.C.E. Examination Board intend to introduce in 1968 an optional examination, initially in a limited number of subjects, for a Certificate of Sixth Year Studies.

491. Examinations for the S.C.E. are also held on the Ordinary grade, which is almost exactly comparable with the Ordinary level of G.C.E. S.C.E. Ordinary grade is normally taken by pupils in their fourth year of secondary education at the age of 16. Below the S.C.E. Ordinary grade there are no public examinations such as those leading to the C.S.E. in England.

492. The examination system in Scotland has implications for the integration of Scottish independent schools with the State system. In the first place, a number of the larger independent Scottish schools, particularly boarding schools, are geared to the English system and prepare secondary school pupils for the G.C.E. If these schools were to be integrated with the public system of education in Scotland, they would have to prepare pupils for the S.C.E. (whether or not they prepared them, as a few schools already do, for the G.C.E. in addition to the S.C.E.). Secondly, the comparative lack of specialisation in the Higher grade of the S.C.E. and the fact that the examination is generally taken by more able pupils in the year immediately after they have taken, or would have taken, the Ordinary grade examination, may limit or modify the respects in which a "Sixth Form College" would be a suitable role for a Scottish independent school to fulfil. Thirdly, if our recommendation in paragraph 278 that entry to the majority of schools should be based on a wide spread of ability is accepted, means will have to be found in Scotland of defining the lower limit other than by reference to the level of ability required for examinations leading to the C.S.E. We allow for this kind of situation, however, in paragraph 278 (footnote).

Denominational schools

493. Scotland has no "aided", "controlled", nor "special agreement" schools. Since the Act of 1918, denominational schools have been provided by the education authorities on the same basis as non-denominational schools, except that the denomination concerned has reserved rights in the teaching and inspection of religious knowledge, and approval, as to religious belief and character, of teachers appointed to these schools. But the appointment and payment of teaching staff and the maintenance of denominational schools, as well as the building of new schools, are wholly in the hands of the local education authorities. We note these arrangements in view of our recommendation in paragraph 297 for a new type of aided status for boarding schools. We have no reason to suppose, however, that the lack hitherto of any arrangements for aided status in Scotland should complicate their introduction in respect of boarding schools.

"Academies"

494. In Scotland the term "academy" is incorporated in the title of many state secondary schools. We note this in view of our recommendation in paragraph 288 concerning the possible establishment of "academies" which might cater for pupils having special gifts in particular fields. Any special aptitude school that might be established in Scotland would no doubt require a more distinctive name.

BOARDING EDUCATION IN THE STATE SECTOR

School hostels

495. There are no education authority boarding schools as such in Scotland. Where, due to a sparse and scattered population, there is a clearly recognised need for boarding facilities (as in the Highland counties, where large numbers of children have to live away from home at varying stages of their secondary school career), it has been met by the provision of hostels from which the children attend a local day school. Pupils in school hostels are pupils who have received their primary education and sometimes the early years of their secondary education in small local schools but who can complete their secondary education only by attending a central school serving a wide area and attended predominantly by day pupils whose homes are within daily travelling distance. The cost of enabling pupils from remote areas to attend central secondary schools—including the cost of travel to and from home as well as the cost of hostel accommodation (or lodgings)—is met by the local education authorities in whose areas the children's parents reside. There are 21 schools with hostels, accommodating 598 boys and 696 girls.

496. A major school hostels building programme for the Highlands and Islands has recently been put in hand by the Scottish Education Department in co-operation with the National Building Agency and the seven local education authorities concerned—Argyll, Caithness, Inverness-shire, Orkney, Ross and Cromarty, Sutherland and Zetland. The programme, which is likely to be in two or three phases, provides for the erection of a total of between 20 and 30 purpose-built school hostels. The complete programme is expected to provide an additional 1,700 residential places.

497. While the hope is that the new hostels will be run in such a way as to provide some of the benefits of boarding education, the main purpose at present conceived for them is not to provide boarding education as such but to cater as comfortably and informally as possible for the residential needs of children who are obliged to leave home in order to attend suitable central day schools. The Scottish Education Department has begun consulting education authorities about arrangements for staffing the new hostels and for operating them in such a way as to extract the maximum educational advantage from them. At the present moment there is little uniformity of outlook and practice in running school hostels. Among the more important questions to which answers have still to be found and generally accepted are whether the persons appointed to be in charge of hostels should be professional teachers or not and whether they should be responsible to the head teacher of the school or, as is generally the case at present, directly to the education authority.

498. The establishment in the remote north and west of Scotland of residential schools as such has been suggested from time to time. But the desire of the great majority of parents is that their children should spend as much time in the home environment as can be reconciled with adequate educational opportunity. For this reason they have preferred the establishment, wherever practicable, of four year "junior high" schools from which children can return home if not daily, at least at weekends. Apart from this consideration, there would be a danger, given the small number of school children throughout the area, that the establishment of residential schools would undermine the viability of the few existing comprehensive day schools which rely on the attendance of hostel pupils.

Residential schools for special purposes

499. A small number of residential boys' schools for special purposes are managed by education authorities. These combine secondary courses with agricultural courses or the latter stages of secondary with further education courses and provide places for 300 boys.

Assistance from education authorities for boarding places at fee-paying schools

500. Education authorities have power under Section 49 of the Education (Scotland) Act 1962 to grant assistance, entirely at their own discretion, towards "the fees and expenses payable in respect of persons attending schools at which fees are payable". We understand that, in the session 1965-66, 137 school fee grants were given at a cost of some £21,000. Of these, only 7 were granted in respect of boarding pupils (two being primary pupils) at independent schools, and 3 in respect of boarding pupils at grant-aided secondary schools. Education authorities made 72 awards in respect of pupils attending fee-paying day schools managed by education authorities or receiving special education and 55 in respect of secondary pupils attending grant-aided day schools. This power, therefore, is seldom used. When it is used, it is normally as a result of individual cases of social and educational need, e.g. when a pupil at a fee-paying school is bereft of his father, and therefore loses the means of support, at a critical stage in his schooling.

Assistance from the Scottish Education Department

501. The main evidence of the nature of the demand for boarding education in Scotland comes from statistics assembled by the Scottish Education Department from their records of applications for assistance with boarding fees. "Central awards" are administered by the Scottish Education Department under the authority of the Students' Allowances (Scotland) Regulations, 1962, at an annual cost of about £20,000. These awards are available for boarding school education in the United Kingdom if the parents are not resident in the area of a particular education authority and if it would be unreasonable to expect an authority to use its discretionary power to make an award. These prerequisites are met in cases where both a child's parents are temporarily resident overseas because of the father's employment. In considering applications for central awards in respect of boarding education the Scottish Education Department follow closely the principles recommended in the report of the 1960 Working Party (see paragraph 154) for the guidance of local education authorities. The scale of parental contributions is also in line with that recommended in the report (see Chapter 15).

502. The figures show that the demand for assisted boarding education in Scotland is extremely low. In 1966-67 the number of children receiving central government grants towards boarding education was 118 (as against 160 who had applied). The majority of central awards granted by the Scottish Education Department in respect of boarding education are for the children of parents who are resident overseas for business reasons. A small proportion of boarding awards are in respect of servicemen's children and the majority of these are the children of commissioned officers. Applications for assistance with boarding education are preponderantly in respect of places at independent schools but a sizeable proportion relate to grant-aided schools. The proportion of awards granted to applications made is high. Details for the period 1960-67 are given in Appendix 17.

Independent schools

503. We observed at the beginning of this chapter that, as compared with England and Wales, the independent schools in Scotland play a very small part in educational provision. Only 11 of the 134 independent schools in Scotland (and one of these has just closed) fell within the definition of "public school" in our terms of reference. Although in the independent sector the distinction between primary and secondary education is not clearcut, a broad classification on the basis of pupils' ages shows that a slight majority of the independent schools in Scotland are primary schools: 47 primary to 42 secondary, with 45 covering both stages of education. A division into day (or mainly day) schools and boarding (or mainly boarding) schools gives a majority of 82 day to 52 boarding schools. Most of the day schools are co-educational and most of the boarding schools are for boys only. In January 1967 there were 9 boys', 15 girls' and 58 co-educational day schools; and 40 boys', 6 girls', and 6 co-educational boarding schools.

504. A feature of the Scottish independent schools is that they include very few large schools. There are only two with rolls of over 800 and both of these are predominantly day schools with primary as well as secondary departments. There are no schools in the 601–800 range; seventy-eight per cent of the schools are in the size range "up to 200". Details are given in Appendix 17. Apart from the public schools there is only one independent and wholly boarding school in Scotland which has more than 200 pupils and that is the Queen Victoria School, Dunblane, which is not an independent school in the accepted sense of the term. It provides primary and secondary education for the sons of servicemen, operates under a Royal Charter and is largely financed from public funds under the control of the Ministry of Defence. If schools with less than 50 per cent boarding places are included, eight further independent schools with rolls of over 200 can be added. They are all girls' schools—five in Edinburgh and the remainder in Ayrshire, Perthshire and Stirlingshire.

505. The public schools in Scotland are listed in Appendix 17, Table I, and details of fees are given in Tables J and K. The concentration of public schools in and near Edinburgh is noticeable. None of the schools is of great antiquity. Five were established in the first half of the nineteenth century, four in the second half; and the remaining two belong to the present century. The largest of the boys' boarding public schools has 447 pupils, and the one remaining girls' boarding public school in Scotland (with nursery and primary as well as secondary departments) has 496 pupils.

506. The way in which independent schools' share of pupils at school increases with the age of the pupil is shown in Table L of Appendix 17, and the relationship, over a period, of numbers of 17 year olds in independent schools to numbers of 17 year olds in grant-aided and education authority schools is illustrated in Table M.

507. In terms of pupil numbers, independent schools are roughly equivalent to each of the two other selective, fee-paying sectors in Scotland—grant-aided schools and education authority fee-paying schools. Table N gives details of the numbers of secondary schools in each of these categories and Table O the number of pupils.

508. As we said in paragraph 500, education authorities have power under Section 49 of the Education (Scotland) Act to grant assistance towards the fees of pupils attending independent or other fee-paying schools. They also have power under Section 25 of the Act to contribute to the maintenance of any school not under their own management which may be included in their scheme of educational provision. In fact, however, these powers are now rarely used in respect of independent schools. There is no tradition, as there is in some parts of England, of education authorities paying the fees of a substantial number of pupils attending independent schools in their area.

Recognition as "efficient"

509. Independent schools in Scotland are subject to inspection and are required to be registered under statutory provisions broadly the same as those in Part III of the 1944 Act for England and Wales. But there are no arrangements for recognising the schools as "efficient".

Availability of boarding places

510. Table F (Appendix 17) shows the number of boarding pupils at independent schools in Scotland in 1967 as 7,155. A breakdown of the figures for independent schools shows that in January, 1967 the 11 public schools together provided 2,883 boarding places, 2,282 for boys and 601 for girls. In round figures the ratio of independent boarding places to total school population (excluding special and approved schools) works out at one place for every 125 pupils. Grant-aided schools in Scotland, again on the basis of actual pupil numbers, provide a total of 1,492 boarding places, 979 for boys and 513 for girls. A summary of the number of boarding places at present available in Scotland is as follows:

Table 32

Boarding places available in Scotland, January 1967

	Boys	Girls	Total
Independent schools	5,441	1,714	7,155
Grant-aided schools	979	513	1,492
Education authority schools and hostels	898	696	1,594
	7,318	2,923	10,241

In addition (see paragraph 496 above), the current school hostels building programme is expected to make available a further 1,700 residential places. This would increase the total to 11,941 places.

Conclusions

511. We have drawn attention to certain features of the Scottish educational system of which special account will have to be taken if Scottish independent schools are to be integrated under our proposals with the State system in Scotland.

512. None of these features need present an insurmountable obstacle to the implementation of our main proposals. We are, however, conscious of the

fact that the Scottish boarding schools, in number, size and geographical location, offer comparatively limited scope for a scheme of integration designed to meet need for boarding education in Scotland and that, so far as the content of their courses is concerned, most of the public schools are orientated towards the G.C.E. At the same time, whether as a consequence of the separate historical development of Scottish education in the public sector, or of a greater tradition of egalitarianism among the people, the demand for boarding school education appears to us to have been much more limited than in comparable classes of society in England. Where the need for boarding facilities has, as in the Highlands and Islands, stemmed from low density of population and remoteness, they have been or are being provided by the education authorities concerned.

513. In these circumstances we do not wish to offer any firm recommendation on the question whether special arrangements should be made or separate legislation enacted to integrate independent schools in Scotland with the Scottish State system. A different kind of scheme would be acceptable provided that the main objects were achieved. What is important is that a sufficiently wide range of educational opportunities should be available to all children who might qualify for boarding places on the basis of social or educational need. We do not think there should be any statutory or other barrier to prevent assisted pupils crossing the Border in either direction for their education. In general, however, we would expect the majority of assisted places in integrated Scottish schools to be allocated to pupils resident in Scotland and that all the schools concerned would gear their curriculum to the Scottish pattern of examinations whether or not they also chose to cater for pupils wishing to sit the G.C.E. examinations.

514. If the proportion of boarding need estimated in Chapter 7 for England and Wales in 1980 (80,000 places within a school population of 10,491,200) were applied to Scotland, the equivalent figure would be 8,756 places (for a school population of 1,148,200). But in the case of England and Wales, our conclusions in Chapter 8 had the effect of reducing the total by 17,000 because it seemed unrealistic to assume that either less able pupils, or girls at any level of ability, could have their full needs for boarding met within the next 15 years. If an equivalent reduction is made in the Scottish figure, the total boarding need in 1980 would be about 6,900 places. This compares with a total of about 2,100[1] places (including those at hostels and farm schools) which are already provided by education authorities or at which pupils are assisted from public funds—to which should be added the 1,700 further hostel places now planned. There would thus be a shortfall of about 3,000 places. However, as we have suggested, different traditions may affect attitudes towards boarding education in Scotland, and the effective need will not

---

[1] *Footnote:*

These 2,100 places are made up as follows:

Pupils at hostels	1,294
Pupils at farm schools etc.	300
Pupils at independent and grant-aided schools	
assisted by education authorities	10
assisted by Scottish Education Department	118
assisted by other government departments	400 (estimated)
	2,122

necessarily develop in the same way as in England and Wales. The figure of 3,000 should therefore be treated with caution; we do not want to lead Scottish opinion in this matter in directions which may appear either alien or irrelevant. It will be for those responsible to decide how many boarding places should be provided in the public sector, and how many taken up at independent schools. In 1967, there were 7,155 boarding places in all at independent schools in Scotland. Solely for costing purposes we have allowed (in Chapters 8 and 16) for a take-up of 2,000 independent boarding school places by 1980. This would mean the integration of a substantial proportion of suitable schools.

515. We note that in Scotland there is no specific legislation on charities equivalent to the Charities Act in England and Wales and that the legal basis of educational endowment schemes is different from that obtaining south of the border. These are matters, however, which should not, in our view, present any insuperable difficulty in the context of our financial proposals.

WALES

Special considerations

516. Wales has educational legislation and financial arrangements in common with England. Throughout this report, the figures we have given have referred to England and Wales without distinction. Similarly, our proposals are intended to apply to both equally. Nevertheless there may be a special problem for Wales in this as in some other aspects of education.

517. The proportion of all pupils attending schools in Wales who are attending recognised independent schools is 2 per cent, compared with 3·9 per cent in England and Wales as a whole. The percentage of boarding pupils in such schools as a proportion of all pupils at school in Wales is 0·8, compared with 1·5 in England and Wales as a whole. An analysis of provision in recognised schools which cater mainly for boarders is given in the following table.

Table 33

Recognised efficient schools in Wales, January, 1967
(*including public schools*)

	A	B	C			
	Total No. of schools	No. of mainly boarding schools (half or more boarders)	No. of boarders and day pupils in schools at B			
			Boarders		Day pupils	
			Primary[1]	Secondary[2]	Primary[1]	Secondary[2]
Boys	22	15	255	1,592	57	208
Girls	21	9	126	1,353	53	178
Mixed	13	—	—	—	—	—
Totals	56	24	381	2,945	110	386

Source: Department of Education and Science annual returns.
   [1] Pupils aged 10 and under.
   [2] Pupils aged 11 and over.

518. Equivalent figures for the public schools included in our main terms of
reference (which are included in the figures in Table 33) are as follows:

Table 34

Public schools in Wales, January, 1967

	A	B	C			
	Total No. of schools	No. of mainly boarding schools (half or more boarders)	No. of boarders and day pupils in schools at B			
			Boarders		Day pupils	
			Primary[1]	Secondary[2]	Primary[1]	Secondary[2]
Boys	4	4	4	821	1	76
Girls	4	4	66	956	11	100
Mixed	—	—	—	—	—	—
Totals	8	8	70	1,777	12	176

Source: Department of Education and Science annual returns.
[1] Pupils aged 10 and under.
[2] Pupils aged 11 and over.

519. In offering evidence, the Welsh Joint Education Committee, representing
local education authorities, addressed itself to the general issue of our terms
of reference rather than to any specifically Welsh problems. It considered
that "the terms of reference should have reflected more closely the Government's declared policy to eliminate separatism in secondary education; and
that, accordingly, the Commission should have been asked to recommend
ways and means of absorbing the public and independent schools within the
maintained sector by a specified date".

520. The headmasters of two public schools in Wales suggest in their evidence
that their schools are already integrated with the State system, in that a
substantial proportion of pupils come from maintained schools and from a
wide range of homes, including some pupils assisted by local education
authorities. They see the possibility of the growth of a new boarding tradition,
which could in particular help to supplement the sixth form provision in rural
secondary schools.

521. A voluntary body, the New Wales Union, however, submitted evidence
which reflected what was said by our predecessors on the Fleming Committee
nearly a quarter of a century ago. The Union would like more boarding
places to be made available, particularly weekly boarding places for children
of secondary school age, in view of the long travelling distances in sparsely
populated areas; but its concern is that the existing public and preparatory
schools in Wales may have too little contact with Welsh life to be suitable for
this purpose.

522. We have ourselves formed the impression that the social class problem
of the public schools is predominantly an English phenomenon which does
not bite deeply into the national life of Wales any more than of Scotland. Just
as a number of Welsh children cross the border for independent boarding

education, so we understand that a proportion of places in Welsh public schools are taken by pupils no longer living in Wales. There appears in Wales also to be the difficulty which was well expressed in the following paragraphs in the Fleming Report.

"285. It must be recognised that the small community is a much more important factor in the life of Wales than in that of England, and a Welsh boy or girl would lose a great deal by being cut off from the main stream of communal and family life, and by having no part in those things which distinguish it—its festivals, social functions, peculiar beliefs, and its attitude towards language. From a specifically Welsh point of view this is the heart of the question, since men are Welshmen chiefly in virtue of their participation during the period of youth in the adult life of the home and the community. The culture of minorities can only be preserved from becoming a mere "museum-piece" by being maintained as a practical response to practical needs, and though the exceptional individual may successfully resist the cultural amnesia which so easily overtakes a youth or child in new surroundings, it is from his educational environment that the average individual, and certainly the average child, must acquire the way of life which must distinguish his manhood, and, if there is no place in that environment for the values which the community in general holds, the child will necessarily find that his education has ill-adapted him for a useful adult life in his own country.

286. . . . On this score any form of Boarding School life in Wales before the decisive formative years, or for any considerable number of years, would have its perils unless the schools in Wales adapt themselves to the needs of Welshmen and to the national culture".

523. Since these words were written nearly twenty-five years ago national sentiment has expressed itself still more vigorously on the need to deepen and sharpen the relevance of school to life, and to Welsh life in particular, in its widest cultural implications, a concern which has led, in recent years to the establishment of "Welsh" secondary schools and a growing demand for more of these.

524. The general recommendations of an accepted scheme of integration would of course apply to Wales as to England, and it would be open to a parent in Wales, as in England, to apply for the admission of his child to any boarding school in England or Wales. It is reasonable, however, to suppose that for the most part Welsh parents would wish to apply for a school in Wales. In exercising such a choice, which involved the use of public funds, they might reasonably and properly require that such a school should provide opportunities for Welsh studies. To return to the Fleming Report: "it would be anomalous and indeed to Welsh sentiment intolerable, if the extension of boarding school opportunities in Wales, with the assistance of public funds, should involve the sacrifice of the language".

525. Most independent schools in Wales have hitherto offered little opportunity for studies of the Welsh language and culture. This is not to say that there could be no place for them in a scheme of integration; it may well be that they will wish to continue to serve the limited aim of meeting the interests of parents from across the border or from the anglicised areas of Wales who do not identify themselves with Welsh cultural aspirations. In a few of these

schools, however, the facts of Welsh life and language have won more than formal acknowledgement in the activities and curricula offered to the pupils. Indeed in one of these, a public school with a long-standing scheme of co-operation with the local education authority, the terms of its foundation charter charge it explicitly with the duty of teaching the Welsh language and making its pupils conversant with Welsh history and culture.

526. It has been represented to us that there is need in Wales of a national maintained boarding school which would give expression to the ideals of a bilingual education. The discussion of this many-sided issue does not lie within the terms of reference of the Commission, but if there is a need for new departures of this kind, they could both contribute to and benefit from the scheme of integration we propose.

Conclusion

527. It will be for Parliament to decide to what extent our proposals for integration may be generally applicable to Wales—as indeed to Scotland. What is clear is that the opportunities for children in Wales to have boarding education according to their needs should be no less than in England. But to regard our task as concerned only with boarding education, and with the provision of boarding education on a national scale, would be to distort our terms of reference. Our main function is to make recommendations for the integration of public and similar independent boarding schools. In recommending that under-provided parts of England should have more maintained boarding provision, we have deliberately geared this recommendation to the concept of an integrated system, in which independent and maintained schools should be complementary. The case for building more maintained boarding schools arises because independent schools are insufficient in certain areas, rather than because they are potentially unsuitable. It is possible that the same should be done in Wales; if so, we would support this. But whether the independent schools in Wales, in general, can usefully serve the purposes and interests of Welsh Wales is a matter which the responsible authorities in Wales, and those whose interests are directly involved, must decide.

Part Seven

Recognition as Efficient

CHAPTER 19

Recognition as efficient

528. Although our terms of reference were directed primarily to the public schools, we were asked also to recommend "whether any action is necessary in respect of other independent schools, whether secondary or primary". We have, as our recommendations show, regarded all independent boarding schools with 25 per cent or more of boarding pupils, and which are recognised as efficient, as being eligible for integration, although not all may prove acceptable. There remains a further category—those schools not recognised as efficient—which we have excluded from our proposals for integration. What, if anything, should be done about them?

529. Under Part III of the Education Act, 1944, which came into force in 1957, all independent schools must be registered. If the Secretary of State, on the advice of H.M. Inspectors, is not satisfied that a school is suitable to be registered, he may issue a Notice of Complaint on one of four grounds:

1. Unsuitability of the premises.
2. Deficiencies of accommodation, having regard to the number, ages and sex of the children.
3. Deficiencies of the instruction.
4. Unsuitability of the head teacher or staff to be in charge of children.

Subject to the right of appeal to a Tribunal, a school can be closed if the Secretary of State's requirements are not met.

530. In addition to registration a school may also seek to be "recognised as efficient" under Rules 16. Recognition, which is granted only after full inspection, is given to schools which reach at least a standard equivalent to that expected in a maintained school. Apart from the higher status which results, there is a material benefit in that the staff of recognised schools may join the national teachers' superannuation scheme. Recognised schools must be of a size to permit adequate staffing, have a reasonable range of subjects and offer at least a three year course. Registered schools which are not recognised as efficient vary from bare tolerability to a standard approaching that of recognised schools.

531. There were in January, 1967, 3,119 independent schools registered under Part III of the Education Act, 1944. Of these 1,497 were recognised as efficient by the Secretary of State (including all public schools in England and Wales). 305,179 children (135,989 of primary, 169,190 of secondary age) attended recognised schools other than nursery schools, and 129,866 (97,198 of primary, 32,668 of secondary age) attended unrecognised schools. There were 120,854 boarders in recognised schools, 9,847 in unrecognised schools.

532. To the uninitiated parent, there is undoubtedly a good deal of misunderstanding of the descriptions "registered" or "recognised" which schools use in their brochures. The question is whether there is any justification for

continuing to allow children to attend schools which are not recognised by the Secretary of State as efficient. Parental freedom of choice is not at issue. The overriding consideration must be the welfare and education of the children. Children may be obliged, for example, to live in sub-standard housing because their parents have little or no choice in the matter. But no child of compulsory school age need attend a school not recognised as efficient. Such schools are not always inadequate, nor are the parents necessarily conscious of the choice they are making, because of possible confusion between the terms "registered" and "recognised". But if a registered school is in fact worthy of recognition as efficient, there is no difficulty in putting the matter beyond doubt by applying for recognition.

533. The Plowden Council came out against the compulsory closure of schools not recognised as efficient, for three reasons. The first was that "there are undoubtedly registered schools of higher quality than some maintained schools". We do not regard this as a conclusive argument; there is everything to be said for maintained schools also being obliged to reach a minimum standard of efficiency. The second was that "schools are constantly changing, and there is a need to retain a grade for those schools which might in time become recognised". We would agree the need for some kind of provisional registration. A school newly opened could not be regarded as efficient until it had proved its worth, and some period of build-up would have to be allowed. Equally, a school once recognised under any compulsory "efficiency" scheme ought to be put back on the "provisional" list for a limited period if its standards declined at any time after recognition. The third reason was that "some feel an objection in principle to extending the Secretary of State's powers in this way". While respecting this view we do not fully accept its logic. The Secretary of State already has powers to check the worst abuses under the rules governing registration, and the rightness of this is not disputed. No new issue of principle would in our view arise if he had the power to insist on a higher rather than a lower minimum standard of efficiency.

534. The difficulties are not ones of principle. Most people would agree that schools ought all to be efficient according to some recognisable standard, and that the standards at present required for registration do not ensure this. Many see practical difficulties in defining standards of educational provision in terms which can be legally prescribed and enforced. We accept that there are difficulties of definition and enforcement, but we are nevertheless persuaded that a start should be made in raising standards compulsorily above the level required for registration.

535. Difficulties of definition—of determining and prescribing minimum levels of material provision and competence in teaching—will arise whatever standard is aimed at. The related problem, of enforcing standards at particular schools, with the demands on the Inspectorate (and on the administration) which this would entail, would be less if the number of schools to which the standards should be applied were limited in the first instance. How to limit the number in order to provide a manageable basis for starting the process of raising the standards of unrecognised schools? We have considered whether it would be reasonable to apply a new standard to secondary schools only. This would not be impossible; but it would be both unfair and untidy. Schools have a wide variety of age boundaries, and there is no clear distinction between independent primary and secondary schools. Also, it would

make little sense on educational grounds to allow primary but not secondary children to continue to attend schools which are not recognised as efficient. Primary education is no less important than secondary.

536. There is, we feel, a dividing line which would be at once more manageable and more justifiable than that between primary and secondary schools. The more significant effects of really bad schooling are likely to be encountered by children in boarding schools rather than day schools. There are few influences at work on a child in boarding school during term time other than those of the school; and if the school is unsatisfactory the effects are correspondingly more pervasive than in a day school, from which the child returns home every evening and every weekend. We want all schools to be efficient; but to be within the reach of practicability, and to make an impression on the problem where it is most acute, we believe that, as a start, all schools, whether primary or secondary, with *any* boarding pupils in residence, should either be recognised as efficient within a stated period or be required to close.

Conclusion

537. In the event, the then Secretary of State for Education and Science (The Rt. Hon. Patrick Gordon Walker, M.P.) decided to act in advance of our recommendations in this report, following consideration of the problem by a Departmental inquiry headed by a Minister of State (Mrs. Shirley Williams, M.P.). He announced his decision in the House of Commons on 3rd November, 1967, in the following terms:

"I wish to announce a decision which I have made about independent schools. Following the trial and conviction on charges of cruelty and assault of the joint principal of an independent school registered under Part III of the Education Act, 1944, my predecessor announced on 10th May that he had asked my hon. Friend the Minister of State to conduct a Departmental inquiry. The inquiry was to cover the circumstances of the particular case and, more generally, the adequacy of existing statutory provision relating to proper standards of education and welfare in independent schools.

My hon. Friend has completed her report—but I cannot yet publish it, because the particular matters which gave rise to it are now the subject of appeal and are, therefore, *sub judice*.

On the general point, I have been giving much thought to independent schools. I would dearly like to take measures to ensure that all these schools reach a proper standard of efficiency within a relatively short time, but to achieve this would involve a very substantial enlargement of the Inspectorate —larger than we can afford or perhaps could recruit.

I have, therefore, decided to concentrate first on the boarding schools. Here, the need for high standards is greatest, both because the children's education and welfare depend during term time entirely on the school and because their parents are often far away, sometimes out of the country.

There are 314 registered boarding schools not now recognised as efficient. I intend to apply the standards required for recognition to every one of these over the next five years. I expect many of them to be capable of the necessary improvements, but I shall take action under the Act against those which fail to meet the requirements, which cover not only the premises and the quality of the education provided but also the arrangements for the general welfare of the pupils.

This special effort on boarding schools, which I am confident will receive general public support, will not reduce the present level of work on day schools, and when the new standard has been secured for boarding schools I hope that we can have a further drive to raise minimum standards in day schools".

Acknowledgements

538. Our work has unfortunately not produced a unanimous report. We understand and respect the reasons why three of our colleagues have felt unable to sign, although we do not agree with them. Our meetings have been friendly throughout; and we, the majority, would like to say how much the report owes to the work which our minority colleagues have put into it. Despite the absence of their signatures, their contribution, both in discussion and in drafting, even at points on which they have registered disagreement, has been invariably constructive. We would like this to be generally known.

539. We could not have written the report without the help of many other people. Despite the wide range of views about the nature of our work, including doubts whether we ought to be undertaking it at all, we have met with unfailing co-operation and courtesy on all sides.

540. We could not have done our job without inflicting questionnaires on many schools—all public schools and some other independent and maintained schools. A number of them have also received us as their guests and have done everything they could to enlighten us about their way of life. To the governing bodies, the heads, teaching and administrative staff, and to the boys and girls we have met, we are most grateful.

541. We have held many formal and informal meetings with representatives of the public schools as well as a number of other educational bodies. Our requests for information have also caused extra work for local education authorities and government departments, in particular the Department of Education and Science and the Scottish Education Department. We appreciate the time and effort they have all given.

542. We are greatly indebted to the large number (and wide variety) of organisations and individuals who either responded to our request for written evidence or came forward of their own accord with statements or comments which were no less valuable. We have found that the shades of opinion on this subject are almost without limit, as we think our Appendix of extracts from the evidence will show.

543. We turn now to those who have worked closely with the Commission and have given us special help. Dr. Royston Lambert was in a sense in the field before we were, with his research into boarding education. He has built amply on this foundation in his subsequent work on our behalf, assisted by an enthusiastic team of colleagues at King's College, Cambridge. When we came to the financial structure of the independent schools, we could have found no better guide to the complexities than Mr. Howard Glennerster at the London School of Economics, and he is responsible for our Appendix on this subject. Mr. Graham Kalton, whose survey of Headmasters' Conference Schools was published shortly after our appointment, has given us access to his working material (by permission of the H.M.C.), and has volunteered a great deal of assistance with statistical queries. To all of these we are grateful.

544. We have been unusual among committees appointed by Education Ministers in having no Departmental assessors associated with our work, but we are indebted to Mr. M. W. Pritchard, H.M.I., for having attended a number of our meetings by invitation. His wealth of experience was already well-known to many of us, and we have been glad to draw on it.

545. No Commission of this sort can conclude its report without a true expression of gratitude to those whose work has made their deliberations and conclusions possible. We have had a relatively small staff to carry the very heavy administrative responsibility. Our thanks go to Mr. G. Etheridge, who has given valuable service as Assistant Secretary, to Mr. R. G. Hostler, who has been responsible for arranging our meetings and travel, and to the team which, under their guidance, has done much of the work of gathering and sorting out the material for the Appendices. There have been changes of staff, but the mainstays of this team have been Miss J. S. Green, Mrs. A. R. Massey and Mr. V. Truscott. The Secretary's task has been greatly eased by having as his own personal secretary during most of the past two years Miss E. M. Anderson.

546. No less than five drafts of the report were produced before the final version, and the sheer volume of writing and re-writing during this period would appal most professional authors. Very few works of scholarship demand such industry and few writers have to satisfy fifteen very different individuals that what they compile is acceptable. The ultimate responsibility has fallen on our Secretary, Geoffrey Cockerill, who has contributed much to our thinking and has retained his equanimity and humour throughout our prolonged discussions. We want him to know how much we appreciate his devotion to our objectives, his charity with our failings and his willing response to the prodigious demands we have made upon him for the last two years.

Signatures

Chairman:	JOHN NEWSOM
Vice-Chairman:	D. V. DONNISON
Members:	ANNAN
	KATHLEEN BLISS
	JOHN C. DANCY
	T. EWAN FAULKNER
	ANNE GODWIN
	WILLIAM S. HILL
	H. G. JUDGE
	G. H. METCALFE
	JOHN VAIZEY
	BERNARD WILLIAMS

Secretary: G. F. COCKERILL

Note of dissent

1. Our terms of reference start with the words:

"The main function of the Commission will be to advise on the best way of integrating the public schools with the State system of education".

The report of the majority rejects the possibility of outright integration and we consider that it is right in so doing.

2. Having rejected outright integration, the report sets out to establish certain priorities within the other fields covered by the terms of reference. Although there is no specific statement to that effect, the clear implication of the report is that the socially divisive influence of the schools concerned should receive the highest priority of treatment. The proposals made direct themselves primarily at this influence and seek to provide only partial remedies to the other problems considered—e.g. boarding need and provision for less able pupils.

We do not concur with this order of priorities. We recognise that the schools do constitute a socially divisive influence, but it seems to us they do so more by way of reinforcing an existing state of affairs than by initiating it. In our judgement of this issue it seems to us unwarrantable to devote considerable sums of public money to a purpose to which we do not attribute a particularly high degree of priority.

3. We are in general agreement with a good deal of the analysis contained in the report and consider that it will allay some of the prejudice and ignorance which have too often surrounded public discussion of these problems. In particular we have been impressed with the urgent need for more sixth form boarding provision for girls and with the arguments in favour of more co-educational boarding schools.

4. Our inability to accept the assessment of priorities in the report is also mirrored in our rejection of the solutions proposed. We consider that the rigidity involved in the 50 per cent principle and most of the patterns of reorganisation envisaged, all backed by underlying compulsory powers, do not represent a realistic means of "ensuring that the public schools should make their maximum contribution to meeting national educational needs". The proposed solutions often seem to us to take too static a view of a rapidly changing society where free and flexible arrangements are likely to be more helpful than comparatively rigid formulae.

5. We are not impressed by either the arguments or the recommendations advanced for the selection of pupils in terms of academic ability. On the one hand, large numbers of pupils are excluded as being unable to cope with the courses envisaged, which undermines the doctrinal basis of the argument for no selection. On the other hand, while many public schools would in fact be able to broaden their existing ability range and still do a very good educational job, a number of others would be altered under these proposals from what in effect they are, exceptionally good grammar schools, into much less effective institutions in terms of their academic facilities and potential.

6. We consider that both the report and its recommendations pay insufficient regard to the continuing interests of the fee-payers whom we do not consider a negligible or undesirable section of the community.

7. We believe that any scheme designed to enable the public schools to make a contribution to meeting "unsatisfied boarding need" through assisted places requires the support of a central agency. Although we may have reservations about some of the details concerning the Boarding Schools Corporation, we believe that some such organisation needs to exist to achieve more rapidly, effectively and extensively what the report rightly recognises has not been achieved since the publication of the Fleming Report. We see the Corporation working in a very flexible way between regional appraisal of the demand arising from boarding need and the supply available within the independent boarding sector.

8. We would like to see the following developments occur as and when the necessary finance is available:

(i) A number of the schools which have plenty of experience in the education of boys and girls of average ability and less might accept substantial numbers of maintained pupils with boarding need. We are certain that many schools would wish to do this.

(ii) A much smaller number of boys' and girls' schools should be frankly accepted for what they are—outstandingly good academic boarding schools. We consider that all of them would welcome the opportunity of enrolling maintained pupils with the appropriate academic potential within the specified boarding need categories. While a number of such pupils might enter at different ages, we see no great point in disturbing the existing age-ranges of such schools.

(iii) Other public schools and independent schools might usefully reconsider their existing roles and decide to offer within the framework of a broad general education a special emphasis on certain disciplines, especially in their sixth forms. Such schools might develop a particularly flexible age-range for admission and could co-operate closely with the maintained sector to meet the needs of children for whom they had special facilities to offer.

(iv) The provision of more co-educational schools in the independent boarding sector.

9. To sum up, we believe that the majority of our colleagues are in danger of trying to achieve the best at the cost of the good. We believe that our more modest proposals will be more acceptable to the schools, much easier to implement, and could set affairs in motion in such a way that this problem will eventually cease to engender the sterile and excessively doctrinaire controversy by which it is at present bedevilled.

T. E. B. HOWARTH
KITTY ANDERSON
JOHN DAVIES.

A note of reservation

1. I dissent from
 (i) the proposals for a Boarding Schools Corporation;
 (ii) the proposals to base the take up of half the places in "integrating" schools on boarding "need";
 (iii) the high priority implicitly assigned to boarding education;
 (iv) the inclusion in the scheme of Scotland and of Wales.

2. The task of this Commission is not one of defining the place of boarding in contemporary education; yet this is, in fact, how the problem of defining the place, if any, of the non-maintained school in our society has been presented to us. In my view, there may be an inherent contradiction arising from this view of the question which will lead to practical difficulties of an overwhelming nature.

3. What is this contradiction? To find it, I must go back to the beginning of the report and, indeed, to the terms of reference. A "private" sector of education, drawing its pupils mainly from certain small, but important, social groups, with teachers drawn from a limited section of the community, is said to be inherently divisive. It is a declining sector. It is probably less divisive than it once was; it is probably becoming less divisive; but that it is divisive is almost tautologically true. Whether or not this divisiveness leads to all manner of other social ills, or springs from them, is largely a matter of personal opinion, rather than of established fact; but I would not dissent in the main from what my colleagues say about it.

4. But on what terms should divisions be brought to an end? Are the terms to be the creation of a separate State sector of *boarding* education?

5. *Boarding.* The main objection to private schools is that they are socially divisive. Some of them happen to have beds. It therefore seems less revolutionary to change the bodies in the beds than to eliminate the beds. It is as though Henry VIII had not dismantled the monasteries, but filled them with social need cases, after an exhaustive social survey of the number of people in the population who felt the urge for a life of contemplation in a cell. There is a degree of confusion in attempting to "solve" a social question by throwing out the middle class and replacing it by a different social group.

6. There is a basic confusion between boarding need and boarding demand. These are quite distinct concepts, requiring different quantitative and evaluative treatment.

7. *Boarding Demand.* It is difficult to see how any valid measure of boarding demand could be devised: certainly, the evidence on which the Commission is relying is tenuous in the extreme.

8. Parents' motives in freely choosing a boarding education for their children are plainly highly complex. The two most important are probably family tradition, and the socio-economic benefits associated, or thought to be associated, with attendance at a public (boarding) school. But even when the

choice is now made, how far is it a choice of boarding education, and how far a choice of a type of education involving the acceptance of boarding as an element in the total package?

9. The problems of measurement are even more difficult if one attempts to assess the potential demand thought to exist amongst parents who do not now regard the choice as open to them. All questions put to them must be hypothetical: they cannot be confronted with a real situation. And it is plainly impossible to frame a question, or even a set of questions, which would disentangle attitudes towards boarding from attitudes towards the total educational package of which boarding is part. No doubt many parents who cannot now afford it, or whose children cannot secure places, would like a free public school education for their sons and daughters. But what value do they attach to boarding as such? How many would in fact prefer a day school if comparable socio-economic benefits (real or imagined) were freely available without having to accept boarding as part of the package?

10. But even if the problems of measurement could be overcome, how should an unsatisfied demand for boarding be evaluated? Should boarding be provided at public expense for all whose parents opt for it? If not, what is the basis for discrimination? What combination of ethical, personal and social criteria could provide a rational basis for separating the chosen from the unchosen? The Commission first rejects educational criteria and then re-introduces them by tying the public schools to examination syllabuses, the G.C.E. and C.S.E.; it then puts forward social criteria which may be relevant to boarding *need*, but are plainly irrelevant to boarding *demand*; and proposes a Corporation with ill-defined terms of reference as the standard British method of pretending that profound ethical problems do not exist. And this latter proposal is put forward on the extraordinary ground that the local authorities could not be relied upon to take up places. This is almost certainly true, but is it not remotely possible that the local authorities' reluctance might stem not from parsimony, but from an unwillingness to become involved in an operation possessing no clear ethical basis or demonstrable social benefit?

11. *Boarding Need.* The evidence that parsimony is not the reason for the local authorities' likely reluctance is, in fact, overwhelming. In their capacities as education and children authorities, local authorities already make generous provision for meeting recognised boarding needs. The children's services do so for about 70,000 children in England and Wales, and are in close touch with a very much larger number of children whose family circumstances *may* give rise to an urgent boarding need: there are 25,000 handicapped children in special schools or equivalent boarding places: local education authorities provide or take up about 11,000 places each year in ordinary independent and direct grant schools, and provide 11,000 places in their own ordinary boarding schools.

12. But the assessment of such needs is a highly expert business, resting on a professionalism painfully built up by the relevant services over a long period of time. And the same professionalism has defined a need for a very wide choice of facilities, ranging from placement with foster parents and use of the ordinary day schools, to the highly specialised educational therapy provided in residential communities for children with very severe behavioural problems.

13. I know of no evidence which suggests that there is some large unrecognised area of boarding need which the local authorities are not meeting—though there are obviously deficiencies in particular areas of need, and in particular parts of the country, which require to be remedied through the normal development of these services. And even if there are unrecognised types of need, they will be brought to light by the local personal services, and should be met by expanding the residential facilities which these services have at their disposal. They will not be discovered by a Boarding Schools Corporation totally lacking in relevant expertise or local resources. Nor would the public schools be suitable places in which to place all but a small minority of such children. The Home Office evidence is incontrovertible on this point: and it is a plain inference from this evidence that the children's services would not want to take over the public schools even if they were abolished as educational communities, and made available simply as premises for adaptation. These services are already sufficiently embarrassed by their legacy of over-large, geographically isolated, Poor Law Institutions and Approved Schools.

14. There is, however, one area of boarding need for which the public schools, while they continue to exist, provide an answer. This is to provide for the education of children, typically of quite well-to-do middle class parents, who cannot attend day schools because their parents work abroad, or have occupations which involve frequent changes in the family's home base, of whom about 18,000 or so are helped by the Government as employer. But there is little evidence that present arrangements have failed to discover, or to meet, legitimate needs which are of this kind. The point would, therefore, require consideration only if the dictates of logic were to be followed, and the Commission proposed the abolition of the public schools.

15. *An Alternative.* In order to achieve a 'fair' representation of children from all parts of the Kingdom in the boarding schools, and in order to allay the fears of the schools that they might be 'municipalised', the Commission proposes a 'central instrument' operating through regional committees. I take the view that boarding education and child care should remain a direct responsibility of the local education and children's authorities. I realise that there is a wide variation in local availability of places. My reading of the evidence suggests that parents, teachers, councillors and education and children's officers differ widely and legitimately in their attitudes to the desirability of boarding, and the "need" to board also differs from place to place. The diversity of provision may well be a legitimate manifestation of different local priorities. Some local authorities already provide their own "ordinary" boarding schools; others, especially in the north of England, may wish to do so. I would regret anything that discouraged this tendency. At the same time, where an authority, either singly, or jointly with other authorities, sees fit to take up boarding places in independent schools, we should not discourage them from doing so, and a pooling scheme to assist with finance can be established. Further, it seems to me to be unwise to extend any scheme like that proposed by the Commission to Scotland and to Wales where the "problem" appears, on the evidence, to be virtually non-existent.

16. The middle course between the extremes of "abolition" and "leaving them alone" is a compromise of an unusual kind. This compromise inevitably leads the Commission to propose a solution in terms of proportion of the student body. I would ask whether a solution to a social dilemma can ever be answered

neatly in these terms. The logic of abolition is clear. The argument runs that the schools are divisive; that they must be changed; and the pupils evicted from them will go to their local schools, or emigrate. But a half-way house prompts the question—where will the fee-paying pupils go whose parents would formerly have opted for the fee-paying sector, but whose places are now pre-empted? It seems to me probable that either the private day sector will be enlarged at another point, or that the pupils who are to be publicly subsidised will be drawn from those groups for which their parents now pay fees. Either consequence is exactly the opposite of what the Commission says it wants to see.

17. It will be objected, however, that it is incumbent upon those who dissent from the majority point of view to propose an alternative course of action. In a sense this is, of course, unfair since, like the Irishman in the bog who was asked the way, I would not have started from here. I do not think that the central question of the public schools is finding enough poor children to fill their beds; I believe, rather, it is what is the future of independent educational institutions drawing their pupils from a restricted social group, in con- temporary England (for it is not a problem in Scotland or Wales). Thus, the major part of the relevant analysis of the situation will, in my opinion, appear in the second report. But, nevertheless, the question about boarding has been put and an answer has to be given.

18. All that is needed till then in my opinion is a central office, working to the existing bodies of local authorities, in order to keep them informed of the general state of play of the boarding situation throughout the country, and in order to help the local authorities, or their consortia, in placing arrangements. This body could receive requests from overseas parents and pass them on, and do such other work as the local authorities asked it to do. The financial question can be solved by a pooling arrangement built in to the structure of the General Grant, or alternatively by a pooling arrangement on the same lines as those now prevailing for other parts of the further and higher edu- cation system: though I prefer to leave the matter for individual authorities to pay for.

19. This will not be popular with those boarding schools who look to central government payments in order to bolster up their enfeebled finances. I have already explained that I think that the Commission's solution is likely to lead to insuperable difficulties. My solution seems to me both what is likely to happen and the only solution that is commensurate with the principle to which I attach the highest importance, that decisions about the educational future of individual children should be taken by local authorities and parents in the context of an established set of priorities in educational expenditure.

20. The merits of this solution, it seems to me, are many. In particular, it would enable the public authorities totally to resist the pressure from the boarding schools, if such pressure there be, to find candidates for empty places. Furthermore, it enables local authorities to make arrangements for those children whom the majority has left on one side, i.e. those children of lower than C.S.E. ability.

JOHN VAIZEY.

METHOD OF WORKING

1. We obtained information and evidence in a variety of ways:
 (i) We sent questionnaires to all independent schools in membership of the Headmasters' Conference (H.M.C.), the Association of Governing Bodies of Public Schools (G.B.A.) and the Association of Governing Bodies of Girls' Public Schools (G.B.G.S.A.) and to a sample of other independent secondary schools and maintained secondary boarding schools. In the case of Headmasters' Conference schools, the questions were supplementary to those already asked of the schools in a survey sponsored by the H.M.C., the results of which were published in 1966.[1] The replies to our questionnaires are summarised in Appendix 6.
 (ii) We invited evidence from a wide range of bodies having a possible interest in our terms of reference. Copies of the letter of invitation and accompanying questionnaires, a list of bodies which responded and a selection of extracts from the evidence received are all included in Appendix 7.
 (iii) We obtained information about the recruitment and careers of former public school pupils and others from H.M. Treasury, H.M. Diplomatic Service, the Ministry of Defence and a selection of employing and professional bodies. Some of the information is embodied in the report (Volume I) and some is set out in Appendix 8.
 (iv) We asked local education authorities, government departments, and a selection of nationalised industries and other employers for information about assistance given to parents towards the cost of boarding education. The results are referred to in Part Three of the report (Volume I).
 (v) We visited a cross-section of schools (independent and maintained) and had discussions with staff and pupils. A list of schools visited is in Appendix 3.

2. When we were appointed, Dr. Royston Lambert was already engaged at King's College, Cambridge, on research into boarding education sponsored by the Department of Education and Science. His initial findings, including those published in "The State and Boarding Education"[2] provided us with valuable background information. We thought it necessary to reinforce this by asking the Department to sponsor further research by Dr. Lambert and his colleagues at the Research Unit into Boarding Education as a continuation and development of his original project, to include girls' schools, preparatory schools, and further studies into the need and demand for boarding education. The results of his research will be published separately and are not therefore included as Appendices, with the exception of a paper on need and demand for boarding education, reproduced as Appendix 9.

3. In order to be informed also about the finances of independent schools, we associated ourselves with research into the finance of education already being undertaken by the Unit for Economic and Statistical Studies on Higher Education at the London School of Economics. Mr. Howard Glennerster has been directly responsible for this aspect of the Unit's work. His findings are reproduced as Appendix 12.

---

[1] "The Public Schools:—A Factual Survey": Graham Kalton (Longmans, Green & Co. Ltd. 1966).
[2] Methuen, 1966.

LIST OF SCHOOLS INCLUDED IN
TERMS OF REFERENCE

Our terms of reference included all independent schools in membership of the Headmasters' Conference (H.M.C.), the Association of Governing Bodies of Public Schools (G.B.A.) and the Association of Governing Bodies of Girls' Public Schools (G.B.G.S.A.). Membership of these bodies (independent schools only) when we were appointed is shown in Section 1 below. Changes in membership since our appointment are shown in Section 2.

Section 1

Notes

1. In the following list of public schools, the religious denomination of the schools is shown in the second column. Denominational character has been determined in the following way: first, if the school's instrument of foundation prescribes a denominational character, this denomination is taken; secondly, if it cannot be determined in this way, the denomination is taken as that of the school's weekday services. The category "Inter-denominational" has been used for those schools which specifically provide for more than one denomination in their arrangements for worship. Following is a key to the abbreviations:—

C.E.	Church of England	J.	Jewish
Ch.S.	Christian Science	Meth.	Methodist
C.W.	Church in Wales	Mor.	Moravian
C.S.	Church of Scotland	R.C.	Roman Catholic
Cong.	Congregational	S.F.	Society of Friends
Ep.	Episcopalian	U.	Undenominational
Int.	Interdenominational		

2. Details of the numbers of pupils and the fees charged in January, 1967, at each boarding school in England and Wales are set out in Appendix 14. References to Appendix 14 are given in the third column of the following list— a letter for the region and a number for the school. Details of schools in Scotland (marked x) are given in Appendix 17. Details of day schools (marked †) will be given in our second report. Schools which had ceased to be public schools (as defined) in January, 1967, are marked *.

	Denom.	Ref. No. App. 14		Denom.	Ref. No. App. 14
Boys					
Abbotsholme School, Uttoxeter, Staffordshire	U.	E.6	Ampleforth College, York	R.C.	A.5
Aldenham School, Elstree, Hertfordshire	C.E.	G.34	Ardingly College, Haywards Heath, Sussex	C.E.	G.98
Allhallows School, Lyme Regis, Dorset	C.E.	H.4	Beaumont College, Old Windsor, Berkshire	R.C.	G.4

Section 1

	Denom.	Ref. No. App. 14		Denom.	Ref. No. App. 14
Bedford School, Bedford	C.E.	G.2	Downside School, Stratton-on-the-Fosse, Somerset	R.C.	H.32
Berkhamsted School, Hertfordshire	C.E.	G.35	Dulwich College, London, S.E.21	U.	G.61
Bishop's Stortford College, Hertfordshire	U.	G.37	Durham School, Durham	C.E.	A.2
Bloxham School, Banbury, Oxfordshire	C.E.	G.74	Eastbourne College, Sussex	C.E.	G.101
Blundell's School, Tiverton, Devon	C.E.	H.5	Edinburgh Academy, Edinburgh, 2	Int.	x
Bootham School, York	S.F.	B.1	Ellesmere College, Shropshire	C.E.	E.1
Bradfield College, Berkshire	C.E.	G.5	Epsom College, Surrey	C.E.	G.84
Brighton College, Sussex	C.E.	G.99	Eton College, Windsor, Berkshire	C.E.	G.18
Bromsgrove School, Worcestershire	C.E.	E.19	Felsted School, Dunmow, Essex	C.E.	G.24
Bryanston School, Blandford, Dorset	C.E.	H.11	Fettes College, Edinburgh, 4	Int.	x
Canford School, Wimborne, Dorset	C.E.	H.12	Forest School, London, E.17	C.E.	G.63
Carmel College, Wallingford, Berkshire	J.	G.75	Giggleswick School, Settle, Yorkshire	U.	B.8
Charterhouse School, Godalming, Surrey	C.E.	G.80	Glasgow Academy, Glasgow, W.2	U.	x
Cheltenham College, Gloucestershire	C.E.	H.20	Glenalmond, Trinity College, Perthshire	Ep.	x
Chigwell School, Essex	C.E.	G.23	Gordonstoun School, Elgin, Morayshire	Ep.	x
Christ College, Brecon	C.W.	I.1	Grenville College, Bideford, Devon	C.E.	H.6
Christ's Hospital, Horsham, Sussex	C.E.	G.111	Gresham's School, Holt, Norfolk	C.E.	F.4
City of London School, London, E.C.4.	U.	†	Haileybury and Imperial Service College, Hertford	C.E.	G.39
Clayesmore School, Blandford, Dorset	C.E.	H.13	Harrow School, Middlesex	C.E.	G.64
Clifton College, Bristol, Gloucestershire	C.E.	H.22	Highgate School, London, N.6	C.E.	G.65
Colston's School, Bristol, Gloucestershire	C.E.	H.25	Hurstpierpoint College, Sussex	C.E.	G.103
Cranleigh School, Surrey	C.E.	G.83	Ipswich School, Suffolk	C.E.	F.7
Dean Close School, Cheltenham, Gloucestershire	C.E.	H.26	John Lyon School, Harrow, Middlesex	U.	†
Denstone College Uttoxeter, Staffordshire	C.E.	E.7	Kelly College, Tavistock, Devon	C.E.	H.7
Douai School, Woolhampton, Berkshire	R.C.	G.6	King's College School, London, S.W.19	C.E.	G.66
Dover College, Kent	C.E.	G.49	King's College, Taunton, Somerset	C.E.	H.34
			King's School, Bruton, Somerset	C.E.	H.35
			King's School, Canterbury, Kent	C.E.	G.51
			King's School, Ely, Cambridgeshire	C.E.	F.1
			King's School, Gloucester	C.E.	H.27

Section 1

	Denom.	Ref. No. App. 14		Denom.	Ref. No. App. 14
King's School, Macclesfield, Cheshire	U.	†	Queen's College, Taunton, Somerset	Meth.	H.39
King's School, Rochester, Kent	C.E.	G.52	Radley College, Abingdon, Berkshire	C.E.	G.12
Kingswood School, Bath, Somerset	Meth.	H.36	Ratcliffe College, Leicestershire	R.C.	D.6
Lancing College, Sussex	C.E.	G.112	Reed's School, Cobham, Surrey	C.E.	G.89
Langley School, Norwich, Norfolk	U.	F.5	Rendcomb College, Cirencester, Gloucestershire	C.E.	H.28
Leighton Park School, Reading, Berkshire	S.F.	G.9	Repton School, Derbyshire	C.E.	D.3
Leys School, Cambridge	Meth.	F.2	Rishworth School, Halifax, Yorkshire	C.E.	B.11
Liverpool College, Lancashire	C.E.	C.4	Rossall School, Fleetwood, Lancashire	C.E.	C.5
Llandovery College, Carmarthenshire	C.E.	I.3	Royal Masonic School, Bushey, Hertfordshire	C.E.	G.43
Lord Wandsworth College, Basingstoke, Hampshire	U	G.29	Royal Merchant Navy School, Wokingham, Berkshire	C.E.	G.13
Loretto School Musselburgh, Midlothian	C.E.	x	Rugby School, Warwickshire	C.E.	E.13
Malvern College, Worcestershire	C.E.	E.22	Ruthin School, Denbighshire	U.	I.6
Marlborough College, Wiltshire	C.E.	H.46	Rydal School, Colwyn Bay, Denbighshire	Meth.	I.7
Merchant Taylors' School, Northwood, Middlesex	C.E.	G.40	St. Bees School, Cumberland	C.E.	A.1
Merchiston Castle School, Edinburgh, 13	C.S.	x	St. Benedict's School, London, W.5	R.C.	†
Mill Hill School, London, N.W.7	U.	G.67	St. Dunstan's College, London, S.E.6	C.E.	†
Milton Abbey School, Blandford, Dorset	C.E.	H.15	St. Edmund's School, Canterbury, Kent	C.E.	G.54
Monkton Combe School, Bath, Somerset	C.E.	H.37	St. Edward's School, Oxford	C.E.	G.78
Mount St. Mary's College, Spinkhill, Derbyshire	R.C.	D.1	St. George's School, Harpenden, Hertfordshire	Int.	*
Nautical College, Pangbourne, Berkshire	C.E.	G.10	St. George's College, Weybridge, Surrey	R.C.	G.92
Nottingham High School, Nottingham	U.	†	St. John's School, Leatherhead, Surrey	C.E.	G.93
Oratory School, Woodcote, Berkshire	R.C.	G.77	St. Lawrence College, Ramsgate, Kent	C.E.	G.55
Oswestry School, Shropshire	C.E.	E.3	St. Paul's School, London, W.14	C.E.	G.72
Oundle School, Peterborough, Northamptonshire	C.E.	D.7	St. Peter's School, York	C.E.	B.6
Prior Park College, Bath, Somerset	R.C.	H.38	Scarborough College, Yorkshire	Int.	A.6
			Sebright School, Wolverley, Worcestershire	C.E.	E.25

Section 1

	Denom.	Ref. No. App. 14		Denom.	Ref. No. App. 14
Sedbergh School, Yorkshire	U.	B.12	*Girls* The Abbey School, Malvern Wells,		
Sevenoaks School, Kent	U.	G.57	Worcestershire	C.E.	E.17
Sherborne School, Dorset	C.E.	H.16	Abbot's Hill School, Hemel Hempstead, Hertfordshire	C.E.	G.33
Shrewsbury School, Shropshire	C.E.	E.4	Alice Ottley School, Worcester	C.E.	E.18
Silcoates School, Wakefield, Yorkshire	Cong.	B.13	Ancaster House School, Bexhill, Sussex	C.E.	G.97
Solihull School Warwickshire	C.E.	E.15	Ashford School, Kent	U.	G.46
Stonyhurst College, Whalley, Lancashire	R.C.	C.6	Atherley School, Southampton, Hampshire	C.E.	†
Stowe School, Buckingham	C.E.	G.21	Badminton School, Westbury-on-Trym, Gloucestershire	U.	H.19
Strathallan School, Forgandenny, Perthshire	U.	x	Bedford High School, Bedford	U.	G.1
Sutton Valence School, Kent	C.E.	G.58	Bedgebury Park School, Goudhurst, Kent	C.E.	G.47
Taunton School, Somerset	Cong.	H.43	Benenden School, Cranbrook, Kent	C.E.	G.48
Tettenhall College, Staffordshire	Int.	E.9	Berkhamsted School for Girls, Hertfordshire	U.	G.36
Tonbridge School, Kent	C.E.	G.59	Brentwood School, Southport, Lancashire	C.E.	*
Trent College, Long Eaton, Nottinghamshire	C.E.	D.5	Bruton School for Girls, Sunny Hill, Somerset	Int.	H.31
Truro Cathedral School, Cornwall	C.E.	H.2	Burgess Hill P.N.E.U. School, Sussex	U.	G.106
University College School, London, N.W.3	U.	†	Casterton School, Carnforth, Lancashire	C.E.	A.4
Uppingham School Rutland	C.E.	D.11	Channing School, London, N.6	U.	G.60
Warwick School, Warwick	C.E.	E.16	Charters Towers School, Bexhill, Sussex	U.	G.100
Wellingborough School, Northamptonshire	C.E.	D.9	Cheltenham Ladies' College, Gloucestershire	C.E.	H.21
Wellington College, Crowthorne, Berkshire	C.E.	G.17	Christ's Hospital for Girls, Hertford	C.E.	G.38
Westminster School, London, S.W.1	C.E.	G.73	City of London School for Girls, London, E.C.4	U.	†
Whitgift School, Croydon, Surrey	U.	†	Claremont School, Esher, Surrey	Ch.S.	G.81
Winchester College, Hampshire	C.E.	G.32	Cleveland School, Stockton-on-Tees, Co. Durham	U.	†
Worksop College, Nottinghamshire	C.E.	D.10	Clifton High School for Girls, Bristol, Gloucestershire	U.	H.23
Wrekin College, Wellington, Shropshire	C.E.	E.5			
Wycliffe College, Stonehouse, Gloucestershire	C.E.	H.30			

Section 1

	Denom.	Ref. No. App. 14		Denom.	Ref. No. App. 14
Convent of the Holy Child Jesus School, Edgbaston, Warwickshire	R.C.	E.10	Gardenhurst School, Burnham-on-Sea, Somerset	C.E.	H.33
Convent of the Sacred Heart School, Hove, Sussex	R.C.	*	Godolphin School, Salisbury, Wiltshire	C.E.	H.45
Convent of the Sacred Heart School, Woldingham, Surrey	R.C.	G.82	Greenacre School, Banstead, Surrey	U.	G.85
			The Grove School, Hindhead, Surrey	C.E.	G.86
Cranborne Chase School, Tisbury, Wiltshire	C.E.	H.44	Guildford High School, Surrey	C.E.	†
Croft House School, Shillingstone, Dorset	C.E.	H.14	Harrogate College, Yorkshire	C.E.	B.9
Croham Hurst School, South Croydon, Surrey	Int.	†	Hawnes School, Haynes Park, Bedfordshire	U.	G.3
Derby High School for Girls, Littleover, Derbyshire	C.E.	†	Headington School, Oxford	C.E.	G.76
Downe House School, Newbury, Berkshire	C.E.	G.7	Heathfield School, Ascot, Berkshire	C.E.	G.8
Durham High School, Durham	C.E.	†	Hollington Park School, St. Leonards-on-Sea, Sussex	C.E.	G.102
East Anglian School for Girls, Bury St. Edmunds, Suffolk	Meth.	F.9	Howell's School, Denbigh	U.	I.4
			Hull High School, Yorkshire	C.E.	B.2
Edgbaston C. of E. College, Birmingham, Warwickshire	C.E.	E.11	Hunmanby Hall Girls' School, Filey, Yorkshire	Meth.	B.3
Edgbaston High School, Birmingham, Warwickshire	Int.	†	Huyton College, Liverpool, Lancashire	C.E.	C.3
Ellerslie School, Malvern, Worcestershire	C.E.	E.20	James Allen's Girls' School, London, S.E.21	U.	†
Elmslie Girls' School, Blackpool, Lancashire	C.E.	†	Kent College, Pembury, Kent	Meth.	G.50
Eothen School, Caterham, Surrey	U.	†	Kingsley School, Leamington Spa, Warwickshire	C.E.	E.12
Esdaile School, Edinburgh, 9	C.S.	x	Lady Eleanor Holles School, Hampton, Middlesex	C.E.	†
Farnborough Hill Convent College, Hampshire	R.C.	G.28	Lawnside School, Malvern, Worcestershire	C.E.	E.21
Farringtons School, Chislehurst, Kent	Meth.	G.62	Lewes High School, Sussex	U.	†
Felixstowe College, Suffolk	C.E.	F.6	Lillesden School, Hawkhurst, Kent	U.	G.53
Francis Holland School, London, N.W.1	C.E.	†	Lowther College, Abergele, Denbighshire	C.E.	I.8
Francis Holland School, London, S.W.1	C.E.	†	Malvern Girls' College, Worcestershire	C.E.	E.23
			Micklefield School, Seaford, Sussex	U.	G.104

Section 1

	Denom.	Ref. No. App. 14		Denom.	Ref. No. App. 14
Moira House School, Eastbourne, Sussex	Int.	G.105	Royal School, Bath, Somerset	C.E.	H.40
Moreton Hall School, Oswestry, Shropshire	C.E.	E.2	St. Albans High School, Hertfordshire	C.E.	†
The Mount School, London, N.W.7	U.	G.68	St. Audries School, West Quantoxhead, Somerset	C.E.	H.41
The Mount School, York	S.F.	B.4	St. Brandon's School, Clevedon, Somerset	C.E.	H.42
Newcastle-on-Tyne Church High School, Northumberland	C.E.	†	St. Catherine's School, Bramley, Surrey	C.E.	G.91
Northwood College, Middlesex	U.	G.69	School of St. Clare, Penzance, Cornwall	C.E.	H.1
Oakdene School, Beaconsfield, Buckinghamshire	C.E.	G.19	St. Dunstan's Abbey School, Plymouth, Devon	C.E.	H.8
Ockbrook School, Derbyshire	Mor.	D.2	St. Elphin's School, Darley Dale, Derbyshire	C.E.	D.4
Overstone School, Northamptonshire	U.	D.8	St. Felix School, Southwold, Suffolk	C.E.	F.8
Parson's Mead School, Ashtead, Surrey	Int.	G.87	St. George's School for Girls, Edinburgh, 12	Int.	x
Penrhos College, Colwyn Bay, Denbighshire	Meth.	I.5	St. Helen's School, Northwood, Middlesex	C.E.	G.71
Piper's Corner School, High Wycombe, Buckinghamshire	C.E.	G.20	St. Hilary's School, Alderley Edge, Cheshire	C.E.	C.1
Polam Hall School, Darlington, Co. Durham	S.F.	A.3	St. James's School, West Malvern, Worcestershire	C.E.	E.24
Princess Helena College, Hitchin, Hertfordshire	U.	G.41	St. Joseph's Convent School, Reading, Berkshire	R.C.	G.14
Prior's Field School, Godalming, Surrey	U.	G.88	St. Leonard's-Mayfield School, Mayfield, Sussex	R.C.	G.108
Queen Anne's School, Caversham, Berkshire	C.E.	G.11	St. Leonard's and St. Katherine's School, St. Andrews, Fife	U.	x
Queen Ethelburga's School, Harrogate, Yorkshire	C.E.	B.10	St. Margaret's School, Exeter, Devon	C.E.	H.9
Queen Margaret's School, Escrick, York	C.E.	B.5	St. Martin's School, Solihull, Warwickshire	C.E.	E.14
Queen's College, London, W.1	Int.	G.70	St. Mary's Convent, Ascot, Berkshire	R.C.	G.15
Queenswood School, Hatfield, Hertfordshire	Meth.	G.42	St. Mary's Convent, Shaftesbury, Wiltshire	R.C.	H.47
Roedean School, Brighton, Sussex	C.E.	G.107	St. Mary's Hall School, Brighton, Sussex	C.E.	G.109
Royal Masonic School for Girls, Rickmansworth, Hertfordshire	U.	G.44	St. Mary's School, Calne, Wiltshire	C.E.	H.48
The Royal Naval School, Haslemere, Surrey	C.E.	G.90			

Section 1

	Denom.	Ref. No. App. 14		Denom.	Ref. No. App. 14
St. Mary's School, Gerrards Cross, Buckinghamshire	C.E.	†	Uplands School, Parkstone, Dorset	C.E.	H.18
St. Mary's School, Wantage, Berkshire	C.E.	G.16	Upper Chine School, Shanklin, Isle of Wight	C.E.	G.45
St. Michael's School, Limpsfield, Surrey	C.E.	G.94	Upton Hall Convent School, Wirral, Cheshire	R.C.	C.2S
St. Michael's School, Petworth, Sussex	C.E.	G.113	Wadhurst College, Sussex	C.E.	G.110
St. Monica's School, Clacton, Essex	C.E.	G.26	Welsh Girls' School, Ashford, Middlesex	C.E.	G.96
St. Paul's Girls' School, London, W.6	C.E.	†	Wentworth Milton Mount School, Bournemouth, Hampshire	U.	G.31
St. Stephen's College, Broadstairs, Kent	C.E.	G.56	West Cornwall School, Penzance, Cornwall	Meth.	H.3
St. Swithin's School, Winchester, Hampshire	C.E.	G.30	Westonbirt School, Tetbury, Gloucestershire	C.E.	H.29
St. Winifred's School, Llanfairfechan, Caernarvonshire	C.E.	I.2	Westwood House School, Peterborough, Northamptonshire	C.E.	F.3
School of St. Mary and St. Anne, Abbots Bromley, Staffordshire	C.E.	E.8	Winceby House School, Bexhill, Sussex	C.E.	*
Sherborne School for Girls, Dorset	C.E.	H.17	Winterbourne, The Collegiate School, Bristol, Gloucestershire	Int.	H.24
Skellfield School, Thirsk, Yorkshire	C.E.	A.7	Wycombe Abbey School, High Wycombe, Buckinghamshire	C.E.	G.22
Stonar School, Melksham, Wiltshire	Int.	H.49	York College, York	C.E.	†
Stover School, Newton Abbot, Devon	C.E.	H.10			
Stratford House School, Bickley, Kent	U.	†			
Sunderland Church High School, Co. Durham	C.E.	†	*Mixed*		
Surbiton High School, Kingston-upon-Thames, Surrey	C.E.	†	Ackworth School, Pontefract, Yorkshire	S.F.	B.7
Tormead School, Guildford, Surrey	U.	G.95	Bedales School, Petersfield, Hampshire	U.	G.27
Trinity Hall School, Southport, Lancashire	Meth.	C.7	Friends' School, Saffron Walden, Essex	S.F.	G.25
Tudor Hall School, Banbury, Oxfordshire	C.E.	G.79			

Section 2

Changes in the membership of the three organisations since we were appointed are detailed below:

 (i) *Schools which have ceased to be members* (or whose headmaster has ceased to be a member)
   (a) *Schools closed or about to close*
       Beaumont College, Old Windsor, Berkshire. (G.B.A. and H.M.C.)
       Brentwood School, Southport, Lancashire. (G.B.G.S.A.)
       Convent of the Sacred Heart school, Hove, Sussex. (G.B.G.S.A.) (merged with Convent of the Sacred Heart School, Woldingham, Surrey)
       Esdaile School, Edinburgh, 9. (G.B.G.S.A.) (closure subject to statutory processes)
       Gardenhurst School, Burnham-on-Sea, Somerset. (G.B.G.S.A.)
       West Cornwall School, Penzance, Cornwall. (G.B.G.S.A.)
       Winceby House School, Bexhill, Sussex. (G.B.G.S.A.)
   (b) *Other reasons*
       St. George's School, Harpenden, Hertfordshire. (G.B.A.) (now a voluntary aided school)
       St. Joseph's Convent School, Reading, Berkshire. (G.B.G.S.A.)
 (ii) *Schools whose headmasters have become members of the H.M.C.*
       Milton Abbey School, Blandford, Dorset.
       Reed's School, Cobham, Surrey.
       Rendcomb College, Cirencester, Gloucestershire.
       (These three schools were already members of the G.B.A.)
(iii) *Schools whose governing bodies have become members of the G.B.A.*
       Belmont Abbey School, Hereford.
       Frensham Heights School, Farnham, Surrey.
       Millfield School, Street, Somerset.
       Redrice School, Andover, Hampshire.
       Royal Wolverhampton School, Staffordshire.
       St. Peter's School, Bournemouth, Hampshire.
       Sidcot School, Winscombe, Somerset.
       Tettenhall College, Wolverhampton, Staffordshire. (Headmaster already a member of H.M.C.)
       Wells Cathedral School, Somerset.
(iv) *Schools whose governing bodies have become members of the G.B.G.S.A.*
       Clarendon School, Abergele, Denbighshire.
       Colston's Girls' School, Bristol, Gloucestershire.
       New Hall School, Chelmsford, Essex. (formerly known as the Convent of the Holy Sepulchre School).
       Farlington School, Horsham, Sussex.
       Lansdowne House School, Edinburgh, 12.
       Runton Hill School, Cromer, Norfolk.
       St. Denis School, Edinburgh, 10.
       St. Hilary's School, Edinburgh, 10.
       St. Margaret's School, Bushey, Hertfordshire.
       St. Margaret's School for Girls (Newington), Edinburgh.
       St. Mary's School, Baldslow, St. Leonards-on-Sea, Sussex.
       Wroxall Abbey School, Warwickshire.

INDEX

Unless otherwise stated, references are to paragraph numbers. The Appendices in Volume II have not been indexed in detail but a few major references are included in this index. The introduction and summary of conclusions and recommendations have not been indexed.

LIST OF APPENDICES WHICH WILL APPEAR IN VOLUME II

1. Method of working
2. List of schools included in terms of reference
3. Schools visited
4. Foundations of boys' public schools.
5. Trends in numbers of pupils and schools
6. Questionnaires to schools—a survey of the replies
7. Evidence—lists of bodies and individuals submitting evidence and quotations from it
8. Careers of former public school pupils
9. Need and demand for boarding education—by Dr. Lambert and Mr. Woolfe
10. Schemes of government
11. Group arrangements
12. The finances of the public schools—by Mr. Glennerster and Miss Wilson
13. Assessment of parental contributions for the purpose of university awards
14. List of schools with boarding places in England and Wales and regional summary tables
15. Map of England and Wales showing position of public schools with boarding places
16. Map of England and Wales showing density of boarding places
17. Scotland statistics and map showing public schools with boarding places

Printed in England for Her Majesty's Stationery Office by McCorquodale & Co. Ltd., London
HM 2382   Dd. 138567   K160   6/68   McC.   3309